Religious Explanations

A Model from the Sciences

—

Edward L. Schoen

Duke University Press   Durham 1985

© 1985 Duke University Press
All rights reserved
Printed in the United States of America
Library of Congress Cataloging in Publication Data
Schoen, Edward L., 1949–
Religious explanations.
Bibliography: p.
Includes index.
1. Religion and science—1946–   . I. Title.
BL240.2.S32   1985   200'.1'5   84–24237
ISBN 0–8223–0616–6

For Shirley

Contents

Introduction   vii

I   The Problem   1

II   The Possibility of Religious Explanations   24

III   Scientific Explanations   51

IV   Religious Explanations   81

V   The Plausibility of Religious Explanations   121

VI   Plausible Religious Explanations   149

VII   Explanations and Religious Life   186

Notes   209

Index   223

Introduction

—

DURING THE HEYDAY of logical positivism, there seemed to be only three options open for religion. Some philosophers thought that the religious enterprise was outmoded, that it should be abandoned entirely. A second group was less negative about the significance of religious practice, but because they were impressed with the enormous prestige and power of the natural sciences, members of this group tried to carve an important role for religion along nonscientific lines. Most moved in a decidedly noncognitivist direction. A final group remained entrenched in the conviction that religious belief was epistemically sound. Theorists of this sort argued that the cognitive integrity of religious truth claims could be salvaged by showing that such claims are capable of meeting the most rigorous of scientific standards for theoretical adequacy. Since the positivists had offered a listing of supposedly proper scientific standards, members of this last camp tried to show that assorted religious claims could live up to positivist expectations by being verifiable, falsifiable, or otherwise empirically testable.

Over the course of the last few decades, positivism has fallen into disrepute. But in many ways, the prestige of the natural sciences is even greater now than it was during the height of that movement. Since the sciences have continued to play such a prominent role in contemporary life, the plight of religion appears to be about the same. There are still some who believe that religious practice is nothing more than a superstitious remnant of earlier and darker prescientific times. Others remain convinced of the theoretical superiority of the sciences. Although purely noncognitive characterizations of religion are fairly rare these days, the insistence that religious belief be structured along specifically nonscientific lines is still strong. Finally, a few have continued in the struggle to show not only that religious truth claims can be patterned along strictly scientific lines, but also that such claims are capable of meeting rigorously scientific standards for theoretical adequacy.

My own deepest sympathies lie with the last camp, though I carry some affection for the other two as well. With the first group, I am convinced that the rise of modern science has driven certain religious traditions and certain kinds of religious truth claims from the field. Part of the sixth chapter of this book is devoted to a characterization of a few of the sorts of religious beliefs that have been rendered untenable by the growth of the natural and social sciences. I find myself in agreement with the second group, that certain of the more significant aspects of religion are nonscientific, perhaps even noncognitive, in character. The burden of this study, however, is to show that there is at least one important kind of religious affirmation that can be scientifically structured and that can meet even the most rigid of scientific tests for theoretical adequacy. More precisely, it will be argued in the following pages that certain religious explanations can be formulated in the same way as explanations in macrophysics. The force of this argument will be directed toward showing that there is no philosophical or scientific reason why at least some of these explanations should not be pursued and others accepted.

While my sentiments remain with the third camp, I must confess that I am somewhat uneasy with its current status. I have not been entirely satisfied with many of the recent attempts to show that certain stretches of religious discourse can be scientifically structured. The reasons for my dissatisfaction are several. In the first place, while many philosophers in this group claim to be postpositivist in their commitments, powerful traces of verificationism as well as other bits of positivist doctrine tend to persist. Disappointingly, the avowal of postpositivist thinking is much more frequent than its practice. Second, the results of many of the more determined efforts to chart parallels between the cognitive structures of the sciences and those of religion have been undermined by one of two problems. Either the basic characterization of the sciences that has been used as a model for religious discourse has been seriously flawed or else the discussion of the close parallels between scientific and religious cognitive structures has been more suggestive than precisely delineated. Finally, even in those rare cases where comparisons between the sciences and religion have been carefully structured and carried through to detailed completion, there often has been a dearth of practical results.

This collection of disappointments originally stimulated my own thinking about the cognitive rehabilitation of religious discourse and finally led to the course of argumentation developed here. In the initial chapter, the problems to be addressed are isolated and clarified. While the recent history of skeptical attack upon the epistemic integrity of religious discourse is peppered with all sorts of seemingly unconnected arguments, two powerful currents of thought can be uncovered that unify this apparent chaos. Both of these currents spring directly from an appreciation of contemporary science. First, the extraordinary sweep of scientific advance over the past few centuries has encouraged the supposition that the scope of human inquiry is exhausted fully by the various physical and social sciences. Following the lead of such writers as Thomas Huxley and Sigmund Freud, many contemporary thinkers have submitted to the conclusion that the sciences are able to fill any theoretical roles that previously might have been thought to fall within the purview of religion. Not all critics have committed themselves to this vision of the epistemic sufficiency of the sciences, however. Some have been influenced by a second line of thought. Convinced of the epistemic potential offered by the investigative and explanatory strategies utilized in the physical sciences, many have come to the conclusion that any religious theory or explanation that cannot be patterned along rigidly scientific lines must be epistemically inferior, if not cognitively worthless.

In order to address both of these currents of contemporary skeptical challenge as directly as possible, it will be necessary to follow a very specific strategy. To meet the second line of objection, it must be shown that at least some of the theoretical structures employed in religious contexts are rigorously analogous to those used in the most uncontroversial branches of the natural sciences. This beginning step toward the cognitive rehabilitation of religious discourse can be taken by showing that certain religious accounts may be modeled in strict conformity with epistemically impeccable scientific patterns. Once this first step has been taken, it will be possible to challenge the contention that the sciences exhaust the scope of human cognitive inquiry. It can be shown that scientifically structured religious discourse is capable of making a genuine contribution to the human intellectual enterprise.

Like the first chapter, the second is preparatory in nature. It is devoted to demonstrating that recent discoveries in the philosophy of science and in the foundations of logic have rendered problematic the implementation of traditional strategies for the rehabilitation of the cognitive integrity of religious discourse. With the demise of the positivist vision of scientific explanation has gone the conviction that some deductively patterned ideal can be taken as a standard for determining the acceptability of explanatory structures. With the introduction of the possibility of alternatives to classical systems of logic, it would appear that standard logical constraints upon explanations must be questioned as well. Thus, if an acceptable basis for judging the epistemic integrity of religious explanations is to be found, it is necessary first to undertake a fresh investigation of the nature of properly constructed scientific accounts. In this way an adequate set of criteria for evaluating the possibility or plausibility of religious explanations can be assembled.

The third chapter is devoted to a renewed quest for usable scientific models. Unfortunately, there are strong reasons for believing that several distinct sorts of explanatory strategies are utilized in the various sciences. Since one of the major motives behind this investigation of scientific explanatory structures is to find a model for religion that can withstand the assault of recent skeptical attack, the field of acceptable candidates can be limited by turning attention exclusively toward those scientific strategies of untarnished epistemic merit. In order to remain on the safest ground possible, only those explanatory types employed in macrophysics will be considered. Of these, there is one sort that turns out to be particularly fertile in its religious implications. Under this strategy, explanations are constructed for patterns of events rather than for individual occurrences. In formulating an explanation for some specific pattern of events, the scientist seeks an analogous range of phenomena for which the governing mechanism already is understood. Using the known mechanism as a guide, he fashions a conception of a new explanatory entity along precisely determined lines. If the characterization of this new entity is properly formulated, an acceptable scientific explanation can be offered for the selected range of patterns.

There are a number of advantages in concentrating upon this particular sort of scientific explanation. Some of these are enumerated in the fourth chapter. For example, when carried over into religious contexts, this particular explanatory strategy can be used to provide a functional definition of 'God'. Such a definition has several attractive features. Just as the physicist can govern his research toward a finer understanding of subatomic particles by defining them as those entities that account for such-and-such patterns of physical phenomena, so a correctly developed functional characterization of 'God' can be used to direct research toward a clearer conception of God. Furthermore, since the explanatory strategy under consideration here utilizes a clear logic of discovery, a precise research program can be specified for anyone interested in filling out a specific functional definition of 'God'. Properly constructed functional definitions also can be used to generate individuating and identifying criteria for God. They even can be used to develop definitions of 'God' that do not require any appeal to peculiarly religious terminology. With such features as these, functional definitions of 'God' can be used as a foundation for assembling an effective series of responses to a wide range of skeptical challenge. It is possible to disarm objections that depend upon the claims that God cannot be identified, cannot be individuated, or cannot be defined in nonreligious terminology.

While it might be possible to generate religious explanations in strict conformity with patterns used in the sciences, it would not follow that such explanations were true or even worthy of serious pursuit. The fifth and sixth chapters offer an attempt to move beyond the question of the possibility of scientifically structured religious explanations to the question of their plausibility. An explanation reaches the level of initial plausibility if it is properly formulated. Since the third chapter offers a detailed specification of the manner in which one sort of scientific explanation must be constructed, it is not difficult to delineate a precise set of criteria by which the initial plausibility of religious explanations modeled after the pattern of that chapter can be assessed. Of course, properly formulated explanations, though initially plausible, may turn out to be false. Therefore, before any religious explanation can be entertained seriously, it must meet additional plausibility constraints. After considering a variety of possible additional requirements, two distinct sets are extracted from an analysis of the writings of Thomas Kuhn and Larry Laudan. Since these two sets of plausibility requirements are not mutually compatible, each is used independently of the other to assess the plausibility of a representative sampling of scientifically structured religious explanations.

Among the candidates considered are included examples from both "rivalist" and "nonrivalist" religious traditions. Rivalist explanations are those religious accounts that are offered in competition with scientific ones. Nonrivalists, on the other hand, do not intend their explanations to oppose those of the sciences. By appealing to the phenomenon of explanatory overdetermination, nonrivalists are able to suggest religious accounts for ranges that already may be explainable by scientific means. Among the religious explanations considered, rivalist accounts for natural patterns of phenomena as well as rivalist explanations for broad historical patterns turn out to be wildly implausible. Under certain special conditions, however, rivalist accounts for personal patterns may be worthy of pursuit or even of acceptance. Generally speaking, nonrivalist explanations fare much better. In fact, no philosophical or scientific reason can be given against the acceptability of certain nonrivalist explanations for natural, historical, or personal patterns of phenomena.

The final chapter of this book is an attempt to show how scientifically structured religious explanations may be carried over into religious contexts without losing their uniquely religious character. Some philosophers have pressed the claim that any religious discourse patterned after that of the sciences must of necessity prove defective. Taking inspiration from the writings of Ludwig Wittgenstein, they would argue that scientifically structured religious explanations are never truly religious. To counter this line of objection, two sorts of response are developed. First, the force of such "Wittgensteinian" objections is considered on a case by case basis. Each is found wanting in some respect. Second, a sketch of the kinds of roles that scientifically structured explanations might play in the life of vibrantly committed religious communities is provided in order to show that such accounts would not detract from any of the important cognitive or noncognitive activities of genuinely religious believers.

One last point that must be emphasized involves the use of personal pronouns throughout this book. In earlier drafts, I tried a number of different strategies in the hope of avoiding sexist language. In the end, I decided to use masculine forms in general examples under the traditional assumption that the use of masculine forms in such contexts involves no sexual implications. Although I realize that this solution is not entirely satisfactory, it seemed to be the least problematic of the alternatives available.

Acknowledgements

During the summer of 1979 I was given the opportunity to attend a National Endowment for the Humanities summer seminar directed by William Alston. This particular seminar, entitled "Talk about God," was devoted to a consideration of problems surrounding the nature and structure of religious discourse. As part of my work that summer, I began a study of the relationship between religious and scientific explanatory strategies that eventually evolved into the argument developed here. I am extremely grateful to Professor Alston, not only for the invaluable stimulation of that summer, but also for his continued interest. My thought has improved immensely under the pressure of his sustained, but always supportive, criticism. While I am fully confident that he always will be able to find ways of improving my thought, I am also quite certain that my argument would not have developed to this point without the benefit of his careful comments on earlier drafts. I am indebted to Professor Jude Dougherty as well. While he does not share the perspective represented in these pages, he was kind enough to read my work and offer needed support and advice along the way. I must also mention my debt to the referees for Duke University Press. Their careful and incisive criticisms have helped to strengthen my argument considerably. Finally, I must note that Western Kentucky University granted me a reduction in my teaching load in order to permit me time to finish this study, and that my graduate assistant, Robert O'Connor, was kind enough to check the accuracy of quotations as well as the details of documentation.

1

The Problem

—

OVER THE PAST CENTURY or so, the extraordinary successes of the sciences together with reflections upon those successes have given rise to a powerful series of skeptical arguments that have been used to cast serious doubt upon the possibility of asserting truths about God. Some thinkers, energized by their own accomplishments in the various sciences, have moved directly to sweepingly antireligious themes. Others, reticent to push their conclusions too far, have been embraced by more vigorous followers eager to press the case against religion. Although this welter of deeply influential critiques of religious belief and practice has emerged from a surprisingly wide diversity of disciplines, only the briefest glimpse at a few writers is required to capture something of the rich variety of ways in which convictions about the nature and findings of the sciences have led to profound doubts concerning the theoretical adequacy of religious belief.

One of the most persuasive attacks took its start from the text of Charles Darwin's *The Descent of Man*, page after page of which is devoted to a detailed compilation of comparisons between human beings and other living creatures. Darwin's extensive comparisons led him to the conclusion that not only does the physiological structure of man bear striking resemblance to structures found in other species, but human behavioral, emotional, and intellectual capacities can be found in less developed forms among many other species as well.[1] Finding such similarities so numerous and so compelling, Darwin finally concluded that "we ought frankly to admit their community of descent; to take any other view, is to admit that our own structure, and that of all the animals around us, is a mere snare laid to entrap our judgement."[2]

As his conclusion indicates, Darwin was not willing to rest content with a simple list of noticed resemblances among species. Instead, he pressed his case to the conclusion that his scientific gleanings were so damning to nineteenth-century Christian dogma regarding the nature of God's creative acts that, were one to persist in the supposition that God separately created each distinct species, there would be no way of avoiding the additional conclusion that God must be held blameworthy for maliciously designing the biological world so as to mislead careful investigators into serious error. Nor did Darwin help to placate those of his contemporaries lodged in schools of theology when he reserved a few pages for showing that dogs and monkeys are capable of anger, jealousy, and pride.[3] Though brief, his comments on this subject chafed painfully against the traditional Christian doctrines of original sin and the uniqueness of man's sinful nature.

Surprisingly, Darwin himself does not appear to have been tempted to push his findings to the extreme. Rather than moving to attacks against the truth of Christianity, he took the more conservative tack of suggesting relevant theological reforms. For instance, near the end of *The Descent of Man* he counseled moderation in the face of mounting evidence against simplistic interpretations of Genesis by arguing:

I am aware that the conclusions arrived at in this work will be denounced by some as highly irreligious; but he who denounces them is bound to show why it is more irreligious to explain the origin of man as a distinct species by descent from some lower form, through the laws of variation and natural selection, than to explain the birth of the individual through the laws of ordinary reproduction. The birth both of the species and of the individual are equally parts of that grand sequence of events which our minds refuse to accept as the result of blind chance.[4]

But where Darwin was hesitant to tread, many of his admirers boldly strode. T. H. Huxley, one of the most vocal, took Darwin's attack on popular doctrines of creation as but the latest example in a distinguished history of scientific progress over superstitious religion and wrote:

Extinguished theologians lie about the cradle of every science as the strangled snakes beside that of Hercules; and history records that whenever science and orthodoxy have been fairly opposed, the latter has been forced to retire from the lists, bleeding and crushed if not annihilated; scotched, if not slain. But orthodoxy is the Bourbon of the world of thought. It learns not, neither can it forget; and though, at present, bewildered and afraid to move, it is as willing as ever to insist that the first chapter of Genesis contains the beginning and the end of sound science; and to visit, with such petty thunderbolts as its half-paralysed hands can hurl, those who refuse to degrade Nature to the level of primitive Judaism.[5]

V. I. Lenin's famous critique of religious belief arose out of his intense interest in socioeconomic problems. Convinced that talk about God is untrue, he concluded that religion can serve only one important function within human society. Religion "is the opium of the people. Religion is a kind of spiritual gin in which slaves of capital drown their human shape and their claims to any decent human life."[6] While his argument against the truth of religious belief was drawn from speculation about social economics and political theory rather than from reflections upon modern controversies in biology, Lenin, like Huxley, deeply rooted his attack in powerfully held convictions about the procedures and discoveries of the sciences. As he put it, "Our programme is entirely based on the scientific, that is , the materialistic world outlook. The explanation of our programme therefore necessarily includes an explanation of the true historical and economic roots of religious obscurantism."[7] Regardless of the controversial nature of his views about the structure and results of scientific investigation, this passage makes it clear that Lenin was in agreement with Huxley on one very fundamental point: the paths of true science and religion are diverging ones. Impressed with the power of true science, Lenin concluded that the way of science must be sought eagerly while religion must be tolerated, at best, as a bothersome distraction from that right path.[8]

Sigmund Freud may have been more tolerant in his approach to religion than Huxley or Lenin, but he was no less skeptical of religious truth claims nor less thoroughly entranced with a vision of the supremacy of true science. Although he explicitly stated that *The Future of an Illusion* was a psychological investigation in which he took no interest in assessing the truth value of religious assertions,[9] Freud still could not resist making a few comments about the plausibility of various theological doctrines. For example, he believed that his discovery that religious doctrines are, psychologically speaking, illusions

strongly influences our attitude to the question which must appear to many to be the most important of all. . . . We shall tell ourselves that it would be very nice if there were a God who created the world and was a benevolent

Providence, and if there were a moral order in the universe and an after-life; but it is a very striking fact that all this is exactly as we are bound to wish it to be.[10]

Of course, Freud was not enticed into the simple conclusion that merely because one's wishes mesh so nicely with certain beliefs, such beliefs must be false. As he readily acknowledged, in his sense of 'illusions', illusions "need not necessarily be false. . . . For instance, a middle-class girl may have the illusion that a prince will come and marry her. This is possible."[11] But with regard to religious illusions, he was rather more pessimistic. With respect to their truth value, Freud argued that some religious illusions "are so improbable, so incompatible with everything we have laboriously discovered about the reality of the world, that we may compare them . . . to delusions."[12]

Concerning less obviously absurd religious doctrines, Freud officially took a more agnostic stance, though he left little doubt about the eventual fate of such illusions. He wrote:

Of the reality value of most of them we cannot judge; just as they cannot be proved, so they cannot be refuted. We still know too little to make a critical approach to them. The riddles of the universe reveal themselves only slowly to our investigation; there are many questions to which science to-day can give no answer. But scientific work is the only road which can lead us to a knowledge of reality outside ourselves.[13]

It would appear, then, that while Freud's interests, background, and studies were widely different from those of Huxley or Lenin, he came to share a common conviction with them: the realm of science is the realm of truth. Furthermore, Freud seems to have joined Huxley and Lenin in the belief that science and religion develop along quite different lines. While science draws steadily toward the clear light of truth, religion is destined to suffer the indignities of a long, terminal illness.

During the 1920s and 1930s a somewhat novel twist was added to the more traditional line of skeptical argument exemplified in these passages taken from the writings of Huxley, Lenin, and Freud. Spurred by the evident successes of the sciences, many critiques of religious belief and practice were driven beyond the mere repudiation of religious assertions as outmoded falsehoods to the more radical conclusion that talk about God and his nature is cognitively meaningless. A. J. Ayer's *Language, Truth and Logic* provided one of the most popular formulations of this more radical critique. Ayer argued that "to say that 'God exists' is to make a metaphysical utterance which cannot be either true or false. And . . . no sentence which purports to describe the nature of a transcendent god can possess any literal significance."[14]

According to Ayer, the problem with sentences like 'God exists' or 'God is wise' is that they, while seemingly used to make straightforward truth claims, are actually nothing more than metaphysical sentences. Unfortunately, any metaphysical sentence is "a sentence which purports to express a genuine proposition, but does, in fact, express neither a tautology nor an empirical hypothesis."[15] Since he believed that metaphysical sentences, unlike scientific ones, stand in no evidential relation whatever to the actual or possible course of human experience and that "every empirical hypothesis must be relevant to some actual, or possible, experience,"[16] Ayer concluded that religious utterances cannot be empirical hypotheses. Moreover, because no theologian would wish to admit that his utterances should be construed as mere vacuous tautologies or, worse yet, as downright contradictions, Ayer argued that there can be no alternative but to dub religious utterances as cognitively meaningless since "all propositions which have factual content are empirical hypotheses."[17]

Obviously, this argument would remain glaringly incomplete unless Ayer could link factual content, empirical hypotheses, and cognitive meaning. In his attempts to find a plausible criterion for cognitive meaningfulness in terms of direct experience, Ayer hoped to forge the requisite links. His initial approximation to such an acceptable criterion can be found in the first chapter of *Language, Truth and Logic* where he wrote:

We say that a sentence is factually significant to any given person, if, and only if, he knows how to verify the proposition which it purports to express—that is, if he knows what observations would lead him, under certain conditions, to accept the proposition as being true, or reject it as being false.[18]

Ayer sharpened this particular formulation a few pages farther along by distinguishing a strong from a weak sense of verifiability:

A proposition is said to be verifiable, in the strong sense of the term, if, and only if, its truth could be conclusively established in experience. But it is verifiable, in the weak sense, if it is possible for experience to render it probable.[19]

This distinction allowed Ayer to opt for a weak verifiability criterion for cognitive meaningfulness which he embraced in a somewhat defective formulation.[20]

Subsequent recognition of the defects in his original formulation led Ayer to a more sophisticated version of his criterion which he set down in the introduction prepared for the second edition of *Language, Truth, and Logic*. There he argued that "a literally meaningful statement, which is not analytic, . . . should be either directly or indirectly verifiable."[21] With regard to direct and indirect verifiability, he wrote:

A statement is directly verifiable if it is either itself an observation-statement, or is such that in conjunction with one or more observation-statements it entails at least one observation-statement which is not deducible from these other premises alone; and . . . a statement is indirectly verifiable if it satisfies the following conditions: first, that in conjunction with certain other premises it entails one or more directly verifiable statements which are not deducible from these other premises alone; and secondly, that these other premises do not include any statement that is not either analytic, or directly verifiable, or capable of being independently established as indirectly verifiable.[22]

Unhappily, even this more refined formulation appeared to buckle under the strain of critical scrutiny.[23]

Ayer was not the only one having trouble formulating a plausible criterion for cognitive meaningfulness sufficient to support an attack against the factual meaningfulness of religious utterances. Attempts to provide criteria in terms of falsifiability rather than verifiability seemed to fall prey to the same kinds of objections that bedeviled Ayer. Even translatability criteria—whereby statements were deemed cognitively meaningful if and only if they could be fully, or even partially, translated into certain proposed ideal empiricist languages—appeared to be insufficient for the task. The dismal array of failures catalogued in Carl Hempel's well-known "Problems and Changes in the Empiricist Criterion of Meaning," particularly when supplemented with his additional remarks of 1958,[24] and the constant deluge of critical literature that has appeared over the last few decades,[25] seem to have doused permanently any flickers of hope that some adequate positivist criterion for cognitive meaningfulness might eventually be found.

Nevertheless, in spite of this general failure to link clearly cognitive meaningfulness, factual content, and the course of human experience, the suspicion that religious utterances may be factually or cognitively meaningless has persisted. Antony Flew nicely captured this tenacious suspicion in his famous falsifiability challenge. Before introducing his challenge, Flew noted that "it often seems to people who are not religious as if there was no conceivable event or series of events the occurrence of which would be admitted by sophisticated religious people to be a sufficient reason for conceding 'There wasn't a God after all' or 'God does not really love us then.'"[26] In light of this peculiarity, Flew went on to pose his challenge to the believer: "'What would have to occur or to have occurred to constitute for you a disproof of the love of, or of the existence of, God?'"[27]

As Kai Nielsen has argued, it is not necessary to presuppose any specific positivist criterion of cognitive meaningfulness in order to feel the sting of Flew's challenge.[28] No particular precise or adequately articulated link between the actual or possible course of human experience and cognitively meaningful utterances must be assumed. Rather, to feel the force of Flew's challenge, one only need make the much weaker assumption that there must be at least some evidential relation of some sort between the actual or possible course of human experience and cognitively meaningful assertions. Hence, granting the acceptability of this weaker assumption, if the believer hopes to salvage the cognitive meaningfulness of his religious utterances, he is required to show that at least one actual or possible human experience is evidentially relevant to their truth or falsity.

In view of the repeated failure of attempts to formulate any plausible verifiability, falsifiability, or translatability criterion for cognitive meaningfulness, it might be very easy for the believer to succumb to the temptation to reject brusquely Nielsen's suggested weaker assumption, thereby hoping to undermine once and for all the critical force behind Flew's challenge. Alvin Plantinga is one who has moved in this direction. In his rebuke of positivistically inspired critiques of religious discourse, he has argued that if "the notion of verifiability cannot so much as be explained, if we cannot so much as say what it is for a statement to be empirically verifiable, then we scarcely need worry about whether religious statements are or are not verifiable."[29]

Unfortunately, this sort of reply has one rather serious limitation. It fails to counter Nielsen's weaker assumption in any direct way. Now if his weaker assumption carried no ring of plausibility or if it did not trace its roots back to the writings of some of the most venerable figures in the history of philosophy, then perhaps the mere failure to delineate precisely specific evidential relations between the course of experience and truth claims would cast Nielsen's weaker assumption under a cloud of doubt. But for many thinkers, both past and present, there can be almost nothing so obviously, if not even trivially, true than that cognitively valuable truth claims must stand in some evidential relation with the possible or actual course of human experience.

It does not take much investigation into the recent history of philosophy to see just how deeply Nielsen's weaker assumption has influenced philosophical thought about religion or to see just how persistent that assumption still remains. In the early 1920s Rudolf Carnap undertook a rational reconstruction of the sciences in which one of his primary goals was to provide a clarification of the meaning of central scientific concepts. This clarification was to be accomplished through a constructional system whereby higher-level concepts could be reduced to more basic ones. As Carnap saw it:

A constructional system undertakes more than the division of concepts into various kinds and the investigation of the differences and mutual relations between these kinds. In addition, it attempts a step-by-step derivation or "construction" of all concepts from certain fundamental concepts, so that a genealogy of concepts results in which each one has its definite place. It is the main thesis of construction theory that all concepts can in this way be derived from a few fundamental concepts.[30]

Carnap did not envision this construction of higher-level scientific concepts out of more fundamental ones as an isolated epistemological project. Instead, he began to reveal something of the wider significance of his process of meaning clarification and analysis by writing, "It makes no logical difference whether a given sign denotes the concept or the object, or whether a sentence holds for objects or concepts. . . . Thus, in construction theory we sometimes speak of constructed objects, sometimes of constructed concepts, without differentiating."[31] With this merger of concepts expressed with objects denoted, Carnap's intention moved beyond the simple elucidation of meanings. Constructional systems were expected to map patterns of reference as well.

The collapse of questions of meaning into questions of reference becomes fully explicit in Carnap's comment that

If, in the course of the formation of the constructional system, a new object is "constructed", then this means, according to our definition of construction, that it is shown how statements about it can be transformed into statements about the basic objects of the system or the objects which have been constructed prior to the object in question. Thus a rule must be given which enables us to eliminate the name of the new object in all sentences in which it could occur; in other words, *a definition* of the name of the object must be given.[32]

The most important epistemological consequence of this coincidence of patterns of meaning with patterns of reference was driven home in Carnap's discussion of the most basic level of his constructional system, the level out of which all higher levels of scientific conceptualization were to be constructed. About this level, Carnap argued, "Since we wish to require of our constructional system that it should agree with the epistemic order of the objects . . . , we have to proceed from that which is epistemically primary, that is to say, from the "given", i.e., from experiences themselves in their totality and undivided unity."[33] More precisely, he said, "We choose as basic elements of the system 'my experiences'. . . . We choose a system form with an 'autopsychological basis'."[34]

With his particular selection of constructional base and by adopting a correspondence theory of truth,[35] Carnap was able neatly to link matters of meaning, reference, truth, and verification by claiming:

Only the construction formula of the object—as a rule of translation of statements about it into statements about the basic objects, namely, about relations between elementary experiences—gives a verifiable meaning to such statements, for verification means testing on the basis of experiences.[36]

Given this careful connection of meaning with reference, truth, and verification, any successful Carnapian construction of a system of concepts for the sciences would result not only in extensive meaning clarification, but also in the disclosure of the exact evidential links between scientific truth claims and the course of possible and actual human experience. This latter goal, more than the former, really seemed to interest Carnap. As he confessed with regard to his motivation in the attempt to rationally reconstruct the sciences:

Epistemological analysis is an analysis of the contents of experiences, more precisely the analysis of the theoretical content of experiences. We are concerned only with the theoretical content of the experience, that is, with the possible knowledge that is contained in the experience.[37]

All this rational reconstruction with its attendant elucidation of constructional systems of meaning and its complicated tracing of evidential relations between high-level scientific statements and the course of experience could never have been sustained by Carnap were he not supported and encouraged by a very specific, visionary commitment. In "The Constructional or Empirical Problem of Reality," Carnap explicitly acknowledged the motivational role of his guiding image, the vision that:

Ultimately, all knowledge goes back to my experiences, which are related to one another, connected, and synthesized; thus, there is a logical progress which leads, first, to the various entities of my consciousness, then to the physical objects, furthermore, with the aid of the latter, to the phenomena of consciousness of other subjects, i.e., to the heteropsychological, and, through the mediation of the heteropsychological, to the cultural objects.[38]

So there it was. Beneath all the details lurked the conviction that all of scientific knowledge must be grounded evidentially in the course of human experience. Carnap ultimately was concerned to tease out the specifics of the evidential relations between the highest levels of scientific theory and the course of experience by decisively tracing the intricacies of scientific discourse to a theory-independent experiential base. If successful in his reconstruction, he would be able not only to determine the meaning of scientific terminology, but also to show how the truth value of particular scientific assertions could be assessed.

There was a second element in Carnap's guiding image of the structure of the sciences which he tacked onto the end of the passage just cited. Not only was he convinced that scientific truth claims must stand in some relatively straightforward evidential relation to the course of experience, he went on to add that *"this is the theory of knowledge in its entirety."*[39] In short, not just the sciences, but all human knowledge must stand in certain straightforward evidential relations to the course of human experience. That is, all truth claims, no matter what their origin or subject matter, must be evidentially supported by experience in exactly the same ways as scientific truth claims are supported. Of course, this move from the scientific realm to the full scope of human cognitive endeavor was facilitated by the fact that Carnap found no difficulty in accepting the belief that the sciences exhaust the entire range of human theoretical interest and activity.[40]

This Carnapian vision of the sciences both as evidentially linked to the course of human experience and as exhaustive of human knowledge was shared widely by others who sought positivistically acceptable theories of cognitive meaning. For example, in his characterization of the features he believed to be essential to any epistemologically adequate grounding of the sciences, Moritz Schlick nicely mirrored the convictions of Carnap. In his discussion of the required protocol base, Schlick wrote:

What was originally meant by "protocol statements," as the name indicates, are those statements which express the *facts* with absolute simplicity, without any moulding, alteration or addition, in whose elaboration every science consists, and which precede all knowing, every judgement regarding the world. . . . If we succeed therefore in expressing the raw facts in "protocol statements," without any contamination, these appear to be the absolutely indubitable starting points of all knowledge.[41]

Like Carnap, Schlick was guided by the belief that all human knowledge rests upon an evidential, observational base. Furthermore, he was willing to add that this observational base could provide an indubitable grounding for human knowledge. Finally, with Carnap, Schlick betrayed his conviction that human knowledge is exhausted by the sciences. Since the scope of science and the scope of human knowledge were coextensive, nothing of cognitive or theoretical value was left outside the realm of the sciences. In summing up the vision of Carnap, Schlick, and like-minded thinkers, Carl Hempel tersely remarked that the "fundamental tenet of modern empiricism is the view that all non-analytic knowledge is based on experience."[42]

This fundamental conviction, Hempel's "fundamental tenet of modern empiricism," is fossilized now in Kai Nielsen's weaker assumption and has hung on persistently through thick and thin to give Flew's challenge its lasting sting. Attempts to provide positivistically adequate criteria for cognitive meaningfulness have been abandoned. Attempts at the rational reconstruction of the sciences in the spirit of Carnap have been given up as well. But none of this appears to have shaken the conviction that all human knowledge must be grounded in experience. Even the facts that no uncontroversial, theory-independent foundational base adequate evidentially to support the sciences has ever been found and that there is some reason to believe no such base can be found have been impotent to unsettle the widespread faith in Hempel's fundamental tenet.[43] In the face of the general failure to provide verifiability, falsifiability, or translatability criteria for cognitive meaningfulness and in full recognition that a theory-independent evidential base for the sciences remains as elusive as ever, seemingly countless thinkers still are willing to stand behind A. J. Ayer in his candid confession: "I believe in science. That is, I believe that a theory about the way the world works is not acceptable unless it is confirmed by the facts, and I believe that the only way to discover what the facts are is by empirical observation."[44]

Because of this widespread and deeply entrenched commitment to Hempel's fundamental tenet of modern empiricism, Kai Nielsen recently has been able to mount an extremely influential, skeptical attack against religious belief crucially based upon nothing more than his own particular formulation of quite familiar and popular themes. According to his variation on these themes, a "putatively factual statement actually has factual significance (is factually meaningful, has factual content) only if some differential experience is relevant to its truth or falsity."[45] Here again are those old connections between meaning and verification, but with a difference. The key term here is "relevant." By introducing this noncommittal term, Nielsen's characterization of cognitive meaning requires nothing more than a simple adherence to Hempel's tenet. No official stance whatever with regard to the detailed nature of the evidential link between truth claims and experience is required.

Nielsen, with this weak confessional stance, reformulated Flew's original challenge with considerable persuasive force. He argued:

It must be possible (logically possible) with respect to any religious truth-claim, on the one hand, to describe two empirically identifiable but distinct situations or states, one of which actually obtains when the religious statement in question is true, the other when it is false or, on the other hand and less determinately, at least if one situation or state obtains, we will have good grounds for saying the religious statement in question is true, and if the other obtains, we have good grounds for saying that it is false.[46]

With this reformulation, Nielsen was able to capitalize on those underlying assumptions that have continued to hang on through the recent history of positivist failures. His formulation depended neither upon the success of some particular attempt to rationally reconstruct the sciences nor upon the plausibility of any specific criterion for cognitive meaningfulness. Of course, Nielsen would have to concede that the detailed evidential relations between scientific assertions and the course of human experience have yet to be displayed convincingly, but by pleading patience with so complex and intricate a problem, he can retreat to a common ground of commitment to Hempel's fundamental tenet. Given this commitment, it is but a few easy steps to the argument that if all human knowledge must be based in experience in the ways that the sciences are based, then religious assertions, if they are to be taken seriously, must be judged by the same kinds of standards operative in the sciences.

With this assemblage of skeptical arguments offered by thinkers like Ayer, Flew, and Nielsen coupled with the more traditional attacks in the spirit of Huxley, Lenin, or Freud, any serious attempt at the rehabilitation of religious belief and practice must take a stand against one, or perhaps several, distinct claims. From the more traditional line of skeptical argument came the claim that religious belief must be relegated to the dustbin of outmoded truth claims. With the rise of modern science, religious truth claims slowly are being shown to be false. One by one they are falling and will continue to fall to the advances of the sciences. From the more recent and radical line of argument offered by Ayer, Flew, and Nielsen, religious assertions turn out to be cognitively meaningless. Religious truth claims fail to meet the most basic test of meaningfulness employed in the sciences: they fail to be evidentially linked to the course of human experience in any straightforward way. From both the more traditional line of skeptical argument and the more recent one has emerged a vision of the supremacy of science. Science is conceived as the paradigm of human knowing, the standard by which all other cognitive disciplines must be judged, if not the only genuine theoretical enterprise to which all others must be reduced.

Probably the most restrictive response that can be mustered by anyone interested in salvaging religious belief or practice is to concede the full force of both more traditional and more recent skeptical arguments. Surprisingly, it is possible to concede that religion is incapable of thwarting the encroachment of the sciences in the quest for knowledge as well as to concede that religious utterances are incapable of standing up to the rigorous tests for cognitive integrity employed in the sciences and still maintain that there is a meaningful role for religion in human life. Religion is salvaged by the simple expedient of getting out of the truth claiming business altogether in the hope of finding some significant role for religious utterances that falls outside the cognitive or theoretical sphere.

Oddly enough, one of the first to point out the possibility of an escape into the realm of the noncognitive was Rudolf Carnap. He opened this door for the believer with the note that the

proud thesis that no question is in principle unsolvable for science agrees very well with the humble insight that, even after all questions have been answered, the problem which life poses for us has not yet been solved. . . . the mastery of life requires an effort of all our various powers; we should be wary of the shortsighted belief that the demands of life can all be met with the power of conceptual thinking alone.[47]

As might be expected, many theologians impressed with the discoveries and powerful methods of the sciences have felt pressed to take the alternative suggested by Carnap. Rudolf Bultmann provides a nice example. In *Jesus Christ and Mythology*, he registered a sensitivity to the stress placed upon the credibility of religious texts by the discoveries of modern science when he said, "The contrast between the ancient world-view of the Bible and the modern world-view is the contrast between two ways of thinking, the mythological and the scientific."[48] Bultmann not only believed that the findings of science conflict with traditional Judeo-Christian teachings but also concluded that it is religion, not science, that must succumb. Thus he argued that the existence of Satan, heaven, and hell as well as Jesus' divinity must be rejected as mythological since "de-mythologizing takes the modern world-view as a criterion."[49]

In full accord with Carnap's suggested line of escape, Bultmann did not allow his conclusions concerning science and religion to lead to a total repudiation of the theological enterprise. Instead he argued that true religion remains outside the scientific sphere. To be sure, he believed that where the tentacles of science reach, they prove deadly to religious orthodoxy. But since they do not reach everywhere, Bultmann concluded that there are important aspects of human religious life that remain insulated forever from the progress of science. As he put it:

To de-mythologize is to reject not Scripture or the Christian message as a whole, but the world-view of Scripture, which is the world-view of a past epoch, which all too often is retained in Christian dogmatics and in the preaching of the Church.[50]

Thus, while the believer must give up any hope of salvaging the historical truth claims of orthodox Judeo-Christianity, whatever remains outside the critical range of the sciences may be retained confidently. According to Bultmann, this safe residuum of "Christian preaching is *kerygma*, that is, a proclamation addressed not to the theoretical reason, but to the hearer as a self."[51]

In a more strictly philosophical vein, R. M. Hare employed the same basic Carnapian strategy when he replied to Flew's original challenge. Like Bultmann, Hare conceded that religious utterances served certain explanatory functions in the past that in modern times have been usurped by the sciences. Thus, like Bultmann, Hare concluded that if religion is to play any important role in human life, it must find its place outside the realm of scientific concern. Chiding Flew for not recognizing what he thought any clear-headed believer would take for granted, Hare wrote:

The mistake of the position which Flew selects for attack is to regard this kind of talk as some sort of *explanation*, as scientists are accustomed to use the word. As such, it would obviously be ludicrous. We no longer believe in God as an Atlas—*nous n'avons pas besoin de cette hypothèse.*[52]

Beyond this conclusion that religious utterances cannot be used explanatorily, Hare also appeared willing to concede the more radical point that talk about God is not even assertive. In Hare's view, to have a religious commitment is to have a *blik* and "Flew has shown that a *blik* does not consist in an assertion or system of them."[53] Nevertheless, Hare stopped short of Bultmann's conclusion that true religion bears absolutely no relation whatever to "theoretical reason."[54] Instead, he argued that while a *blik* itself is neither assertive nor explanatory, "without a *blik* there can be no explanation; for it is by our *bliks* that we decide what is and what is not an explanation."[55]

The main problem with the course of response to the modern skeptic's challenge suggested by Carnap and taken by Bultmann and Hare has nothing whatever to do with difficulties surrounding things like *bliks* or the *kerygma*. To adopt Hare's convictions that religious discourse is neither assertive nor explanatory or to embrace Bultmann's even more sweeping conclusion that talk about God falls entirely outside the realm of the theoretical is to fly in the face of an extraordinary amount of actual linguistic practice. Of course, it cannot be denied that many believers use language within a religious context in ways that are not explanatory, theoretical, or even assertive. For instance, "hallelujah" might be used for praising while "amen" could be uttered to signify the completion of some particular ritual or, in less formal contexts, might be used by members of a congregation as an indication of enthusiastic agreement with the preacher. Similarly, confessions of sins, pleadings for forgiveness, and psalms of adoration usually involve the use of language in ways that could not naturally be construed as theoretical or assertive. Perhaps it also would have to be admitted that certain whole congregations or sects never use their religious utterances assertively for any theoretical or explanatory purpose. Certainly ministers deeply influenced by the writings of Bultmann would find few occasions for the theoretical use of language within their own sanctuary walls. Probably charismatic or other anti-intellectual groups could also be expected to slight theoretical or assertive religious discourse.

Nevertheless, there is an extremely broad spectrum of believers from a wide diversity of religious traditions who do appear to use their religious discourse in theoretical ways, not only assertively, but also for providing explanations. For the sake of familiarity, consider any of the major branches of Protestant or Roman Catholic Christianity. Within such traditions, there are certainly frequent occasions upon which the sentence 'God exists' is used intelligibly to express surprise (as when an unexpected check arrives in the mail) or to express wonder (as when the intricate interdependencies among assorted plants and animals in a meadow's ecosystem first are noted) or to express awe (as when gripped by the splendor of icy torrents plunging from snow-capped peaks) or even sarcastically to express rage (as when a young child is found to have cancer). There are also frequent occasions upon which the sentence 'God exists' seems to be used with complete propriety to express the straightforward truth claim that there is a certain entity of a rather special and particular sort. In fact, were it impossible to use 'God exists' in this assertive way for making ontological claims, the above-mentioned uses of 'God exists' would become odd in the extreme. Each such use appears to be parasitic upon the more basic, ontological use. After all, it is the fact that various people, not necessarily the speaker, have supposed that there is a being who provides good things for his creatures, who is the designer and sustainer of the universe, and who faithfully rewards those who serve him that allows the sensible and appropriate use of 'God exists' to express delighted surprise at good fortune, wonder at nature's complexity, awe at natural phenomena, and even dismay or rage at undeserved misfortune.

'God exists' is not the only sentence that seems to have an obvious, assertive function. Frequently, believers will begin by affirming the existence of an entity purportedly referred to by the name 'God' and then go on to use such sentences as 'God is omnipotent' and 'God is a person' in a descriptive way to make truth claims concerning the nature, character, or properties of their chosen entity. Indeed, the observation that many religious believers often affirm the existence of some particular entity by saying 'God exists' and then go on to describe that divine being in assorted ways by asserting 'God is wise' or 'God is good' appears so obvious and trivial as to require little in the way of evidential support. If supporting evidence is desired, however, it easily can be collected from the range of ordinary linguistic behavior commonly manifested by believers. Consider, for example, the reactive behavior of "native" religious speakers when provoked by questioning. To the believer's utterance that God is wise, one might ask, "Does that mean that he knows how to solve problems?" Typically, the believer will respond in a clarifying way. Were his initial use of 'God is wise' to be taken as something other than a truth claim descriptive of some divine entity, such question-and-answer behavior would be anomalous in the extreme. Similarly, unless 'God is wise' could be used assertively for theoretical purposes, much theological debate and controversy would be rendered inexplicable. There would seem to be no way of satisfactorily explaining what a theologian is doing when he utters 'God is wise' together with several supporting arguments, arguments that are subsequently sharpened and refined in light of elaborate critiques.

Even religious doubt or repudiation would be difficult, if not impossible, to explain unless talk about God could be assertive. Typically, when asked why they have begun to doubt or why they are no longer willing to say 'God is good' troubled believers will respond with something like, "If God were good, he would not have let my baby die." A response of this sort seems to indicate not only that the course of human events impinges evidentially upon the truth of 'God is good' but also that 'God is good' stands in important conceptual relations with sentences like 'God will never allow unnecessary suffering' or 'God will never allow useless death'. In these cases, the believers' doubts or repudiations seem to be just that, doubts or rejections of truth claims on the basis of some recalcitrant experience or theoretical difficulty.

The wealth of linguistic data that can be assembled by even the briefest survey of major branches of Protestant and Roman Catholic Christianity goes well beyond the mere support of the general conclusion that much talk about God is assertive. A broad stretch of linguistic behavior within religious contexts undergirds the more specific conclusion that religious communities will use theological language to explain specific behavior. When asked why they attend church on Sunday, it is not uncommon for believers to explain by making reference to God's wants or desires. At other times, believers will account for the occurrence of particular experiences by making reference to divine activities. Funny feelings in the night, quiet whisperings of direction, or dramatic visions often are explained by citing God's intervention. In similar fashion, believers may use theological language for the explanation of certain patterns of events, the meaning of life, or the essential purpose of humanity.

Beyond the straightforward citation of specific instances in which the linguistic behavior of various religious believers appears to indicate that talk about God is being used assertively or even explanatorily, a rather large body of indirect evidence can be assembled that also seems to lead to the conclusion that religious devotees rely heavily upon the assertive or explanatory force of their utterances. For example, when confronted with an evolutionary account of life, many believers feel threatened. Likewise, when provided with psychological or sociological accounts of religious experience, some sincere believers squirm uneasily. The only plausible reason why evolutionary accounts of the origin of life or naturalistic explanations of religious phenomena can make so many believers uncomfortable seems to be that such believers take evolutionary, sociological, or psychological theories to be offering explanations in stiff competition with their own. Of course, this competition could not be felt unless members of religious communities believed that their religious convictions carried an explanatory force of their own. Along slightly different lines, the traditional problem of evil also can be brought as indirect evidence in support of the contention that many believers use their talk about God explanatorily. When confronted with persuasive formulations of this problem, believers often recoil in shocked befuddlement. Under interrogation, such believers usually remark that their unsettled attitudes are a result of the fear that there is no way in which the fact of evil in the world can be explained from within their religious framework. This reaction can only be taken to mean that such troubled believers think their religious commitments are capable of explaining some occurrences but incapable of explaining others.

Given a good dose of ingenuity it might be possible to dismiss this and other linguistic data as misleading by offering an alternative analysis of the behavior of believers in such contexts. Perhaps it could be argued with some plausibility that such believers only seem to be using religious discourse in an assertive way while, in actuality, they are doing something quite different. Less radically, dismissal of this range of data might be achieved in a more Bultmannian fashion by declaring that many believers are suffering from a lack of religious sophistication. Failing to realize that a cognitive or theoretical use of religious utterances is no longer possible, these believers have persisted in blundering along in the crude fashion of their ancestors. While it might become necessary to resort to such desperate measures as these in order to save a legitimate role for religion in contemporary life, it certainly would be preferable to begin by taking a more directly confrontational approach to current religious skepticism. If the challenges of traditional as well as the more recently radical lines of skeptical argument could be squarely faced and adequately rebuffed, then the broad range of linguistic data just outlined could be naturally interpreted to be of cognitive significance. It also might be possible to salvage certain theoretical or explanatory functions for discourse about God.

Not surprisingly, many writers have taken this more direct approach. For instance, John Hick developed a widely respected response to Flew's original challenge. In his reply, Hick began with the clear concession that the verifiability criterion

is a valid criterion of factual meaning. Accordingly, in order to be either veridical or illusory the mode of experiencing that we call religious faith must be such that the theological statements which express it are either verifiable or falsifiable. It must make an experienceable difference whether they are true or false.[56]

Here Hick affirmed his agreement with Carnap, Ayer, Nielsen, and the rest that all truth claims, whether scientific or not, must be evidentially linked with the course of human experience in some rather straightforward manner. However, he differed from them in his convictions about religion. According to Hick, religious utterances could meet this criterion. To support his conviction, Hick tried to provide a specification of the sort of experience that could be used to verify the Christian faith by describing a situation in which someone dies and is recreated in a new spatial setting with a new body, one that is similar in certain respects to the old body but is composed of material other than physical matter.[57] Unfortunately, Hick was forced to conclude that even all of this would be insufficient for his purposes. As he noted, "Survival, simply as such, would not serve to verify theism. It would not necessarily be a state of affairs which is manifestly incompatible with the nonexistence of God. It might be taken just as a surprising natural fact."[58] So, to make his verifying situation more fully adequate, Hick felt constrained to add two additional features to his story. He suggested

first, an experience of the fulfillment of God's purpose for ourselves, as this has been disclosed in the Christian revelation, and second, in conjunction with the first, an experience of communion with God as he has revealed himself in the person of Christ.[59]

Kai Nielsen, perhaps the most consistent advocate of the belief that religious discourse stands in no evidential relation whatever to the course of human experience, has considered Hick's reply to Flew's challenge and, after lengthy analysis, finally has concluded that this proposal fails to meet successfully even the weakest possible reformulation of the original challenge.[60] Reviewing Nielsen's extended reply to Hick, Basil Mitchell decided that only one of Nielsen's arguments carried any damaging force against Hick. With Nielsen, Mitchell concluded that

Hick has not succeeded in meeting the stated requirement; for the experiences in question are all described in theistic terms ('the fulfiillment of God's purpose', 'communion with God', 'the person of Christ')and it is precisely this sort of language whose intelligibility is in dispute. Hick has failed to describe, in terms which are intelligible to theist and atheist alike, the experiences which would remove all rational doubt about theism.[61]

But Mitchell believed that this flaw in Hick's proposal could be easily remedied by describing "in non-theistic terms the situation which he has been describing in theistic terms."[62] To strengthen Hick's description, he substituted the supposition that

the individual is aware of having survived death and finds himself in a situation which, if not literally identical with traditional representations of the blessed in heaven, is such that he can recognise it as what they were attempting to represent. He is in the company of men who display all the signs of intense happiness and deep mutual affection. They are in the presence of a figure who is recognizable as Jesus and they accept his authority.[63]

With this sort of systematic substitution, Mitchell believed he was able to provide a depiction of a set of experiences that relied on no uniquely theistic descriptive terminology. Furthermore, he argued that anyone confronted with such a set of experiences would have enough evidence to put the truth of traditional Christian theism beyond any reasonable doubt.[64]

There are two important reasons why a direct confrontation with the challenges of Flew or Nielsen, such as this one, should not be pursued. In the first place, even were Hick's original proposal or Mitchell's modification of it undeniably successful, little would be done to thwart the deeper convictions that underlie such challenges and give them their lasting sting. Although some particular verifiability, falsifiability, or translatability criterion obviously would be met, the basic conviction common to Nielsen, Bultmann, Huxley, Freud, and the rest—the belief that all the cognitive or theoretical needs of humanity fall within the scope of the various sciences—would not be touched. It is simply not enough to show that a few isolated experiences can, somehow or other, evidentially impinge upon one or two religious truth claims. Something more must be done. To resurrect fully the cognitive integrity of religious utterances, it is necessary to provide a detailed analysis of the ways in which they can play significant theoretical and even explanatory roles in human life. Moreover, if the modern skeptic's deep conviction about the paradigmatic nature of the scientific enterprise is to be respected, it is necessary to show that the ways in which religious claims fulfill full-blooded cognitive roles are able to parallel precisely the theoretical structures employed in the hardest of the sciences. That is, it must be shown that religious truth claims are able to be developed, tested, and modified in precisely the same ways as scientific claims are elaborated and evaluated.

Second, there is little reason to pursue Hick's line of response because even the weakest skeptical challenge that relies upon the specification of some evidential relation between the course of experience and isolated truth claims appears to be drastically misguided. Recent writings of Thomas Kuhn, W. V. Quine, and others have provided a great deal of evidence in support of the contention that no single event, or even manageably small series of events, is sufficient to confirm or disconfirm any particular truth claim with any degree of probability whatever.[65] Consider, for example, even the most seemingly unproblematic of truth claims: an assertion of "This brick is red." Suppose this claim were challenged by people who report, "This brick is blue." The original claimant could reply that the other reporters were the poor victims of mass hallucination. Should some fancy apparatus be produced that registered that wavelengths near the blue end of the spectrum were being reflected by the brick, the original claimant could adopt the conviction that the machine was broken. Should the machine turn out to pass the severest of inspections, the entrenched claimant could argue that, far from showing the brick was not red, the scientific community was privileged to have witnessed a succession of events demonstrating that current optical theory is seriously defective. In short, there is no single event or manageably small series of events that would tend to disconfirm the isolated claim that this brick is red. Since there are all sorts of ways in which to save the claim by suitably adjusting other theoretical commitments, it would appear that the course of experience does not evidentially impinge upon truth claims taken in isolation. Only portions of theory larger than individual truth claims can be evidentially related to the course of experience and even these evidential relations are not the traditional ones of simple confirmation or disconfirmation.

In *The Justification of Religious Belief*, Basil Mitchell tried to utilize these kinds of postpositivist reflections upon the nature and structure of scientific theories in an attempt to rehabilitate the cognitive aspects of religious discourse.[66] After an extended consideration of procedures used for formulating and evaluating theories in historical investigation and literary criticism as well as in the natural sciences, Mitchell finally concluded, "In its intellectual aspect, traditional Christian theism may be regarded as a world-view or metaphysical system which is in competition with other such systems and must be judged by its capacity to make sense of all the available evidence."[67]

Unfortunately, while there is a great deal of importance in Mitchell's work, his rehabilitation proves disappointing in two ways. First, very little is done to show precisely how theories make sense of available evidence. Although numerous examples provide fertile hints at the way in which evidence might be related to theory, Mitchell ultimately concedes that even in the case of the sciences

it is not possible to specify precise rules in accordance with which such decisions are to be made; scientists have to rely on such 'values' (to use Kuhn's word) as consistency, coherence, simplicity, elegance, explanatory power, fertility.[68]

Clearly, this rehabilitation would be enhanced considerably if a more precise analysis of the ways in which scientific theories make sense of data could be evolved. Much stronger and more persuasive parallels could then be drawn between precisely delineated features of scientific theories and similar features in religious thought.

The second disappointment in Mitchell's work comes with his rejection of any parallel between scientific and religious explanation. He says that "it has to be conceded that theological explanations cannot be of a scientific kind."[69] Certainly, talk about God might be cognitively meaningful and even explanatory without being able to provide explanations of the sort that science can furnish, but if religion could be shown capable of the same kinds of explanations as can be offered by the sciences, a more potent response to the sorts of criticisms found in Huxley, Freud, Nielsen, and the like could be mustered.

In the hope of continuing in Mitchell's spirit of rehabilitation, the remaining pages shall be devoted to a very specific strategy. First, while occupied with the task of showing that discourse about God can be cognitively meaningful, any discussion of 'cognitive meaningfulness' or 'factual meaningfulness' will be strictly avoided. The danger of becoming inextricably tangled in the unprofitable and hopelessly difficult task of developing a plausible definition of 'cognitive meaningfulness' or 'factual meaningfulness' can be skirted safely by making one simple assumption. It shall be assumed that any stretch of language that can be used successfully to provide genuine scientific explanations must be factually or cognitively meaningful. With this assumption, attention may be turned to the more tractable problem of showing how religious discourse may be used successfully to provide explanations strictly parallel with those offered in the sciences. Furthermore, by accepting this assumption, attention is forced in the direction of the relation between religious and scientific explanatory strategies and structures in a manner that should help counter the claim that religious commitments are impotent when measured by the rigorous standards employed in the sciences. An investigation into the nature of one particular sort of scientific explanation with the intention of drawing analogies with the religious sphere will help to insure that the problem of the possibility of religious explanations will be explored without compromising the theoretical constraints operative in even the most uncontroversial branches of physics. Once this exploration of religious explanations constructed in conformity with procedures used in the sciences is completed, some of the ramifications of this investigation with regard to the realistic utilization of religious explanations will be sketched.

The Possibility of
Religious Explanations

—

THE BELIEF THAT RELIGIOUS utterances can never be used for the provision of genuine explanations has been, and still remains, an extraordinarily pervasive one. As was noted in the first chapter, Huxley, Lenin, and Freud were joined by the Vienna Circle in the conviction that religious discourse must find its purpose outside the domain of the rigorous sciences. While they thought that the natural as well as certain social sciences could offer credible explanatory theories, the possibility that religion might fulfill explanatory as well as other theoretical functions was denied universally. They were convinced that if religion were to perform any useful human function at all, it would have to find its validation beyond the reaches of any theoretical or explanatory enterprise. The only shred of hope that religious commitments might be able to find some meaningful, though noncognitive, place in the elaborately diverse course of human activity rested with the recognition that human beings have psychological, social, and emotional needs beyond the theoretical ones met by the continual advancement of the sciences.

It also was noted in the first chapter that skepticism regarding the theoretical usefulness of religious utterances is not limited to the ranks of those generally unsympathetic with the religious enterprise. Furthermore, even thinkers who are committed seriously to the task of rehabilitating the cognitive usefulness of religious discourse have shied away from full-blooded claims concerning the explanatory adequacy of religious convictions. As was seen, Basil Mitchell, though he devoted *The Justification of Religious Belief* to an extended argument for the theoretical integrity of religious belief, finally conceded that religious explanations must be reduced to a second-class status far beneath the place held by explanations in the physical sciences. As he put it:

It has to be conceded that theological explanations cannot be of a scientific kind. In so far as they succeed in achieving a gain in intelligibility they do so not by suggesting a hypothesis from which deductions are made which are subject to strict experimental test, but by placing what has to be explained in a fresh conceptual framework in relation to which answers are possible to questions of a different kind to those asked in the sciences.[1]

There still remain a few who have been willing to explore beyond the weak claims of Mitchell. One of these, Ian Barbour, began very strongly in *Myths, Models and Paradigms* with the assertion that "Despite the presence of distinctive functions and attitudes in religion which have no parallels in science, there are also functions and attitudes in common, wherein I see differences of degree rather than an absolute dichotomy."[2] He then proceeded to outline his detailed conception of the theoretical structure of the sciences with special attention to the nature of theoretical models in the hope of illuminating the realm of religious theoretical activity. In his discussion of scientific models, Barbour wrote:

Theoretical models, such as the 'billard ball model' [*sic*] of a gas, are not merely convenient calculating devices or temporary psychological aids in the formulation of theories; they have an important continuing role in suggesting both modifications in existing theories and the discovery of new phenomena.[3]

As is evident from this passage, Barbour was not willing to rest content with an instrumentalist view of models.[4] He was convinced that theoretical models must play a stronger role than the theoretically dispensable one of useful "calculating devices for correlating observations and making predictions."[5] But he also was unwilling to take the position of naive realism because he believed that the naive realist took "*a literalistic view of models*. Models were taken as replicas of the world, 'pictures of reality'."[6]

In his attempt to strike a balance between the instrumentalist and the naive realist, Barbour embraced

Critical realism. Like the naive realist (and unlike the instrumentalist), the critical realist takes theories to be representations of the world. He holds that valid theories are true as well as useful. . . . Unlike the naive realist, however, the critical realist (along with the instrumentalist) recognizes the importance of human imagination in the formation of theories.[7]

In this view, models "are neither pictures of reality nor useful fictions."[8] More precisely, models

are partial and inadequate ways of imagining what is not observable. They are symbolic representations, for particular purposes, of aspects of reality which are not directly accessible to us. They are taken seriously but not literally.[9]

In order to understand how theoretical models can be taken seriously but not literally, Barbour's connection between models and metaphors must be drawn. In his interpretation, theoretical models are basically metaphors that have been developed extensively. Therefore, the only important difference between models and metaphors is that "a metaphor is used only momentarily, whereas a model is used in a sustained and systematic fashion."[10] Now, according to Barbour:

A metaphor proposes *analogies* between the normal context of a word and a new context into which it is introduced. Some, but not all, of the familiar connotations of the word are transferred. 'The lion is the king of beasts', but it has only some of the attributes of royalty.[11]

Furthermore, "a metaphor cannot be replaced by a set of equivalent literal statements because it is *open-ended*. No limits can be set as to how far the comparison might be extended."[12] Finally, "A metaphor can order our perceptions, bringing forward aspects which we had not noticed before. One kind of experience is interpreted in terms of the characteristics of another."[13]

For Barbour, theoretical models parallel metaphors in each of these regards. First, models are used to suggest an analogy between an imagined object or process and a real one. As Barbour says:

Models are analogical. Similarities with a familiar situation are posited in some respects (the positive analogy), and differences are posited in other respects (the negative analogy).[14]

Second, "scientific models are not eliminable [*sic*] because they, too, are based on analogies which are open-ended and extensible."[15] Finally, a crucial function of models is to

serve as 'organizing images' which give emphasis, selectively restructuring as well as interpreting our perceptions. Models, like metaphors, may help us to notice particular features of the world.[16]

If stress is placed upon the latter two features of models and metaphors, then it is not too difficult to understand how theoretical models can be "taken seriously but not literally."[17] With regard to

Barbour's example of gaseous particles modeled by analogy with billiard balls,[18] it is certainly clear that particles of a gas cannot be taken literally to be tiny colored-and-numbered ivory balls. Nevertheless, this analogy must be taken seriously since the suggestion that particles of a gas are like billiard balls is able to help structure the scientist's perception of gaseous behavior, emphasizing certain patterns and features of that behavior that would otherwise pass unnoticed. Thus, because of this ability to illuminate patterns, organize experience, and structure the perceptible world, it is perfectly natural to think of models as making important claims "about the world and not simply about human feelings and attitudes."[19]

In any attempt to integrate Barbour's first comment about models and metaphors with these latter two claims lurks a bit of trouble. In his affirmation of the analogical character of models, Barbour suggested that there were both positive and negative analogies between scientific models and the entities they are designed to model. In light of this observation, it would seem very reasonable to conclude that models may be taken as providing at least a partial characterization of those things for which they provide models. Surprisingly, this conclusion appears to be unwarranted. Barbour seems to exclude this implication by commenting that "a model is a symbolic representation of selected aspects of the behavior of a complex system for particular purposes. It is an imaginative tool for ordering experience, rather than a description of the world."[20] This conclusion also seems to be discouraged by Barbour's comments that a model "is not a literal picture of the world"[21] and that

A model is a mental construct and not a picture of reality. It is an attempt to represent symbolically, for restricted purposes, aspects of the world whose structure is not accessible to us. No direct comparison of model and world is possible.[22]

Furthermore, this sweeping repudiation of the descriptive power of models falls into line with Barbour's strong rejection of naive realism with its attendant commitment to a literalistic interpretation of models, under which models "were taken as replicas of the world, 'pictures of reality'."[23]

However, there also seem to be passages in Barbour's work where he appears to encourage the conclusion that models may be taken to provide some partial characterization of existents. For example, he argues that scientists actually do consider theories and models as making tentative truth-claims, beyond their usefulness as tools for classifying phenomena. In particular, they hold that there are entities in the world something like those described in the model; they believe there is some isomorphism between the model and the real structures of the world.[24]

This is not the only passage in which Barbour urges the descriptive role of theoretical models. In his discussion of the billiard ball model of gaseous particles he moves far beyond the mere hint of certain isomorphisms between models and existents to the stronger claim that at least some features of models may be literally identical with certain features of the objects they model. He writes:

The model also intimates that some theoretical terms might be related to observable properties of the gas (for example, the momentum change of the 'particles' colliding with the containing wall might be identified with the pressure of the gas).[25]

In fact, in his comments about certain biological models, Barbour explicitly states that "there is a wide variety even among *theoretical models*. Some, such as the 'double helix' model of the DNA molecule, are closer to observations and can be taken more literally."[26]

At this point, Barbour's dictum that "models . . . should be taken seriously but not literally"[27] begins to slip into obscurity. On the one hand, his continual stress upon the contention that models are unable to provide any accurate description of the entities they model presses into prominence his contention that the true importance of theoretical models is centered in their ability to highlight various significant patterns that are hidden within the welter of experience. On the other hand, Barbour provides a sustained argument to the conclusion that not only can assorted isomorphisms between models and objects modeled be discerned, but also some features of models should be taken as literally identical with features of the objects they model. Thus, for many models, particularly biological ones, taking them seriously requires taking at least some aspects of them literally.

While Barbour's ambivalent stance with regard to the theoretical functions of models may not be crucially destructive in his attempt to apply his gleanings from the sciences to the religious sphere, it is certainly more than trivial. It tends to leave him with a vacillating attitude toward the place of models in religious discourse. For instance, sometimes Barbour places heavy emphasis upon his conviction that the importance of theoretical models rests in their ability to structure the data of experience. This emphasis leads him to suggest that differing models can be used to bring differing patterns of phenomena into prominence and to conclude that the wider the diversity of illuminating models employed, the better. A slightly chaotic proliferation of models, some of which may be incompatible with others, is a fully appropriate aid to sharper perception. When carried over into a religious context, this strand of Barbour's thought evolves into a justification of an ecumenical spirit toward alternative religious perspectives. He writes:

> The approach to other religions which I am advocating is the way of *dialogue*. It respects the integrity of other traditions and the presence of irreducible differences. Yet it seeks to understand and appreciate other ways of life from within. Humility and openness enable learning to occur where defensiveness only narrows one's outlook.[28]

At other times, however, Barbour appears to favor the contention that models should be taken as literally, if only partially, descriptive. This particular theme surfaces most prominently in his discussion of the competitive nature of religious models. In chapter 8, when he considers the comparative merits of divergent models for God, Barbour does not restrict himself to a consideration of the ways in which differing models emphasize assorted patterns in experience. Instead, he evaluates alternatives in terms of their respective abilities to characterize adequately God's nature. When God is envisioned as a clockmaker, for example, his personal agency is slighted, though his wisdom and sovereignty are captured adequately. One model, that of a monarch, implies that God is responsible for suffering in the world and so is repudiated by Barbour for its attribution to God of features which he cannot have. When he finally embraces a process model of God, Barbour does so largely because the conception of God offered by this particular vision of God most fully captures the essential features in God's nature. While it requires a denial of God's omnipotence, it nevertheless provides a God worthy of worship by placing a stress upon God's goodness.[29] In all of these considerations, Barbour appears to be focusing upon the conviction that models are to be taken "as making *a tentative ontological claim* . . . as making tentative truth-claims, beyond their usefulness as tools for classifying phenomena."[30]

Without a clear understanding of the precise role theoretical models play in scientific investigation, it is impossible to determine how Barbour intends religious models to be construed. Should models of God be judged exclusively in terms of their abilities to highlight patterns in experience? If so, inconsistencies among alternative characterizations of God can be easily tolerated. Though models may suggest mutually exclusive conceptions of God's nature, each must be prized for its ability to bring unique patterns in experience to light. After all, models are not to be taken as descriptive of God; they are to be taken seriously, but not literally. On the other hand, if models are to be construed as offering at least a partial description of the actual nature of God, inconsistencies among them will become a problem of much more central concern.

Of course, this problem of imprecision must be admitted to be a relatively minor one in and of itself. If the only difficulty with Barbour's conception of scientific models were one of clarity, it could be overcome easily. Further clarity might be found by pursuing Barbour's own writings in greater depth. Should this tack prove fruitless, then the most promising among his competing conceptions of theoretical models simply could be adopted as normative in order to expedite an insightful move to the religious sphere. Unfortunately, there is some reason to believe that more serious problems lie buried within Barbour's work on scientific models. Consider his claim that models

are neither literal pictures of reality nor 'useful fictions', but partial and provisional ways of imagining what is not observable; they are symbolic representations of aspects of the world which are not directly accessible to us.[31]

Or consider his contention that

A model is a mental construct and not a picture of reality. It is an attempt to represent symbolically, for restricted purposes, aspects of a world whose structure is not accessible to us. No direct comparison of model and world is possible.[32]

In both of these passages, Barbour draws a connection between theoretical models and that which is not directly accessible. Theoretical models are provided only for that which is not directly accessible to us. Furthermore, Barbour seems to be hinting in these passages that the reason theoretical models cannot be taken as literally descriptive of anything is because that which they model is not directly accessible to us. The reason models can be only provisional ways of imagining or symbolic representations is because they cannot be compared directly with the things they model. The suspicion that Barbour's primary reason for rejecting any descriptive role for theoretical models is that the objects they model are inaccessible receives strong confirmation from a quick glance at his repudiation of naive realism. He notes:

With a few exceptions, most scientists until the present century assumed that scientific theories were accurate descriptions of 'the world as it is in itself'. The entities postulated in theories were believed to exist, even if they were not directly observable. Theoretical terms were said to denote real things of the same kind as physical objects in the perceived world. Theoretical statements were understood as true or false propositions about actual entities (atoms, molecules, genes, etc.). The main difficulty with naive realism is that we have no access to 'the world in itself', especially in the sub-microscopic domain; there is no way to compare a theory directly with 'reality'. . . .
    Corresponding to a naively realistic view of theories is *a literalistic view of models*. Models were taken as replicas of the world. . . . The nineteenth-century predilection for picturable mechanical models has been thoroughly undermined by quantum physics which has shown that the atomic world is very unlike the world of familiar objects.[33]

It might be tempting to associate all this talk about what is not directly accessible, what is not directly observable, and what is not directly comparable with Barbour's rejection of any theory-independent givens. After all, since he is constantly reminding his readers that *"all data are theory-laden,"*[34] Barbour's reason for rejecting the descriptive adequacy of models must be simple: as human percipients, we never have any access to the world as it is in itself. That is, because all our perceptions are theory-laden, we never can construct a mirror of nature that accurately depicts it. We only can construct a depiction powerfully shaped and structured by a wide variety of our theoretical commitments.

As tempting as this interpretation of Barbour might be, to equate direct accessibility with theory independence and inaccessibility with the theory-laden would be a mistake. These equations are blatantly incompatible with Barbour's remark that "there is a wide variety even among *theoretical models*. Some, such as the 'double helix' model of the DNA molecule, are closer to observations and can be taken more literally."[35] For Barbour, the directly accessible is the observable and that which cannot be observed is inaccessible. For all of his extended repudiation of the positivists, Barbour's position here is startlingly positivistic. Though he rejects the theory-independence of perception, he seems to embrace a purely observational epistemic base as an ideal in the sciences. That is, he appears convinced that accurate descriptive statements about the world are possible only if they are checkable directly by taking recourse to the actual course of human experience. If no such straightforward recourse is possible, the scientist is doomed to a symbolic, metaphorical, or imaginative use of his models rather than a literally descriptive one. Of course, insofar as the scientist can find a straightforward evidential link between his statements and the course of experience, he can take them as literally descriptive, though perhaps occasionally false.

If it is correct to assume that Barbour presumes at least some scientific statements to stand in some relatively straightforward evidential relation with the course of human experience, then he would seem to be subject to the sorts of Quinean and Kuhnian criticisms raised near the end of the first chapter. There do not seem to be any isolated statements that can be confirmed or disconfirmed by some single or manageably small series of human experiences. In fact, taken in isolation, single statements do not appear to be confirmable or disconfirmable by experience at all. But even if Barbour cannot be accused of this positivist presumption, there is no reason to join him in the assumption that any statement that fails to stand in some rigid evidential link with experience is incapable of being descriptively accurate.

Consider the actual course of scientific investigation. In the first place, Barbour's restriction of theoretical models to the province of the unobserved or unobservable is a highly artificial one. Often in the history of science, models that were introduced originally as representations of unobserved entities continued to be retained and utilized even though the entities such models were taken to represent subsequently became observable. For example, many of the models that were originally proposed to represent various chromosomal structures and activities lost none of their force or importance for genetic studies even though certain of those previously unobserved entities recently have become observable. Furthermore, the primary reason such models were not abandoned was that, once the relevant entities became observable, those models proved to be descriptively accurate. This fact would appear to indicate not only that it was appropriate to take certain genetic models as literally descriptive prior to the availability of observational data, but also that descriptively accurate models can be constructed by using methods that do not require observational access to the entities being modeled.

Second, Barbour's contention that contemporary scientists are willing to rest content with the claim that there is some analogy or vague, unexplicated isomorphism between their models and real existents is simply counterfactual. Obviously, no practicing scientist ever expected every feature of billiard balls to be carried over into a proper characterization of gaseous molecules. No one expected to find little numbers engraved upon the shiny ivory surfaces of molecules. Nevertheless, many characteristics were expected to be found in both billiard balls and the molecules of various gases. In fact, much of the scientific investigation into the nature of gaseous behavior subsequent to the introduction of the billiard ball model was directed toward the discovery of precisely which features should be carried over from the suggested model and which should be stripped away. Much scientific energy was devoted to delineating the precise nature of possible isomorphisms in as much detail as possible. Indeed, not only did scientists spend much time in tracing out such parallels, but it would seem that the ultimate fate of the billiard ball model depended heavily upon the success or failure of those attempted delineations. Had it been discovered that there were absolutely no features of billiard balls that could be carried rigidly over to gaseous molecules, the billiard ball model soon would have been abandoned in favor of some more promising one. Had it been discovered that some alternative model displays even closer parallels with gaseous molecules than does the billiard ball proposal, billiard balls quickly would have been forgotten in the rush to test that new candidate.

What is so troubling about Barbour's dictum that theoretical models should be taken seriously but not literally is that, within the context of scientific investigation, taking a model seriously is simply entertaining the possibility that, at least in some respect, the particular model in question has features that are identical with certain features of whatever observable or unobservable entities are being modeled. That is, in large measure, taking a model seriously *is* taking it literally. Thus, in his concern to test models, the scientist is interested in discovering whether various models actually do have features in common with assorted entities. It is only insofar as various characteristics of selected models rigidly correspond with features of existing things that there can be any legitimate claim that such models provide genuine insight into the nature and functioning of existents. The adequacy of various models can only be tested by investigating suggested parallels between them and assorted existing things.

The hesitancy on the part of scientists to claim final validity for models in current use must not be confused with the role fully adequate scientific models would be expected to play. In general, reflective scientists may be a modest bunch. They may be unwilling to press arrogant pronouncements concerning the unerring adequacy of their currently embraced models, but their ultimate goal is anything but humble. Any fully adequate model would be expected to embody precisely all of those features of existents that are of interest to the sciences. In short, it would be expected to provide a characterization of existents that was descriptively accurate in every scientifically important detail.

While Barbour's extended investigation into the nature of scientific theory construction and evaluation is somewhat obscure at crucial points and appears to be rather defective at others, his general strategy for rehabilitating the cognitive integrity of religious discourse is exactly the one that will be adopted over the course of the remaining chapters. Gleanings from a study of the epistemological structures employed in the sciences will be carried over and applied to the religious sphere. But, in contrast to Barbour, a much stronger role for models within scientific contexts will be suggested. Consequently, the main theoretical functions of religious or scientific assertions will range far beyond Barbour's conviction that they primarily "serve as 'organizing images' which give emphasis, selectively restructuring as well as interpreting our perceptions."[36]

Before turning to the implementation of this particular strategy, it will be useful to take a survey of the sorts of objections that might be raised against the contention that religious utterances are able to serve legitimate explanatory functions. It should be noted, however, that the catalog of skeptical arguments that follows must not be interpreted as a representative cross section of popular arguments against the possibility of religious explanations. Several of the kinds of arguments discussed in the next few pages have never actually been pressed. Instead, the following mélange of skeptical argumentative strategies is assembled with an eye to showing precisely why the argument for the possibility of religious explanations must proceed along the lines that will be taken in subsequent chapters.

It is important to begin with one very poor but bothersome argument against the possibility of religious explanation so that it can be set quickly aside. It might be argued that religious convictions never can be used for the provision of explanations because the beliefs of religious communities are false. Even were it granted that all religious beliefs are false, this objection still would be doomed to failure. Its fault does not lie in the sweeping assumption that all religious convictions are untrue. Rather, the trouble lies in the linking of explanation with truth. If it were necessary for one's beliefs to be true in order for them to be used explanatorily, then it would have to be concluded that outmoded scientific theories never have been used to explain anything. Since Newton's theory recently has been replaced by Einstein's, Newton's theory would have to be judged to be neither a false explanation nor even an approximate one. Because his theory is false, it could never have been an explanation of any sort. Moreover, since current scientists cannot be certain whether present physical theories are true, it would have to be concluded that it cannot be known whether such theories are being used explanatorily. Obviously, it appears as if modern physicists are offering explanations of all manner of events. If theories must be true to be used explanatorily, there can be no alternative but to conclude that until Einstein's theory can be known to be true, it cannot be determined whether his views may be used for providing accurate, flawed, or even thoroughly false explanations. Indeed, if theories must be true to be used explanatorily, the very notion of a flawed or false explanation seems to slip into the realm of the unintelligible.

Of course, it must be admitted that there is some force to this first skeptical argument. Although the contention that all religious convictions are mistaken cannot be used to bar the possibility of religious explanations, it might be used to show that all such explanations are seriously defective. If all religious beliefs were false, then any explanations that might employ them would be fundamentally inadequate. Thus, while it might be of some academic interest to demonstrate that religious explanations are possible, there would seem to be little point in pursuing such explanations.

In careful recognition of the fact that the universal falsehood of religious beliefs would render religious explanations pointless, stress cannot be placed exclusively upon the demonstration of the mere possibility of religious explanations. Attention must also be focused upon the question of the possibility of adequate or true religious explanations. Therefore, for those aspects of the argument offered in the next few chapters that are concerned exclusively with the simple possibility of religious explanations, questions of truth will be ignored. However, when attention is turned to the possibility of adequate or true religious explanations, the contention that all religious beliefs are untrue will have to be considered more carefully.

A second sort of skeptical argument against the possibility of using religious discourse explanatorily might take inspiration from recent psychological investigations into religious activity. It might be argued that recent investigations have revealed that religious believers are deeply confused about the true nature of their commitments. Although members of various religious communities may believe sincerely that they are using their discourse in religious contexts for the purpose of making truth claims or for the provision of explanations, as a matter of fact, such religious devotees actually are doing something quite different. Suppose, for the sake of example, that Freud's work in *The Future of an Illusion* were found to be convincing. In light of his contention that religious ideas are psychological illusions, it might be argued that adherents to various religious traditions are not making assertions or offering explanations when they speak in religious contexts. Instead, they are trying to make their feelings of helplessness in the face of an overpowering physical environment more tolerable or they are manifesting various primal longings for intimacy and close, personal relationships. Should Freud's work on the psychology of religion be considered unsatisfactory, some other psychological study easily could be substituted. By replacing Freud's suggested functions of religious practice with some more favored set of psychological functions, the basic structure of this argument would remain intact. One could claim that since all adherents fulfill these specific psychological functions in religious contexts, then though members of religious communities truly might believe that they can use their religious utterances for making assertions or for providing explanations, in fact these or other theoretical roles can never be played by such linguistic behavior.

Obviously, up to this point there is nothing in this psychologically motivated argument that would preclude conclusively the possibility of using religious discourse explanatorily. Thus far, no reason has been given to suppose that various explanatory or other theoretical functions could not be fulfilled at the same time as certain psychological ones were being carried out. Nor does there seem to be anything that might preclude religious adherents from deserting the psychological functions of religion for explanatory ones. In brief, the mere fact that religious practice might fulfill certain psychological functions for many, or even all, devotees does nothing whatever to eliminate the possibility of using religious convictions in all sorts of other ways as well. To safely draw skeptical conclusions concerning the possibility of using religious discourse explanatorily, psychological surveys of actual religious practice must be coupled with arguments designed to show that it is impossible for believers to use their religious commitments in explanatory or other theoretical ways.

This same deficiency haunts any attempt to generate skeptical arguments from assorted linguistic studies. Suppose it could be shown that the actual linguistic practice of religious communities is completely devoid of any explanatory or theoretical elements. Suppose, for example, that no case could be found in which competent speakers used their religious commitments explanatorily. This would certainly be a rather startling fact about religious communities. But even if it were possible to substantiate this purported dearth of religious explanations, skeptical arguments concerning the possibility of religious explanations could not be developed without a further investigation into the reasons why religious adherents never use their commitments for the provision of explanations. After all, were it discovered that religious communities failed to use their commitments explanatorily simply because they took absolutely no interest in theoretical matters, nothing about this curious discovery would prohibit more interested believers from using their convictions explanatorily. Suppose it were discovered that the reason believers never proffered explanations was because they were rather dull-witted, lacking altogether any theoretical competencies. There would be no reason to conclude from this that more intellectually gifted believers also would be unable to supply religious explanations. Only if it could be shown that there is something in the very nature of religion or something in the structure of religious discourse that destroys the possibility of using religious utterances explanatorily would it be necessary to draw skeptical conclusions concerning the possibility of such explanations.[37]

Should the skeptic desire to supplement these imagined psychological or linguistic studies in a way that would yield the conclusion that religious explanations are impossible, several promising options offer themselves. For instance, it might be argued that the impossibility of providing religious explanations lies in the limitations of religious language. Perhaps it could be shown that religious adherents are concerned primarily with decidedly nontheoretical activities. Since they are interested in praising, invoking divine guidance, confessing sins, worshipping, and the like, and since the structure of their discourse has been shaped by the ways in which they wish to employ it, their religious language lacks the linguistic features necessary for carrying out specifically theoretical tasks. While the language of religious communities may be rich with the potential for expressing the hopes, fears, and confessions of devotees, it bears no potential for explanation.

Unfortunately, this particular line of argument appears hopelessly inadequate. In the first place, it seems to presuppose that there is some unique language, a religious language, that believers employ within religious contexts. But a quick inspection of such "religious languages" reveals that they are not actually separate languages at all. Religious communities in English-speaking countries typically use the English language in religious contexts. In similar fashion, religious communities in other countries usually adopt the native tongues of those lands. Occasionally, of course, religious communities can be found that refuse to utilize their native language. For the sake of tradition or ethnic identity, communities sometimes employ archaic forms of Latin or prefer to conduct services in such "mother tongues" as Italian or German. Nevertheless, it is always some natural language like German or Latin rather than some uniquely "religious language" that is used. Admittedly, religious communities may enrich their native languages by the addition of selected new terminology. But the grammatical structures as well as an overwhelmingly large proportion of the vocabulary of their native language is carried over intact into religious contexts. It would seem, then, that if the English, German, or other natural language embraced by various communities is linguistically sophisticated enough to allow explanations in everyday as well as highly specialized scientific contexts, there is little reason to suppose these same languages will be linguistically insufficient for the provision of explanations in religious settings.

Suppose it were granted that there is something so odd or peculiar about religious contexts that ordinary natural languages carried over into such contexts invariably are transformed into explanatorily impotent shadows of their former selves. Suppose it were true that "religious languages" are incapable of being used for the provision of explanations. There still would be no reason to conclude that religious explanations are impossible. The possibility of such impoverished "religious languages" changing and evolving with the changing interests and needs of religious communities is in no way precluded. Languages constantly are being shaped and reshaped to fulfill new functions. One need only consider the recent history of the English language as it has been molded by the demands not only of subatomic physics, but also of relativistic conceptions of space and time. Or consider the impact of the recent and startling developments in cosmological theory that have been stimulated by the discovery of a cosmic microwave radiation background.[38]

If the evolution of English within scientific contexts appears too exotic, consider the more mundane, though artificial, development of primitive languages found in the early pages of Wittgenstein's *Philosophical Investigations*. He writes:

A is building with buildingstones: there are blocks, pillars, slabs and beams. B has to pass the stones, and that in the order in which A needs them. For this purpose they use a language consisting of the words "block", "pillar", "slab", "beam". A calls them out;—B brings the stone which he has learnt to bring at such-and-such a call.—Conceive this as a complete primitive language.[39]

About all this language is good for is sending and fetching. But several pages farther along, Wittgenstein imagines a language that has been evolved from this primitive one by the addition of the equivalent of a simple number series, the words "this" and "there" used in conjunction with various pointing gestures, and a selection of color samples.[40] This expanded language allows not only the ability to command the fetching of types of building materials but also provides a way of directing laborers in the construction of a building. Laborers can be told how many of various types of building materials are needed and precisely what must be done with those materials.

If even the useful functions of this very elementary Wittgensteinian language can be expanded so powerfully by the addition of a few words and gestures, it is difficult to see why "religious languages" similarly could not be augmented and altered so as to fulfill new functions. Very young children begin with linguistic capacities as severely limited as those of Wittgenstein's builders. Nevertheless, these childish capacities are expanded and shaped in such potent ways that within a few years the linguistic resources of children are sufficient for the most subtle of scientific purposes. On a much grander scale, natural languages are evolving continually from the crudest and most rudimentary of conceptual tools into powerful structures capable of meeting the most sophisticated theoretical needs of contemporary humanity. If the linguistic capacities of Wittgensteinian builders, children, and even entire linguistic communities can evolve and change to meet new linguistic demands, there seems little reason to suppose that "religious languages" could not evolve similarly in ways to make what is currently linguistically impossible into the linguistic commonplace.

In the face of this extremely brief and inconclusive sketch of the evolutionary potential of languages, the skeptic of religious explanation easily might remain unmoved. After all, it might be countered, in the example of the developing child, a crucial point was omitted. The reason why young children can acquire new and more powerful linguistic capacities is because their parents already possess such capacities. Equipped with an elaborately developed language of their own, parents are able to shape the linguistic evolution of their children by drawing upon their own fully articulated linguistic competencies. Furthermore, the Wittgensteinian builders cannot be taken seriously. True, Wittgenstein envisioned his builders as increasing the sophistication of their primitive language without the aid of any previously established, more fully developed set of linguistic structures. Such an evolution of new linguistic capacities *ex nihilo* is impossible, however. What gives Wittgenstein's story its air of credibility is that he, as well as his readers, surreptitiously superimpose well-established linguistic abilities drawn from a long immersion in German or English linguistic communities upon his primitive workers. Thus, in both the developing child example and the Wittgensteinian one, there is no genuine evolution of new linguistic structures. Instead, there is only the commonplace activity of competent native speakers shaping the linguistic capacities of others in conformity with already extant linguistic patterns. Since in the case of "religious language" there is no fully elaborated linguistic structure that can be used as a model for evolution, it is impossible for religious communities to alter their language patterns with the intention of expanding their linguistic capabilities.

Obviously, this form of skeptical reply suffers from some rather severe shortcomings. First, it seems to presuppose that linguistic evolution requires the pre-existence of certain developed linguistic structures. That is, a language cannot evolve into any form or fulfill any new function that is not already extant. This supposition seems to preclude the possibility of the evolutionary emergence of novel linguistic structures. In short, there can be no creation of linguistic structures, only the utilization of previously existing ones. This seems to imply that the most sophisticated linguistic structures employed by current and future human speakers have pre-existed from eternity. Even if this presupposition with its bizarre implications could be granted somehow, there is another problem that must be faced by the proponent of this argument. This skeptical reply rests squarely upon a clearly counterfactual claim. It is simply not true that religious communities are without any elaborately sophisticated fund of linguistic models. Religious devotees do not live in a vacuum. If their concern is to develop ways of providing religious explanations, there is no reason to suppose that they cannot fashion the necessary tools after the models of explanations used in the natural sciences, in the social sciences, or in the course of everyday life.

A slightly different tack might be taken by the skeptic at this juncture. Instead of arguing that religious communities are unable to evolve new linguistic structures more suitable for theoretical purposes than those currently available, it might be argued that the impossibility of religious explanation is rooted in conceptual defects of the systems of belief employed by such communities. In other words, it might be argued that religious commitments are logically incoherent, inconsistent, unintelligible, or conceptually deficient in some other way. Thus, no matter what elaborate linguistic frameworks might be available in the present or evolved in the future, religious communities can never make use of them for theoretical purposes since their systems of belief are themselves cognitively defective.

Even if it could be demonstrated that the conceptual scheme of the religious believer is conceptually flawed in some fundamental way, heart could still be taken by reverting to a strategy employed by Hilary Putnam in "It Ain't Necessarily So." With regard to the concept of time travel, Putnam wrote:

I believe that an attempt to describe in ordinary language what time travel would be like can easily lead to absurdities and even downright contradictions. But if one has a mathematical technique of representing all the phenomena subsumed under some particular notion of 'time travel', then it is easy to work out a way of speaking, and even a way of thinking, corresponding to the mathematical technique.[41]

Putnam's argument here is that time travel may not be consistently explainable from within the conceptual framework of the ordinary American on the street. Nevertheless, recourse to frameworks made available through discoveries in theoretical mathematics can eliminate the conceptual inadequacies of time travel as expressed by way of ordinary, everyday concepts. Therefore, by switching from one system of concepts to another, theoretical defects can be eliminated, making for very smooth sailing indeed.[42] In similar fashion, unless the skeptic can offer some specific reason to the contrary, there appears to be no reason to deny that while the believer may have no way of providing consistent or coherent religious explanations from within current systems of religious concepts, he still has the liberty of switching to more adequate conceptual frameworks in his pursuit of acceptable religious explanations.

Though not yet clinically dead, the proponent of the possibility of religious explanations certainly is becoming increasingly speculative in his responses to skeptical attacks. Vexed by all these hopeful references to dream worlds of yet undiscovered conceptual frameworks and new linguistic structures, the skeptic might be tempted to shatter all such elaborate speculations by arguing that there are certain concepts that are so central to religious commitment that they would have to be retained intact no matter what alternative languages or conceptual schemes might be adopted by religious communities. Furthermore, it might be argued that these central concepts are downright contradictory. Thus, shift as he might among various languages and conceptual schemes, the believer always will be forced to carry along from one framework to another this central set of inconsistent notions. In brief, logical inconsistency will infect the believer's thinking no matter where he might venture.

There have been numerous attempts to argue against religious commitments in just this way. With regard to the orthodox Christian faith, many have argued that the concept of an immaterial, active God, the notion of disembodied existence, and other apparently central Christian concepts, being incoherent, suffer from irremediable logical defects.[43] For example, consider J. J. C. Smart's contention that "A logically necessary first cause . . . is not impossible in the way that giving you the moon is impossible; no, it is *logically* impossible. 'Logically necessary being' is a self-contradictory expression like 'round square'."[44] Suppose Smart were correct in this contention. Suppose also that some religious community were convinced that being a logically necessary first cause or a logically necessary being is so central to the concept of God that these attributes must be carried over into any new conceptual framework that might be adopted seriously by that community. Even at this rather desperate point, such communities might be able to slip through the skeptic's net of argument.

When pressed to similar straits in theoretical physics, where there would appear to be no linguistic or conceptual framework sufficient to allow a logically impeccable explanation of subatomic phenomena, many have suggested revisions in certain of the laws of logic employed by the sciences. In "The Logic of Quantum Mechanics," Hilary Putnam has argued forcefully that "*Logic is as empirical as geometry. It makes as much sense to speak of 'physical logic' as of 'physical geometry'. We live in a world with a non-classical logic.*"[45] Thus, "the *a prioricity* of logic and geometry vanishes as soon as *alternative logics* and *alternative geometries* begin to have serious physical application."[46] While it takes a pretty hefty dose of logical and mathematical acumen to develop genuine alternatives to classical systems of logic, such alternatives are being explored actively with an eye to solving certain very stubborn problems in the natural sciences.[47] Though few, if any, theologians have been adventuresome enough to try this radical path, there does appear to be some glimmer of precedent for this kind of move in the most rigorous of the physical sciences.

With this final maneuver, the contention that religious explanations are possible seems to be slipping into the nebulous realm of uncontestable speculation. Over the last few pages, gleanings from specific psychological or linguistic studies have been seen to be inadequate for skeptical purposes without some additional support from further arguments. Unfortunately, it has become surprisingly difficult to generate the needed augmentations. Arguments based upon purported linguistic or conceptual inadequacies can be dodged easily by appeal to the evolution of new linguistic or conceptual structures more fully adequate for the purposes of religious explanation. Even the powerful accusation of logical inconsistency seems unable to quell the crafty proponent of the possibility of religious explanation. In light of this brief survey of possible skeptical strategies, it is beginning to look as if the skeptic's supply of objections is about exhausted. In fact, it is beginning to look as if nothing whatever could possibly block the determined religious believer from using his commitments explanatorily.

To draw from this particular string of unsuccessful attacks the conclusion that religious explanations lie beyond the pale of critical scrutiny would be to risk serious error. As a matter of fact, there are numerous and rigid requirements that any purported religious explanation must be able to meet if it is to attain the status of genuine explanation. The impotence of the skeptical attack launched to this point lies in its misdirection. Thus far, no appeal whatever has been made to the actual requirements that must be met by any explanation, be it religious or nonreligious. Instead, skeptical arguments have been assembled along quite traditional lines. For example, skeptical strategies based upon standard criteria of consistency and coherence have been proffered. All such strategies have been dismissed rather summarily as misguided.

If the possibility and success of religious explanations are to be assessed adequately and properly, caution must be taken from recent developments in the philosophy of science. The attempt to assess the theoretical adequacy of claims in the physical sciences in light of historically honored canons of criticism has fallen recently upon hard times. With the evolution of alternative geometries, evaluations of physical theories of space and time by reference to the self-evident truths of Euclidean geometry have fallen into disrepute. In view of the intense intellectual effort being put into the formulation of usable alternatives to classical systems of logic, it even has become difficult to place much confidence in critiques that employ traditional logical principles as criteria of theoretical adequacy.

In light of this radical shaking of faith in traditional criteria of evaluation, the question of the possibility of religious explanations must be approached indirectly. Attention must be turned to actual cases of successful explanation in the hope of discovering the true constraints under which such explanations operate. By investigating the nature and structure of uncontroversially adequate explanations, the real basis upon which such explanations are constructed may be illuminated in a way that will shed light upon the question of the possibility of explanations within the religious sphere. Since the physical sciences provide a wealth of paradigmatically successful explanations, the next chapter will investigate the nature of explanations in physics. Subsequent chapters will be devoted to applying insights gleaned from this investigation of physics to the problem of determining whether explanations of the same sort are also possible in religious contexts.

Before turning to a consideration of successful scientific explanations, however, one last form of skeptical argument must be addressed. This type of argument comes from an entirely different angle. It might be argued that religious explanations are impossible because any community that develops and employs the conceptual machinery necessary for providing such explanations is no longer religious in its concerns. Here the claim is not that religious communities are unable to evolve more elaborate conceptual schemes or linguistic structures.

Rather, the claim is that such an evolution would be from religious interests to nonreligious ones. To attempt to provide explanations is no longer to be involved in an activity or practice that is peculiarly religious. Perhaps it is to engage in pseudoscience or superstition. But whatever it might be, it is certainly not religion.

There seems to be a hint of this sort of argument in Wittgenstein's *Lectures and Conversations on Aesthetics, Psychology and Religious Belief* where he remarks:

Suppose, for instance, we knew people who foresaw the future; make forecasts for years and years ahead; and they described some sort of Judgement Day. Queerly enough, even if there were such a thing, and even if it were more convincing than I have described but, belief in this happening wouldn't be at all a religious belief.[48]

While he is not concerned specifically with explanatory uses of language in this passage, Wittgenstein does seem to be arguing that factual talk about a Judgement Day misses the uniquely religious aspect of religious discourse. More pointedly, a few paragraphs later, he argues:

We don't talk about hypothesis, or about high probability. Nor about knowing.

In a religious discourse we use such expressions as : "I believe that so and so will happen," and use them differently to the way in which we use them in science.[49]

Here Wittgenstein seems to be cautioning against too close a parallel between the linguistic activities of scientists and those of religious adherents. Religion just is not the same sort of thing as science. Unfortunately, the brevity of his remarks coupled with the fact that his comments are recorded only at second hand in these passages leaves the details of Wittgenstein's thought on the uniqueness of religious discourse unsatisfyingly sketchy. It is difficult to decide precisely where he found the crucial differences between scientific and religious discourse to lie. Thus it is difficult to determine whether and, if so, why he thought that the attempt to use religious discourse explanatorily is an abandonment of the unique features and purposes of religion.[50]

While the details of Wittgenstein's own thought may remain frustratingly inaccessible, at least one thread in the complicated fabric woven by one of his most avid followers, D. Z. Phillips, does seem to embody clearly this particular line of argument. Like Wittgenstein, Phillips takes great pains to argue that true religion is not like science. In "Philosophy, Theology and the Reality of God" he concludes:

Both logic and science are *public* in so far as it can be decided whether a statement is logical or illogical, or whether a given practice is scientific or not. Illogical and non-scientific statements are refutable. But because of the nature of theology one may only say that a religious statement is refuted by *a* theology. There is no analogy here with either logic or science.[51]

These are only the beginnings of disanalogy that Phillips finds between the sciences and religion. He also believes that although the sciences are concerned with matters of fact and have clear procedures for testing for the existence of various entities, the question of God's existence is neither a question of fact nor is it a question that might be resolved by some generally accepted testing procedure.[52] Furthermore, while the sciences may be able to give answers to causal questions, any attempt to implicate God in causal chains involves a serious misunderstanding of the nature of God.[53] Beyond all this, he argues that while the sciences are concerned with contingent things, God is neither contingent nor a thing.[54]

It should not be thought that Phillips lumps all religious devotees into this nonscientistic camp. He readily acknowledges that there are many misguided believers who are convinced that their religious commitments are analogous in important ways to the scientific enterprise. As he writes:

There are some people the truth of whose religion depends on the way things go in their lives. Things may not go well here and now, but unless the ultimate facts, the eschatological situation, are favourable in some sense or other, faith has been a hoax and a failure. . . . The kind of difference religion makes to life is the difference between a set of empirical facts being or not being the case.[55]

Nevertheless, his opinion of this type of religious commitment is not very high. Phillips argues, "I do not find it impressive religiously. Indeed, I should want to go further and say that it has little to do with religion, being much closer to superstition."[56] His deep dissatisfaction with this type of religious community does not lie simply with the apparently selfish motives of those who are eagerly anticipating an unending, self-indulgent future life. Rather, Phillips is convinced that believers of this sort have misconceived radically the very nature of the religious sphere. As he puts it, "What they have done is to impose the grammar of *another* mode of discourse on religion—namely, our talk about physical objects."[57]

According to Phillips, then, to suppose that religious purposes are in any signficant way analogous to the explanatory or other theoretical concerns of the sciences is to misconstrue the essence of religion. In fact, to think that religion might be able to offer explanations or might be able to fulfill the sorts of theoretical functions fulfilled by the sciences is to lose sight entirely of the uniquely religious element in religion. In the succinct summary of Phillips, "There is no theoretical understanding of the reality of God."[58]

With claims as strong and controversial as these, one would do well to look to their evidential support. In defense of his position, Phillips argues that he is simply drawing his conclusions from a careful examination of actual religious practice. He says:

> "*Who says* that religion is a distinct and separable field . . . ?" I find this question extremely odd. It is not a matter of anyone *saying* that there are differences between modes of discourse, but *looking* to see whether there are any such differences, and if there are, *showing* their character.[59]

A few pages farther along he adds:

> One can only give a satisfactory account of religious beliefs if one pays attention to the roles they play in people's lives. By comparing these roles with others one can bring out the grammar of religious belief. This is what I tried to do by comparing confessing, thanking, and asking in prayer, with confessing, thanking and asking in other contexts.[60]

This rather simple and straightforward confession of philosophical method must be approached with care, however. It just has been seen that Phillips does not regard all religious beliefs and practices with equal seriousness. Instead, many are dismissed quickly as nothing more than superstition. Thus, there must be something more to his method than this appeal to gleanings from actual linguistic practice would seem to suggest.

A glance at the reply that Phillips offers to those who take his affirmations of method at face value quickly confirms the suspicion that there is much more than elementary linguistic surveys behind Phillips's conclusions about the nature and structure of religion. Both Kai Nielsen[61] and John Hick[62] have objected that if one seriously investigates the actual linguistic practice of many believers, conclusions that are at variance with Phillips's will follow. To the surprise of many, Phillips readily conceded this point. He then went on to argue:

> I do not wish to defend those people whose religious beliefs can be described adequately in Hick's terms. I only wish to stress that there is another kind of belief in God. The difference between them could be brought out by comparing the roles which worship plays in the lives of the respective believers.[63]

So, suspicions raised by the simplicity of Phillips's professed method are justified fully. In fact, he does not rely upon just any actual religious practice. Rather, he finds the linguistic behavior of certain religious communities to be laden with insights while the behavior of other communities must be brushed quickly aside as superficial, not truly religious, or even superstitious.

To get a fuller grasp of his methodology, it is helpful to consider the reasons why Phillips so quickly dismissed the importance of Hick's believers. There seem to be two such reasons. In the first place, Phillips is convinced that many of the beliefs of such people are philosophically indefensible. With regard to specific examples, Phillips argues:

> To believe that the only meaning that the immortality of the soul can have is that of survival after death, and that the only meaning eternity can have is that of infinite duration, may have various effects on one's religious beliefs. If, as a philosopher, one believes these things, one may find one's faith being destroyed, because one can see, intellectually, that it makes no sense to speak of surviving death. Because philosophy has shown the belief to be meaningless, one is forced to give it up.[64]

To say the least, these contentions of meaninglessness are controversial ones.[65] Nevertheless, it is sufficient for present purposes to note only that one major reason why Phillips believes large branches of orthodox Christianity can be dismissed from further consideration is because many of their central convictions are either meaningless or false. If it could be shown that these commitments are fully meaningful and at least not obviously false, then this particular source of dismissal effectively would be removed.

The second reason why Phillips finds the suggestions of Hick and Nielsen of so little interest is that he is convinced that devotees to such beliefs misconstrue the essential nature of religion and so fail to recognize the uniquely religious element in their Christian heritage. As he writes, with specific regard to the question of God's reality:

> When God's existence is construed as a matter of fact, it is taken for granted that the concept of God is at home within the conceptual framework of the reality of the physical world. It is as if we said, "We know where the assertion of God's existence belongs, we understand what kind of assertion it is; all we need do is determine its truth or falsity."[66]

But, Phillips contends, this construal of the reality of God along lines modeled on the questions asked and answered in the sciences obscures the truly religious aspect of the conviction that God is real. The question of God's existence has nothing in common with existence questions concerning electrons or chromosomes. In Phillips's view, "Seeing that there is a God in this context is synonymous with seeing the possibility of eternal love."[67] In general then, "Religious beliefs are not a class of second-best statements, hypotheses awaiting confirmation, or conjectures longing to be borne out."[68] Instead, if they are to be fully appreciated in their uniquely religious aspect, such truths must be conceived along quite different lines.

As a brief indication of the direction that must be taken to illuminate properly the genuine nature of religious truth, Phillips writes:

If a person says, "I have come to see the truth of the saying, that it is better to give than to receive," and another person denies this, this is not like a dispute between business partners over whether a proposed venture will in fact materialize in profit. It is a dispute over the worth of generosity. And if someone has come to see the truth of it, that doesn't mean that he has assessed generosity by means of some measure other than generosity. What he has come to see is the beauty of generosity. When he says there is a lot of truth in it, what this comes to in practical terms is that he strives after it and tries to regulate his life accordingly.[69]

It is important to notice that Phillips believes a misapprehension of religious truths along factual or scientific lines not only misrepresents the nature of such truths, it also intolerably skews the performance of religious rituals and ceremonies. Consider a mother who brings her baby to the Virgin Mary. Suppose this particular mother is seeking protection for her child from the Virgin and hopes to induce Mary to watch over her baby, keeping it from various sorts of mishap. According to Phillips, the bringing of the baby to the Virgin under such ritualistic circumstances would be reduced to an act of superstition. In this setting, there are two reasons why "the religious character of the homage paid to the Virgin is completely ignored."[70] He explains:

Firstly, there is the trust in non-existent, quasi-causal connections: the belief that someone long dead called the Virgin Mary can, if she so desires, determine the course of an individual's life. . . . Secondly, the Virgin Mary is seen as a means to ends which are intelligible without reference to her. . . . In other words, the act of homage to the Virgin Mary has no importance in itself; she is reduced to the status of a lucky charm.[71]

As is abundantly clear from the strategy taken throughout the course of the preceding pages, one of the main thrusts of the following chapters will be to offer an argument in direct opposition to these claims of Phillips. The next four chapters will be devoted to an argument that is designed to show not only that religious belief and practice are, in large measure, rigidly analogous to certain aspects of the scientific enterprise, but also that there is at least some possibility that certain religious explanations are actually true. In light of the work of Phillips, however, a final chapter must be devoted to showing that a rigid parallel between religious explanations and certain kinds of explanations offered in the sciences in no way destroys whatever features are essential to a rich and genuinely religious tradition. Before any of this protracted argument can be developed, attention must be turned to a careful scrutiny of the nature of scientific explanations. Unless such explanations are understood clearly, there can be little hope of uncovering ways in which religious belief and practice can be envisioned profitably as importantly analogous to activities in the scientific realm.

III

Scientific Explanations

—

IT IS DIFFICULT TO generate much optimism concerning the possibility of providing religious explanations that are capable of meeting the strict requirements met in the sciences. Outside of the particular skeptical tradition sketched in the first two chapters, one occasionally finds a writer who is sympathetic to the basic claim that religious assertions can be used for the provision of explanations. For example, in his discussion of Alisdair MacIntyre's "Is Understanding Religion Compatible with Believing?" Richard Brandt concedes:

Religious language has to be construed as primarily descriptive or explanatory, like the language of science: explanatory of the existence of a world, of its order, of historical events of large scale, or of significant events in the personal life of the believer.[1]

But while willing to agree that religious utterances may be used explanatorily, such writers usually are pessimistic regarding the possibility of offering religious explanations that are able to satisfy rigorous standards of plausibility. Therefore, although he agrees that religious devotees might offer explanations by making reference to various aspects of their religious commitment, as might be expected, Brandt is rather more impressed with the promise latent in recent developments in the sciences. Convinced that science finally has come into its own, he appears more than willing to conclude that, whatever power religious claims might have enjoyed in past ages, contemporary needs are served best by the various sciences. As he notes with regard to one specific case:

A candid theologian must admit . . . that it would have been reasonable to grade St. Thomas's system more highly, in point of meaningfulness, in his day than in our own. For the explanatory work done by his system in his day was greater than it can do today when, for instance, the theory of evolution does in a more detailed way some of the jobs which St. Thomas's fifth argument allocates to God.[2]

If there is to be any reasonable hope of arguing for the possibility of plausible religious explanations in the face of this deeply entrenched pessimism, something of the nature and structure of scientific explanations must be revealed that can be used as a standard by which to judge the intellectual integrity of purportedly adequate religious explanations. Rather discouragingly, it is difficult to come by any simple standard that is universally acknowledged to be employed in the sciences. Scientific explanations seem to come in a bewildering variety of types. They appear to vary considerably from one context to another. Furthermore, it seems that types of explanations that are accepted uncontroversially within the context of one scientific discipline are rejected immediately as impermissible when introduced into other fields. In fact, even within the confines of one specific discipline, it appears that types of explanations offered by one group of theorists often are looked upon with contempt by competing communities of investigators.

Even the briefest survey of explanations offered in the different sciences quickly discloses the wide diversity among them. Consider, for instance, the powerful ways in which the scientific and cultural climate of his time affected the nature of the explanations offered by Charles Darwin. Finding himself in a culture deeply immersed in the intricacies of Christian religion and realizing that his own discipline was dominated strongly by theistically tinged biological theories, Darwin's evolutionary explanations were designed specifically for his theologically attuned audiences. His prolonged discussion of the similarities between human beings and other biological creatures was shaped carefully not only to allow the explanation of these similarities along evolutionary lines, but also to emphasize the way in which his new explanations cut against traditional Christian claims regarding the uniqueness of the place of human beings in the overall scheme of things.[3] Since his work was undertaken among contemporaries almost as thoroughly infatuated with the work of Thomas Malthus as they were with specifically Christian convictions, many of Darwin's evolutionary explanations also were molded in conformity with popular socioeconomic themes. Thus, many of the struggles for survival depicted by Darwin in explanation of various biologically adaptive phenomena turned out to be thoroughly Malthusian battles for limited food supplies, conflicts triggered by the stresses of overpopulation.[4]

Although current evolutionary theorists are proud to trace their theoretical roots to the work of Charles Darwin, their own biological explanations are in large measure markedly dissimilar to those offered by their forebear. In large part, this difference between the explanations of Darwin and his successors can be attributed to the simple fact that current biological studies are undertaken within an intellectual and cultural setting rather different from Darwin's. Because of the increasing secularization of the sciences, few contemporary biologists find themselves occupied with peculiarly religious or theological concerns. In like manner, since Malthusian economics have fallen from celebrity status, there is little current interest devoted to casting explanations of biological phenomena in Malthusian terms. While economic themes may emerge occasionally in the course of contemporary evolutionary explanations, most current biological accounts are seasoned heavily with genetic and biochemical theory instead. Indeed, few living biologists can claim anything approaching the kind of expertise in Malthusian theory that was enjoyed by Darwin.[5]

It should not be thought, however, that all the differences between the types of explanations offered by Darwin and those suggested by current biological theorists can be attributed to broad and dramatic differences in cultural context. Much less striking differences in context have their influential effects as well. For example, to take a rather common sort of difference among contexts, consider the way in which differences among the composition and needs of various audiences help to shape the exact structure of scientific explanation offered. In giving an explanation of why diamonds are formed under intense heat and pressure, the account given to professional geologists typically differs quite radically from the explanation provided beginners in geological studies. Should the audience shift from geologists to chemists or physicists or to reasonably educated nonprofessionals or to first-graders, the explanation offered would have to be altered even more drastically. In fact, once something of the vast diversity of ways in which shifts in contexts effect shifts in explanatory structure is glimpsed, hopes of systematizing the ways in which explanations are trivially or nontrivially reshaped by alterations in context quickly fade.

This dream of systematic organization seems all the more distant and unrealizable in the face of the recognition that factors other than contextual ones have their influence upon the structures of scientific explanations. Explanatory structures appear to vary from one science to another. Even though cultural climate and audience composition may be kept rigidly invariant, the structure of explanations that are considered rigorously scientific within the confines of one discipline often are looked upon with extreme skepticism or even repudiated when introduced into the sphere of another science. Probably the most thoroughly discussed example of a structure deemed acceptable by one science while being generally rejected by another is the teleological structure of certain explanations offered in biology. In "Goal-directed Processes in Biology," Ernest Nagel tried to capture the basic notion of a teleological explanation. He wrote:

A commonly recognized but loosely delimited trait of biological organisms, a trait that is often said to distinguish living from inanimate things, is the apparently purposive character of living organisms. Teleological language reflects this distinction. Although there is no exhaustive set of criteria for distinguishing teleological locutions from those which are not, the occurrence of certain expressions in statements is usually a fairly reliable criterion that the statements are teleological. For example, the statements "The purpose of the liver is to secrete bile," "The function of the kidneys is to eliminate waste products from the blood," and "Peacocks spread their tail feathers in order to attract peahens," are teleological.[6]

Although there remains much controversy over the precise importance of teleological explanations like these for the purpose of biological investigation,[7] it cannot be denied that nearly all biologists would accept such teleologically structured explanations as perfectly appropriate within the confines of their own scientific discipline. Nevertheless, were a trained physicist to offer explanations of the behavior of rebounding billiard balls or falling weights in terms of the purposes or goals of such objects, he would soon find himself the subject of severe reprimand. Little more would be required to undercut effectively the force of such explanations than the simple remark that billiard balls and falling weights have no purposes or goals.

It might be tempting to conclude from the fact that biologists show this preference for a type of explanation generally repudiated by practicing physicists that all such major differences in explanatory taste stem from basic, interdisciplinary differences. Since even within the same discipline deep differences over acceptable explanatory structures frequently emerge, this particular temptation must be resisted. Consider, for instance, the recent history of theoretical psychology. Many current theorists are influenced powerfully by the thought of Sigmund Freud. In offering explanations of human behavior, such theorists quite typically and naturally make explanatory reference to various unperceived entities and forces like egos and unconscious drives.[8] While Freudians find such references both acceptable and unavoidable, psychologists trained under the influence of B. F. Skinner find them thoroughly objectionable. Unless they can be stripped entirely of essential reference to the unobservable, Skinnerians would argue, such accounts of human behavior must be dismissed as utterly unscientific.[9]

This brief glimpse of the extreme diversity of ways in which scientific explanations can be shaped and altered to meet the exigencies of assorted circumstances should be sufficient to illustrate the need for some sort of limiting principle. Unless some method can be devised whereby this vast range of scientific explanatory types can be narrowed, the task of relating scientific explanations to the religious sphere will never get beyond the promissory stage. Instead, it will become bogged down interminably in an attempt to distinguish among all these available types. Happily, however, the variety of explanatory structures that may stand as candidates for analogy to the religious sphere can be reduced quite drastically in a most natural way.

As has been emphasized repeatedly in the course of developing the themes introduced in the first two chapters, the common element in the religious skepticism of Huxley, Freud, and all the others who fall within that same general tradition is a conviction that religious belief and practice cannot stand up to the standards of intellectual integrity that are expected to be met by the most rigorous of the sciences. Therefore, any attempt to rehabilitate the cognitive integrity of religious commitment will fall seriously short of its goal if standards of intellectual acceptability are drawn from a scientific discipline about which there is any reasonable suspicion concerning its rigorously scientific status. Since there is some dispute over whether the social and perhaps even the biological sciences are properly up to snuff,[10] arguments based upon comparisons between religious explanations and those offered in such suspect disciplines cannot be expected to establish fully the intellectual integrity of religious conviction. But the physical sciences, particularly if attention is turned away from the increasingly problematic branch of quantum physics, generally appear to be regarded as above reproach. Therefore, by limiting the scope of candidates to the types of explanation found in unproblematic branches of physics, it may be possible to respond adequately to the sort of skepticism elaborated in the previous two chapters.

Unfortunately, this restriction to physical explanations still seems to leave a rather broad spectrum of types. For instance, sometimes it is thought that an adequate physical explanation has been provided by the simple recognition that certain things fall into certain categories. This explanatory type clearly would be exemplified in cases where, in explanation of why the materials in certain test tubes do what they do, it is noted that such materials are metallic substances or gases or positively charged particles. Sometimes it seems sufficient for explanatory purposes to cite some general regularity or physical law. Thus, in explanation of why a rubber ball falls at some particular rate of speed, it is usually enough to remark that all solids do that or, more precisely, that some particular law of motion or acceleration is being observed by the ball. On yet other occasions, it may be appropriate to disclose certain hidden connections which obtain. For example, in explaining the behavior of a metal bar on a table, it may be sufficient to reveal that there is a magnet under the table that is moving in some special way. Rather frequently, explanations are offered by making reference to various operative mechanisms. In explaining why the hands of a clock move in the ways they do, it is usually appropriate to discuss the grinding of gears and the tensions of springs.[11]

Numerous attempts have been made to organize this apparent diversity of explanatory structures by reducing such seemingly different types to one, or perhaps several, basic kinds. One of the most famous as well as influential attempts at such simplification originated with the positivist struggle to show that all legitimate forms of scientific explanation can be restructured in accordance with a single rigid pattern. Following in this tradition, Carl Hempel and Paul Oppenheim tried to specify the features that would be possessed by explanations conforming to this ideal type. In the course of constructing their paradigm, they wrote:

We divide an explanation into two major constituents, the *explanandum* and the *explanans*. By the explanandum, we understand the sentence describing the phenomenon to be explained . . . ; by the explanans, the class of those sentences which are adduced to account for the phenomenon. . . . The explanans falls into two subclasses; one of these contains certain sentences C_1,

$C_2, \ldots, C_k$, which state specific antecedent conditions; the other is a set of sentences $L_1, L_2, \ldots, L_r$ which represent general laws.[12]

Among additional constraints which they placed upon their ideal pattern, Hempel and Oppenheim argued that the

explanandum must be a logical consequence of the explanans; in other words, the explanandum must be logically deducible from the information contained in the explanans; for otherwise, the explanans would not constitute adequate grounds for the explanandum.[13]

Although both Hempel and Oppenheim seemed to believe that an explanation following these rather strict lines would provide a perfect example of the most rigorous of scientific explanatory structures, they also appeared to think that this idealized form might be a bit too restrictive. So, while it obviously would be very nice if all scientific explanations would conform to this fixed, deductive pattern, they finally conceded that certain liberalizations would have to be introduced in order to encompass adequately the full range of acceptable explanatory types. By relaxing the requirements for explanatory propriety to permit the introduction of statistical laws in the place of general ones and to allow the relation between the explanans and the explanandum to be an inductive rather than a deductive one, Hempel and Oppenheim hoped they could encompass more fully the range of explanatory types that must be accepted as uncontroversially scientific.[14]

The influence of this particular attempt to characterize adequately the structure of scientific explanations spread well beyond the bounds of the philosophy of science to affect the arguments of numerous thinkers interested in the explanatory capacities of religion. For instance, Basil Mitchell was willing to argue that religious discourse could be used for the provision of explanations, but not for the provision of the rigorous sorts of explanations that are commonplace in the sciences. It is extremely interesting to note the reason why Mitchell rejected the possibility of any scientifically structured religious explanation. In his discussion of one particular sort of religious explanation, Mitchell wrote, "It is a causal explanation of a different kind from that which is customary in the sciences. It does not rely on general laws established by the observation of many instances."[15] More generally, he said:

It has to be conceded that theological explanations cannot be of a scientific kind. In so far as they succeed in achieving a gain in intelligibility they do so not by suggesting a hypothesis from which deductions are made which are subject to strict experimental test.[16]

Though he does not acknowledge explicitly his dependence upon the work of Hempel and Oppenheim, these passages seem to indicate that Mitchell takes their suggested ideal explanatory structure for the sciences as normative. In fact, Mitchell appears to opt for the more restricted and rigid of their suggestions. In Mitchell's view, it is because religious explanations do not involve strict deductions from general laws that they are incapable of meeting the high standards of explanatory adequacy imposed in the sciences. Along similar lines, Frederick Ferré assigns a nonscientific status to religious explanations. Characterizing scientific explanations, he argues that beside the capacity to be tested by experience and the capacity to be expanded to handle new ranges of data, scientific explanations require that there be a "subsumption of the explained phenomenon under a uniformity or, as John Hospers insists, a 'law.'"[17] Because religious explanations cannot conform to the structure of scientific explanations, the structure suggested by Hempel and Oppenheim,[18] Ferré tries to salvage their theoretical usefulness by introducing a second sort of legitimate explanatory structure. He writes:

Perhaps there might be a point to making a verbal distinction between the class of scientific explanations (explanations-A) and the class of all other kinds of explanations (explanations-B) which serve similar functions without employing the same logical criteria.[19]

If religious assertions are to serve any explanatory function at all, it must be as explanations of type B since it is a "fact (a *logical* fact!) that language about a supernatural God cannot function adequately as a scientific explanation."[20] As one final example of this pervasive argumentative strategy, consider the work of Ian Ramsey. With regard to the nature of science, he writes:

Suppose we have discovered . . . the invariant, 100° Centigrade, for boiling water. Then we can *deduce* that this water here and now in this lab at this particular time boils at 100° Centigrade. This is something which can be *verified* precisely. Already we have the three stages characteristic of scientific procedure: the generalization expressing some invariant; the deduction; the verification.[21]

Since this investigative procedure is inappropriate for religious inquiry, it must be concluded that religious explanations cannot be modeled after this Hempelian paradigm. As Ramsey puts it, it is crucial to remember "the logical diversity of science and theology" [22] and so to rest content with the conclusion that "what the scientist does and what the theologian does, each in his own way, is to discover the logical patterns of this divine visual language as best he can." [23]

Had Hempel and Oppenheim's original suggestion or some more liberalized version of it been able to capture adequately the essential structure underlying the apparent diversity of explanatory types used in the physical sciences, it might not be too difficult to follow in the steps of Mitchell, Ferré, or Ramsey. It would be necessary only to determine which idealized structure fully embodies the true nature of scientific explanations, explicate that structure in detail, and then carry the resulting standard over to religious contexts. It then would be fairly easy to determine how well purportedly adequate religious explanations stand up under the pressure of extended scrutiny. Probably, in concert with Mitchell, Ferré, and Ramsey, it would have to be concluded that religious explanations cannot meet adequately the standards of Hempel and Oppenheim.

Disappointingly, this relatively straightforward approach cannot be taken. There appear to be very strong reasons to suppose that the original project of Hempel and Oppenheim as well as any variant sophistications based upon their initial suggestions cannot succeed. [24] In recognition of this generally acknowledged failure of their program, several alternative courses of speculation have arisen. Some theorists have argued that Hempel and Oppenheim were correct in their conviction that some underlying unity of structure can be deciphered from the chaos of extant types. Their only mistake was in the selection of the particular structure they took to be the ideal one. By substituting some other structure, or perhaps some manageably small set of preferred structures, the diversity of sorts of scientific explanation can be organized effectively and coherently. [25] Other theorists have not been so optimistic. Faced with the intimidating complexity of the problem, they have argued that any reasonably simple scheme of organization is not likely to be forthcoming in the foreseeable future. Instead, investigators must rest content with a much more piecemeal approach. Sticking to the plodding, detailed explication of various diverse explanatory structures, inquisitive eyes always should be open to the possibility of discerning broadly underlying structural similarities between explanatory types. But optimism regarding the imminent revelation of pervasive, basic explanatory kinds should remain guarded at best. [26]

Obviously, it would be nice to know whether all scientific explanations can be unified under some single or manageably small set of structural types. It would be even nicer to know, should such unification be possible, precisely which structural types are the basic ones. But, regrettably, given the present state of controversy over these issues, it appears to be impossible to select any one of the several available resolutions with any degree of confidence. So, in order to skirt this matter entirely, a somewhat different tack must be taken. Rather than siding with one particular current option concerning the true nature of scientific explanation and then carrying this particular alternative over to the religious sphere, the question of the possibility of unifying all scientifically acceptable explanations under one or several basic types will be bypassed altogether simply by selecting for special attention one specific sort of explanation that is peculiarly germane to the question of the possibility of religious explanation.

It is important to understand the exact nature of this choice. No claim whatsoever is being made regarding the importance or unimportance of this particular sort of explanatory structure to the theoretical articulation of physical theories. Nor is any claim being made regarding the relative worth of this sort of explanatory structure in comparison with other structural types offered in the sciences. It may very well be that this particular explanatory structure is a relatively unimportant one that is used only on an infrequent basis. Finally, it must be stressed that no claim is being made regarding the ultimacy of this particular sort of explanatory structure. It may very well be that this structure is reducible to some other more central or fundamental one. On the other hand, it is being claimed that this explanatory type is used, at least sometimes, for the provision of explanations in uncontroversial branches of the physical sciences. In fact, it is used frequently in the most reputable of scientific contexts for the purpose of explaining the physical behavior of macroscopic objects. Furthermore, when so used, this particular structure is considered to be above epistemological suspicion. That is, when properly employed, explanations of this type are acceptable as fully adequate and rigorously scientific.

It also should be noted that because the explanatory structure singled out for consideration here is not necessarily the only one that is commonly accepted as rigorously scientific, should the following attempt to carry this particular structure over to the religious sphere fail to provide any constructive insights regarding the possibility of religious explanations, it would not be necessary to conclude that religious explanations are incapable of formulation in accordance with rigorously scientific standards. There might yet be some other pattern that, if carried over to the religious sphere, would allow the formulation of uncontroversially adequate religious explanations. Alternatively, should the presently chosen structure prove fruitful when carried over to the religious case, it must not be assumed that all religious explanations will automatically fall into this one mold. It may be that other explanatory structures, were they to be carried over in a similar way, would permit other sorts of fully adequate religious explanations.

With these few precautionary comments in mind, attention can be turned to the detailed elucidation of our chosen type of scientific explanation. In an introductory way, Romano Harré offers an illuminating preliminary sketch of this particular sort of explanatory structure. He writes:

Theories are seen as solutions to a peculiar style of problem: namely, 'Why is it that the patterns of phenomena are the way they are?' A theory answers this question by supplying an account of the constitution and behavior of those things whose interactions with each other are responsible for the manifested patterns of behavior. . . . This it does . . . by conceiving of a model for the presently unknown mechanism of nature. Such a model is, in the first instance, no more than a putative analogue for the real mechanism. The model is itself modelled on things and materials and processes which we do understand. In a creative piece of theory construction, the relation between the model of the unknown mechanism and what it is modelled on is also a relation of analogy.[27]

Several main points can be extracted easily from this initial characterization. First of all, Harré notes that the scientist in quest of an explanation of this type must begin by delineating as precisely as possible the material he wishes to explain. It should be emphasized that this material is not some set of particular facts. While it must be admitted that scientists are interested occasionally in the explanation of idiosyncratic features of specific occurrences,[28] the sort of case envisioned here is one in which the scientist is concerned primarily to explain why general patterns of phenomena are manifested within the world rather than to account for specific and uniquely occurring events. To put this point by way of an example, the kind of explanation Harré has in mind is one that is designed to explain why all bodies of a certain type rebound in specifiable kinds of ways rather than one designed to provide an understanding of why Jimmy's red ball bounced off his father's head in some peculiar way at noon yesterday.[29]

Second, Harré points out that once the range of patterns to be explained has been selected, the scientist will move toward his explanation out of a conviction that there must be some mechanism that is responsible for the occurrence of the chosen patterns. That is, the scientific quest for an explanation of this sort is guided always by the supposition that patterns of phenomena are neither arbitrarily imposed upon nature by theory-laden observers nor the mere manifestation of pure chance. Instead, due to the operation of governing mechanisms, patterns of phenomena are determined to be just the way they are and not otherwise. In stressing this point, it should be cautioned that Harré's use of "mechanism" must not be taken in an overly restrictive, clockwork sense. Although the grinding gears of clocks certainly would count as mechanisms in Harré's sense, magnetic fields, social institutions, or anything else that might be thought to control or determine patterns of events would fall comfortably under this heading as well.

Third, inspired by the conviction that there must be some mechanism that is responsible for the selected patterns, the scientist must turn to the elucidation of the nature of his hypothesized operative mechanism. In searching for an understanding of the posited entity, the scientist will begin by casting about for some pattern of phenomena that is relevantly analogous to the pattern or patterns for which he seeks an explanation. If some relevantly analogous pattern of occurrences is discovered for which an explanatory mechanism already is known, the scientist then can move to the slightly more precise hypothesis that his chosen patterns of phenomena not only are controlled by a governing mechanism, but that they are controlled by a mechanism similar to the one that governs the relevantly analogous pattern. Once he has characterized his hypothesized mechanism in this initial way, the scientist finally can focus his energies upon honing the suggested mechanism into a more sharply explanatory tool.

Before looking at an example that can be used to put some flesh upon this preliminarily sketched explanatory structure, the relation of Harré's work in the philosophy of science to our attempt to rehabilitate the cognitive integrity of religious discourse must be clarified. It is important to realize that, for our purposes, Harré's subsequent analyses and his resulting substantive philosophical claims need not be embraced. For example, there is no need to conclude with Harré that the sort of explanation he has described is the most fundamental type found in the sciences. Quite to the contrary, it is possible to remain uncommitted on this point by simply noting that, whether or not this specific explanatory structure is basic or crucial to the sciences in some special way, it is nevertheless a kind of explanation that sometimes shows up in the course of scientific research activities. In similar fashion, it is possible to remain uncommitted with regard to Harré's attempt to resolve Humean problems of induction. Although Harré tries to capitalize upon the fact that scientists suppose governing mechanisms determine the occurrence of regularities, this whole controversial issue can be skirted safely by refusing to step beyond the basic claim that scientists do make such assumptions in the course of pursuing explanations of this particular sort. Whether they ever can be epistemologically justified or whether they should be condemned as ultimately irrational can be left unaddressed and unresolved. It is sufficient for our purposes to point out that scientists within this explanatory context are typically so motivated. In short, Harré's initial sketch of this one type of scientific explanation should be taken as nothing more than a convenient point of departure.[30]

With these brief clarifying remarks out of the way, attention can be turned safely to an illustrative example. Suppose there were a scientist who wished to explain the expansion and contraction of balloons at varying altitudes. According to this model of explanation, this theorist would begin by assembling a set of generalizations regarding the pattern of occurrences he was concerned to explain. His generalizations might range from very primitive observations specifying nothing more than that rising balloons expand while descending ones contract to much more refined ones in which changes in various altitudes are mathematically correlated with changes in expansion and contraction. Once his chosen patterns had been drawn together in this fashion, the scientist could then move on to the supposition that there must be some specific mechanism that makes balloons expand and contract as they do rather than expand and contract in other ways, suddenly disappear, melt, turn into gold, or behave in other diverse ways. This supposition would allow him to begin searching for some relevantly analogous pattern of phenomena for which he believes the governing mechanism already is known. Looking to this relevantly analogous pattern, he finally could formulate his hypothesis that the patterns of phenomena for which he is currently seeking an explanation must be governed by a mechanism similar to the one operative in the known case. For instance, had the scientist known that rubber balls become larger as they reach the surface of the Pacific Ocean and smaller as they are forced deeper and, had he believed that it is the differing pressures upon the balls that determines their sizes at varying depths, he could move to the hypothesis that there must be some sea of air that similarly determines the behavior of his balloons.

A bit of reflection on this example quickly reveals that the intelligibility of any explanation of this particular sort depends heavily upon the degree to which the source of analogy is understood. With respect to his balloons, the researcher's sea of air hypothesis provides the basis for an intelligible explanation of their expansion and contraction only insofar as the action of the Pacific Ocean upon rubber balls is comprehended. In extreme cases of ignorance, where the source of analogy is only very sketchily understood, the selection of such a mechanism as a source of analogy may provide little more information than that the patterns of phenomena to be explained are controlled somehow or other by the hypothesized mechanism in whatever ways the relevantly analogous patterns are controlled by the known, but obscurely grasped, mechanism. In cases where the understanding of the analogous mechanism is more intricately detailed, the functioning of the hypothesized mechanism also will be more adequately grasped and so provide much greater explanatory power.

Since there is no requirement of familiarity imposed upon the source of analogy, it should not be thought that this sort of explanation proceeds by way of some kind of reduction of the unfamiliar to the familiar. The relative familiarity or unfamiliarity of the source of analogy is strictly irrelevant to these explanatory purposes. Thus, it is quite conceivable that a thoroughly familiar pattern of occurrence might be explained by taking recourse to relatively unfamiliar patterns of phenomena governed by even more unfamiliar, though understood, controlling mechanisms. In short, it is the degree to which analogous mechanisms are comprehended rather than their degree of familiarity that helps to determine the precise explanatory power of subsequently hypothesized mechanisms.

For the purpose of carry-over to the religious sphere, the exact nature of the scientist's hypothesized mechanism must be emphasized. In positing the existence of his explanatorily useful mechanism, the scientist is suggesting that there is some entity, or perhaps set of entities, that is capable of behaving in specific kinds of ways. His claim is that there are certain special properties possessed by his suggested entities that enable them to behave in just the ways that they do and that allow them to account for the patterns of phenomena to be explained. In fact, it would seem that the explanatory power of the scientist's suggested entities is directly dependent upon the degree to which it is possible to specify which of their properties are the efficacious ones. Beyond the importance of specifying which properties are the explanatorily relevant ones, it also would appear that the intelligibility of the scientist's explanation increases in direct relation to the extent to which the modes of operation of such explanatorily relevant properties can be traced precisely. Thus, in the balloon case, the scientist's explanation by reference to a sea of air would become more fully illuminating by specifying that it is the pressure of the air that is the efficacious property. Additional understanding would be gained insofar as he could supply details about the way in which his sea of air exerts its pressure upon balloons.

It would be convenient for the purposes of later discussion to introduce the term 'explanatory entity' at this point as a label for any entity that is introduced for explanatory purposes in conformity with the procedure just outlined. But to the introduction of this bit of terminology, several cautionary remarks must be appended. First, it should not be thought that explanatory entities are some special kind of existing or subsisting beings. That is, explanatory entities must not be supposed to fall into some unique ontological category. As used here, the category of explanatory entities is to be taken as an epistemological one designed to cut across all ontological distinctions. To say that an entity is an explanatory one is to specify nothing more than that it plays a particular explanatory role. In other words, an explanatory entity is anything to which essential reference is made in the course of providing an explanation of the type under current consideration. Hence, in line with this use of 'explanatory entity', not only may the sea of air be an explanatory entity, but the Pacific Ocean itself, electrons, magnetic fields, rubber balls, and people also may fall into this category.

Obviously, explanatory entities in this sense may be visible or invisible. Some, like electrons, are never seen while others, like assorted physical objects employed in the course of explaining various commonplace phenomena, are constantly seen, touched, and even tasted. It should also go without saying that it is possible for explanatory entities of this type to exist. Indeed, if they are to play any important role in the provision of true explanations of the sort under current consideration, not only must it be possible for such entities to exist, at least some of them actually must exist. Had our theorist not supposed that his sea of air actually existed, his account of the behavior of expanding and contracting balloons would have been obscure in the extreme. Had his sea been thought to be merely imaginary or fictitious, it would have been impossible to understand how it could possess the ability to determine the expansion and contraction of balloons. Of course, since explanatory entities must have specific properties by which they are enabled to determine the patterns of their explanatory ranges, the mere supposition of their existence is hardly sufficient to render them explanatorily efficacious. But entities which do not exist, no matter what characteristic they might be imagined to possess, would be entirely impotent to determine the course of a real world.

To gain further insight into the nature and structure of this particular explanatory type, it is necessary to return to a closer scrutiny of the balloon example. Up to this point, one rather major problem has received no attention whatsoever. It has been observed that the scientist interested in providing an explanation of this sort must begin by specifying the patterns of phenomena he wishes to explain. He then must hypothesize the existence of an operative mechanism modeled upon the mechanisms supposed to determine relevantly analogous patterns of phenomena. But nothing has been said regarding the ways in which scientists are able to decide which patterns of phenomena are relevantly analogous and which are not.

Consider, then, the plight of the scientist who wants to explain why balloons expand and contract as they do with changes in altitude. In the course of his work, he selects the patterns of behavior of rubber balls in the Pacific Ocean as relevantly analogous. Suppose, however, that balls in the Pacific Ocean not only contract and expand with changes in depth, but also change in color and that the scientist has been advised of this striking dissimilarity between the balls in the ocean and his balloons. He quickly would dismiss this particular dissimilarity as irrelevant. Defending his disregard of the discrepancy between the color behavior of the balls and the color behavior of his balloons, he simply would point out that the color behavior of balloons is not his concern. From the outset, he has been concerned to explain the expansion and contraction behavior rather than the color behavior of balloons. Of course, had he been interested in explaining the color constancy of his balloons, he would have shown significantly more interest in this reported dissimilarity between the balls and his balloons.

It would seem, then, that the basis for deciding relevant analogy is determined by the explanatory interest of the scientist in question. Since our imagined researcher never had been interested in explaining the color behavior of balloons, he was not concerned to find cases where the manifested color behavior was similar to that of his balloons. It is the fact that the rubber balls in the ocean manifested the same patterns of expansion and contraction as the scientist's balloons that made them so explanatorily valuable. Had the balls failed to manifest any such expansion and contraction behavior, the scientist would never have found their patterns of behavior to be relevantly analogous to that of his balloons.

Suppose that the balloon case were altered along somewhat different lines. Suppose the balls in the Pacific Ocean did expand and contract, but not in exactly the same ways as balloons do. If the scientist were interested in explaining nothing more than why balloons expand and contract with differences in altitude, the balls in the Pacific Ocean still might be accepted as relevantly analogous. But if it were the intention of the scientist to explain not only why balloons expand and contract, but also to account for the precise ways in which they expand and contract, the differences in the manner of expansion and contraction between balloons and rubber balls in the ocean would provide a basis for rejecting the rubber ball case as relevantly analogous.

The degree of interest in patterns of phenomena as relevantly analogous varies not only with variations in explanatory intention, but also with the degree of optimism the scientist has with regard to finding alternative sources of relevant analogy. Obviously, the scientist's interest in patterns of phenomena will increase in direct proportion to the specificity of the match between those patterns and the patterns he wishes to explain. A perfect match between the two would be ideal. But if analogous patterns fail to match completely with the patterns to be explained, the scientist may refrain from dismissing the analogous patterns as explanatorily irrelevant. If he believes that there is some reasonable possibility of finding other patterns of phenomena that match more closely the ones he intends to explain, he will, of course, abandon his original find. But if there appears to be little hope of finding any closer match, the scientist may choose to salvage the relevancy of his find by lowering his explanatory expectations. For instance, were the balloon researcher to believe that he has very little chance of finding any patterns of expansion and contraction behavior that will match more precisely the behavior of his balloons, he could retain the rubber ball behavior as relevantly analogous by choosing to explain the expansion and contraction of his balloons only to the degree of specificity to which the ball and balloon patterns overlap.

In discussing the selection of patterns of phenomena as relevantly analogous, the possibility of a lucky break should not be overlooked. Occasionally, in the course of seeking for some pattern of phenomena that properly matches the pattern to be explained, the scientist will come across one that matches his original pattern even more closely than his explanatory intentions require. For example, the balloon scientist originally might have intended to explain only the simple expansion or contraction of his balloons with changes in altitude. But suppose that in his subsequent quest for relevantly analogous patterns, he were to discover that rubber balls not only manifest the simple expansion and contraction behavior of his balloons, they also match with great precision the exact ways in which his balloons expand and contract. Counting his lucky stars, this scientist probably would increase the specificity of his explanatory intentions and invoke the patterns of rubber ball behavior as relevantly analogous with respect to the explanation of the specific ways in which balloons expand and contract. Forgetting entirely his more modestly general expectations, he would struggle to capitalize on the high degree of similarity between the behavior of his balloons and rubber balls.

Although the scientist must be concerned to find patterns of phenomena that are relevantly analogous to the ones he hopes to explain, considerations of relevant analogy are not the only ones that help to direct his attentions toward one pattern of phenomena rather than another. The scientist's ultimate goal is to extract a model for his posited explanatory entity from the relevantly analogous case. For this reason, no matter how similar some pattern of phenomena may be to the pattern he intends to explain, if the scientist does not understand the controlling mechanism that determines that pattern, interest will be turned immediately toward the discovery of some other relevantly analogous pattern for which the mechanism is known.

Even should the mechanism controlling some relevantly analogous set of phenomena be known by the scientist, this in itself may not be enough to arrest his explanatory attention. He might very well abandon one pattern of phenomena for a second one were he to discover that the operative mechanism controlling the latter pattern was more completely understood or perhaps more fully compatible with other bits of scientific knowledge than the mechanism governing the former. In fact, were the mechanism behind the latter pattern sufficiently attractive, the scientist might be willing to sacrifice something of the specificity of the analogy between the pattern to be explained and the relevantly analogous one in order to be able to incorporate that more desirable mechanism into his explanatory account. Though he would not be able to provide as precise an explanation of the specific peculiarities of his patterns by so doing, increased understanding or more extensive theoretical integration might more than repay this price of imprecision.

Once the scientist has discovered the operative mechanism behind the pattern chosen as relevantly analogous, energy must be directed to modeling a new explanatory entity. On the most fundamental level, the scientist will begin by simply affirming that his posited mechanism is like the mechanism that determines the relevantly analogous pattern. Beyond this straightforward assertion of similarity, the scientist must move toward honing his characterization of his suggested entity into an ever more sharply explanatory tool.

Probably the simplest method of honing characterizations of explanatory entities is by purging them of irrelevant features. Consider the sea of air hypothesis. The suggestion that it is a sea of air that accounts for the expansion and contraction behavior of balloons can be sharpened considerably by stripping away any characteristics that are explanatorily useless. For instance, while the source of the analogous mechanism in this case, the Pacific Ocean, may be blue, wet, salty, and so on, such properties as these do not play any role in the account of the expansion and contraction of rubber balls. Thus, in moving by analogy to his suggestion of a sea of air, the scientist safely might strip away such useless features by noting that his sea of air need not be blue, wet, or salty in order to make balloons expand and contract. Obviously, however, even this simple purging process cannot be initiated if the explanatorily efficacious characteristics of the source of analogy remain unknown. Unless the scientist knows which features of the Pacific determine the expansion and contraction of rubber balls and which do not, he cannot reasonably purge any of the characteristics carried over to his description of his sea of air without risking the loss of some explanatorily relevant property.

There is one complication worthy of mention that the scientist must face in this purgation. He must realize that the simple explanatory irrelevance of a property is not a sufficient basis for eliminating it from his description of his newly conceived explanatory entities. Such explanatorily irrelevant properties also must be logically as well as theoretically independent of any other properties that turn out to be explanatorily relevant. That is, in deciding whether to drop some particular property from his characterization of an explanatory mechanism, the scientist must first determine whether the property in question plays any explanatory role. If it does not, it then must be determined whether that property is logically connected with any property that does play an explanatory role. If it is so connected, then the purgation of one without the other would violate specific logical canons. Of course, in extreme cases of desperation, the scientist might be willing to sacrifice the integrity of his logical laws. But ordinarily, the more moderate course would be to leave systems of logic intact by refraining from the purgation of properties that, aside from their logical connection with explanatorily useful properties, themselves make no explanatory contribution. In a similar fashion, the scientist must determine whether there is any accepted scientific theory that essentially connects properties to be purged as explanatorily superfluous with other, explanatorily relevant ones. If there is, then the purgation of such properties from his description of an explanatory mechanism without the purgation of those others entails a repudiation of that portion of accepted theory by which they are essentially connected. In cases like this, it is normally less systematically destructive to allow superfluous properties to tag along with explanatorily efficacious ones than to sacrifice bits of accepted theory for the sake of sharpening one's conception of newly hypothesized explanatory entities.

A second way in which the scientist may hone his understanding of explanatory entities is by turning to the explication of explanatorily relevant properties. Consider once more the sea of air example. Since it was the pressure of the Pacific that was taken to account for the expansion and contraction behavior of rubber balls, it must be that very same property that allows the sea of air hypothesis to provide an explanatory account of the expansion and contraction of balloons. Hence, insofar as the scientist is able to clarify his conception of pressure or weight, his explanation will gain explanatory precision. In many cases, this attempt at clarification can lead to additional suggestions of even finer explanatory mechanisms. For instance, in the sea of air case, the manifestation of pressure might itself come to be conceived as the result of an operative mechanism analogous to popcorn smashing against the lid of a popper. But even if the scientist is unable to find some finer mechanism by which to explicate the efficacious nature of his explanatory entities, precision still might be obtained along more modest lines. By providing a detailed study of the ways in which explanatorily relevant properties function under varying circumstances, precision can be increased. Studies designed to yield mathematically precise correlations between the manifestation of explanatorily relevant properties and the occurrence of various sorts of behavior also would be helpful. In the balloon case, it would certainly be useful to know how various air pressures are correlated with balloon sizes. Should this quest for rigidly fixed correlations between the manifestation of explanatorily relevant properties and assorted patterns of behavior prove fruitless, the scientist might seek to uncover statistical laws of correlation instead. Even the emergence of such statistical laws would bring some increase in explanatory precision.

A third way in which the scientist can hone his understanding of explanatory mechanisms is through the purgation of properties that are explanatorily counterproductive. In the sea of air case, some of the properties of the Pacific were just superfluous. For example, because the scientist was interested only in the expansion and contraction of the balloons, the particular color of the Pacific could be excluded safely from the description of the sea of air as explanatorily irrelevant. But any properties of the Pacific that might have actually defeated his explanatory purposes would have to be repudiated as explanatorily counterproductive. Suppose, for instance, that our researcher had found that the saltiness of the Pacific had a corrosive effect upon the plastic in the balloons and that this saltiness actually altered their elasticity over prolonged periods of time. Had he been interested in explaining the uniformity of the expansion and contraction behavior of the balloons over extended periods of time, the scientist would have been forced to exclude saltiness from his conception of the sea of air. Otherwise, his hypothesis would have been found to be explanatorily defective. Since it would have led to the prediction of a variation of expansion and contraction behavior over time, saltiness attributed to the sea of air would have proven to be more than merely explanatorily superfluous. It would have been absolutely destructive.

It should be noted that the distinction between explanatorily relevant, explanatorily superfluous, and explanatorily harmful properties always is drawn relative to the explanatory interest of the scientist. As his interests shift, properties will shift from one category to another. If the sea of air proponent had been interested in explaining nothing more than the simple expansion and contraction of balloons, then the saltiness, cloudiness, and wetness of the Pacific would have been judged to be explanatorily superfluous. But had the scientist also intended to explain why balloons taste rubbery or remain visible at relatively great distances or remain dry when immersed in a sea of air, then saltiness, cloudiness, or wetness would have to be shifted over to the explanatorily disruptive category.

Throughout the course of the discussion to this point, it has been assumed that the scientist is interested only in the explanation of some predetermined and rigidly fixed range of phenomena. Unfortunately, in the course of actual scientific endeavor, explanatory interests are rarely so antiseptically static. Instead, the positing and subsequent explication of explanatory entities usually follows a much more dynamic evolutionary course. For instance, once entities like our sea of air have been used with some degree of explanatory success to account for the occurrence of a limited range of phenomena, theorists frequently will broaden their explanatory expectations. Thus, had some success been enjoyed in accounting for the expansion and contraction of balloons, researchers might have been encouraged to modify and develop their sea of air hypothesis with an eye to providing an explanation of patterns of cloud, barometric, or wind behavior.

One basic strategy that might be employed in the expansion of the explanatory range of hypothesized entities is simply to return to the original source of analogy in order to explore that source more fully. The theorist might return to scrutinize those features he originally carried over in the characterization of his newly hypothesized explanatory entity, looking for other patterns of phenomena determined by those features that might be relevantly analogous to patterns for which his newly suggested entity could be held responsible. Following this particular line, the sea of air theorist might return to the Pacific Ocean with the intention of uncovering ways in which the pressure of the Pacific determines certain patterns of phenomena. In the course of his investigation, he might find that the Pacific is responsible for various patterns of distortion or explosive behavior beyond the simple patterns of expansion and contraction already noticed. Noting such new patterns, he could expand easily the explanatory range of his sea of air by pointing out that his newly posited entity is responsible for patterns of distortion or explosion that are similar to the patterns determined by the pressure of the Pacific Ocean.

Should the scientist exhaust the possibilities of expanding his explanatory range in this manner, he still might return to his original source of analogy for additional insights. Instead of scrutinizing those features of the initial mechanism that have been carried over already in application to his newly suggested explanatory entities, however, the scientist might search for other features of his original source of analogy that are responsible for yet other patterns of phenomena. Should such features be found, they might be carried over to the new case in the hope of expanding the explanatory scope of his posited entities. Thus, should the sea of air theorist exhaust the explanatory possibilities latent in the pressure of the Pacific Ocean, he still might return to the Pacific, turning his attention to the temperature, color, or other features with the intention of finding some property that is responsible for patterns of phenomena relevantly analogous to patterns for which his sea of air might be held responsible.

Of course, in the return to an original source of analogy, it is not necessary to focus exclusive attention upon the explanatorily efficacious features of some known generative mechanism. It is also possible to concentrate upon the discovery of patterns in the flux of phenomena for which there is some reason to believe that the original mechanism can be held to account. Hence, the sea of air theorist might not return to any detailed investigation of the pressure, color, or other explanatorily relevant property of the Pacific Ocean. Rather, he might return to the sea only to cast about for previously undisclosed patterns of phenomena. Finding such patterns, he then might struggle to trace their origins back to some determinate feature of the Pacific, some feature that can be held responsible for the occurrence of those patterns. Were he to discover such an explanatorily efficacious feature, it might be possible to move toward an additional, explanatorily useful, characterization of his sea of air.

Another basic strategy that might be employed in the attempt to expand the explanatory range of hypothesized entities amounts to nothing more than a repetition of the same strategy followed during the evolution of the initial understanding of those entities. Beginning with the precise specification of some new range of patterns to be explained, the theorist then would have to cast about for relevantly analogous patterns of phenomena. Finding such patterns for which the governing mechanism already is understood, he finally would have to try to shape his characterization of his original explanatory posits in conformity with his comprehension of that already understood operative mechanism.

Although these assorted strategies for expanding the explanatory scope of previously posited entities obviously would proceed in ways similar to the ones already discussed, there are a few novel twists that are worthy of special mention. In the first place, it might turn out that the scientist who is trying to expand the explanatory range of his hypothesized entities by looking beyond his original source of analogy is able to find some set of relevantly analogous phenomena that has a governing mechanism whose efficacious properties are ones already possessed by his original explanatory posit. In this sort of case, it would be unnecessary for the theorist to attribute some new characteristic to his explanatory entities in order to expand their explanatory range. Instead, he simply could point out that properties already possessed by his explanatory entities are identical with the efficacious ones in the newly uncovered mechanism. By noting this identity, he could move immediately to the conclusion that the explanatory range of his own entities can be expanded in the desired manner. As an example, consider once again our familiar sea of air theorist. Looking to increase the explanatory scope of his sea of air beyond the simple expansion and contraction of balloons, he might try to explain, say, a certain odd pattern of distortion among his balloons. Finding no relevantly analogous pattern of distortion for which the pressure of the Pacific might be held responsible, suppose this theorist were to venture beyond his original source of analogy. In the course of his quest for relevantly analogous phenomena, he might find that droplets of water submerged in a thick oil undergo similar patterns of distortion. Suppose, finally, that this theorist were to discover, much to his surprise, that it is the pressure of the oil on the water droplets that is responsible for their oddly deformed shapes. Noting that he already has attributed this same characteristic to his sea of air, this fortunate scientist could move immediately to the conclusion that the pressure of the sea of air accounts not only for the simple expansion and contraction of the balloons, but also for their distorted shapes.

Of course, in the attempt to expand the explanatory range of his posited entities, the scientist is rarely fortunate enough to come across an analogously relevant case where the efficacious properties of the operative mechanism are precisely those already possessed by his original entities. Usually, it will be some other features in the analogous case that are the relevant ones. These new features must then be added to those that already are thought to characterize his initial posits if there is to be any expansion of explanatory range.

Disappointingly, the easy step of adding new properties to one's characterization of explanatory entities in order to enrich their explanatory resources cannot always be taken. Before making this move, the scientist must be certain that it is both logically and theoretically permissible to conjoin newly envisioned properties with the characteristics originally attributed to his entities. That is, he must be sure that the possession of all these properties by his entities is prohibited neither by the accepted laws of logic nor by other theoretical commitments. If there are no logical or theoretical constraints upon the conjunction of all these properties in his entities, then he safely can move to the ascription of the newly discovered properties to his previously characterized explanatory entities.

If there is some logical or theoretical prohibition upon the addition of such new properties to the characterization of the entities, the scientist is left with several options. He may return to the search for analogously relevant patterns of phenomena in the hope of discovering some operative mechanism with different efficacious features, features that can be incorporated into his conception of his original entities without logical or theoretical censure. Usually, this first course of action is the most attractive. But should this alternative be rejected, the scientist could take the more drastic course of repudiating the laws of logic or theoretical commitments that prohibit the conjunction of properties he desires. Unhappily, this course of action allows the expansion of the explanatory range of particular entities only at the expense of other, usually very entrenched, convictions. Finally, the scientist simply may abandon his quest to expand the explanatory range of his entities in the directions he had hoped. Facing the disappointment of his failure to expand the explanatory range of his posits, the scientist who takes this course of action easily might be tempted to suggest the existence of some novel set of entities that could account for his new range of phenomena. By so doing, he would not be forced to abandon his discovery of a relevantly analogous range of patterns with its attendant operative mechanism.

Although this account of the nature and development of explanations through the positing and specification of the operative natures of explanatory entities has been abbreviated severely,[31] enough has been said to allow at least a preliminary investigation of the primary bases

upon which explanations of this type are evaluated. While it is difficult, if not impossible, to rank appropriate criteria for explanatory
adequacy in some systematically rigid hierarchy of importance, it is
possible to generate a list of a few of the more significant ones without
too much difficulty. Fortunately, for the purpose of carryover into the
religious sphere, all that is needed is a brief listing of some of the more
central of these criteria together with a few comments concerning their
relative importance.

Due to the specific structure of explanations generated by appeal
to the existence and operation of explanatory entities, there are certain
basic conditions that must be met before any such explanations can be
entertained seriously. Most of these already have emerged indirectly
during the course of the preceding discussion. For example, since
explanations of this type draw heavily upon the efficacious properties
of mechanisms that are known to govern relevantly analogous patterns of phenomena, the range of phenomena chosen as relevantly
analogous really must be relevantly analogous. Similarly, the controlling mechanisms behind relevantly analogous patterns really must
be understood and really must generate their patterns in the ways
described by the scientist. Were it discovered that the chosen phenomena really were not relevantly analogous or that the operative
mechanisms were not understood or that analogous patterns were
generated in ways quite different from those suggested by the scientist,
then explanatory entities posited by reference to such mistaken information would immediately lose their explanatory force. In short,
should it be discovered that the scientist has constructed defectively
his understanding of the explanatory entities by failing to develop a
description of them along proper lines, the plausibility of his explanatory account would be undercut immediately.

If the scientist were to succeed in constructing his depiction of the
entities along correct lines, subsequent tests would have to be passed
before his explanations could be admitted as fully adequate. Some of
the most important of these additional tests are designed to assess the
degree of compatibility between newly constructed conceptions of
explanatory entities and other theoretical and logical commitments.
As has been noted already, descriptions of entities will be judged as
incompatible with other commitments if either the positing of the
existence of those entities or the description of their modes of functioning requires the violation of accepted logical or theoretical convictions. But interest in compatibility ranges far beyond this simple test

for overall logical and theoretical consistency. For instance, newly posited explanatory entities will be considered more explanatorily adequate insofar as the ways in which they operate are closely similar to the modes of operation of widely accepted governing mechanisms. Thus, within the natural sciences, all other things being equal, new explanations that appeal to mechanisms of a physical or chemical sort will be considered much more adequate than explanations that make reference to more controversial Freudian types of mechanisms. Because some kinds of mechanisms are much more deeply entrenched in various sciences than others, the more closely new mechanisms mirror uncontroversially accepted ones, the more fully they can rest on the prestige of entrenched theoretical fashion. Obviously, since fashions change and what is fashionable in one science may not be so in another, this particular criterion for explanatory adequacy depends heavily upon current trends in specific intellectual circles. For this reason, Freudian mechanisms that may be looked upon with disdain by chemists and physicists might be expected to prevail in certain psychological circles.

A somewhat similar test for compatibility involves the relation between newly posited explanatory entities and established scientific laws. If newly suggested entities operate in conformity with widely accepted laws of chemistry, physics, or some other science, they are more likely to be judged to be explanatorily adequate than entities that require the introduction of novel laws. In the same way, entities that are purported to possess characteristics foreign to other already accepted entities are less likely to be viewed as explanatorily adequate than would be entities supposed to possess commonly recognized properties.

A different, though nevertheless important, kind of criterion for evaluating the explanatory adequacy of newly introduced entities requires an investigation of the degree of explanatory precision they offer. The more precise the explanatory account, all other things being equal, the more adequate it will be considered. This precision can be investigated along two distinct lines. In the first place, an explanation is precise insofar as the ways in which the operative mechanisms that govern the patterns of phenomena to be explained are traced fully. That is, the more detailed the account of precisely how the mechanisms in question control the phenomena to be explained, the more precise the resulting explanation. Thus, an explanation that noted only that the pressure of a sea of air somehow controls balloon sizes would be judged less adequate, on this criterion, than one that provided a detailed tracing of the exact process of governance. Second, the more specific the patterns of phenomena to be explained are, the more precise the explanatory account. So, an explanatory entity that could account only for the simple fact that balloons expand and contract at differing altitudes would be judged less precise than one that could account for the specific ways in which balloons expand and contract at varying altitudes.

The last way in which the explanatory adequacy of newly introduced entities can be assessed that is important enough to merit special attention involves the consideration of the adequacy of competitors in the field. Obviously, if two explanations are both able to account for the same patterns of phenomena, but one is able to do so more precisely or is more compatible with accepted commitments in the sciences or in some other way more fully meets the criteria for explanatory adequacy, it will be accepted as explanatorily superior to its competitor. But there are also less obvious ways in which the introduction of one explanatory entity may be judged superior to the introduction of another. For example, if some entity can account not only for the same range of phenomena as its competitor, but also can be used to explain some additional patterns of occurrences, it normally will be judged as explanatorily preferable to the more limited entity. Similarly, if it were discovered that some already accepted entity can, perhaps with some descriptive modification, be used to account for a range of phenomena for which it had been thought the introduction of a new explanatory entity was required, the positing of such a new explanatory entity normally would be repudiated as theoretically superfluous. The scientist typically will choose to place any new explanatory burden upon the shoulders of old entities not only for the sake of theoretical economy, but also because the encompassing of diverse explanatory functions within the purview of a single set of explanatory entities allows the unification of diverse bits of science into a more inclusive, integrated theoretical structure. For these same reasons of overall simplicity and unity of theory, the scientist typically will repudiate the introduction of new explanatory entities if some way can be found to account for new explanatory ranges by chopping them up into distinct parts, each of which is explainable by reference to some already accepted entity or other.

Although much more could be said about the articulation, evolution, and evaluation of scientific explanations, enough has been sketched to provide an initial characterization of this particular sort. While very incomplete, it still should prove sufficient to show the promise of this one specific explanatory strategy for religion. If nothing more, a bit of reflection upon the nature of this sort of scientific explanation will indicate the misdirection of the concerns of writers like Mitchell, Ferré, and Ramsey. Each of these writers was convinced that any attempt to provide religious explanations of a rigorously scientific type must be abandoned as a hopelessly impossible task. As was noted earlier, Mitchell wrote:

Theological explanations cannot be of a scientific kind. In so far as they succeed in achieving a gain in intelligibility they do so not by suggesting a hypothesis from which deductions are made which are subject to strict experimental test.[32]

If the model of scientific explanation presented by Hempel and Oppenheim is taken seriously, Mitchell's comments here have a telling force against the possibility of religious explanations. On the stricter model offered by Hempel and Oppenheim, the explanandum must be deducible from the explanans.[33] Furthermore, in their view, as Mitchell concedes in the passage just cited, "The explanans must have empirical content; i.e., it must be capable, at least in principle, of test by experiment or observation."[34] But on the model of scientific explanation offered in the preceding pages, Mitchell's worries simply turn out to be misguided. In the provision of explanations by reference to explanatory entities, never is any requirement about the deducibility of explananda from explanans imposed. Similarly, though such explanatory hypotheses are subject to all sorts of tests, they never are subjected to any simple test by experiment or observation.

Like Mitchell's worries, the objections against the possibility of scientifically rigorous religious explanations raised by Ferré and Ramsey turn out to be quite groundless when pressed against the model envisioned in these pages. Ramsey argues that a truly scientific explanation is one that is constructed by generalizing from the experience of particular occurrences. If such generalizations are to be genuinely explanatory, it must be possible to deduce particular instances from them whose occurrence can be precisely verified.[35] Ferré agrees that true scientific explanation requires the subsumption of particulars under general laws. He also agrees that such generalizations must yield predictions that are precisely verifiable.[36] Since religious explanations are incapable of meeting such strict requirements, they cannot be of a fully scientific kind. Once again, while these objections might carry some force when pressed against explanations conceived along the lines of Hempel and Oppenheim, they prove irrelevant when scientific explanations of the sort considered here are taken as models. The explanatory strategy outlined here does not require that an explanans be constructed by generalizing from particular instances. Indeed, the construction of explanatory hypotheses with their essential dependence upon the specification of explanatory entities proceeds along entirely different lines. Furthermore, though explanatory hypotheses can be tested, modified, refined, and abandoned, verifiable predictions are not crucially necessary in this process. Finally, in this model of scientific explanation, it is patterns of phenomena rather than specific occurrences that are explained. In short, the model of scientific explanation proposed here is at such wide variance with the standard employed by Mitchell, Ferré, and Ramsey that if the true possibility of religious explanations is to be assessed adequately, an entirely fresh start must be taken.

IV

Religious Explanations

—

THE BULK OF THE PRECEDING chapter was occupied with a consideration of the ways in which one type of scientific explanation is able to draw explanatory power from special appeals to the nature and operation of governing mechanisms. It was argued that any scientist interested in the explanatory invocation of such mechanisms must begin work by drawing together the set of generalizations he hopes to explain. Once the patterns of phenomena to be explained have been chosen, attention can be turned to locating some set of relevantly analogous phenomena for which the operative mechanism already is understood. Upon finding such an analogous set, a conception of new explanatory entities can be molded in conformity with that understanding of the active nature of the known mechanism. In order to properly shape his characterization of the new explanatory posits, the scientist must work toward carrying over explanatorily efficacious features from the relevantly analogous case while stripping away superfluous as well as detrimental ones.

If there is to be any genuine rehabilitation of the cognitive integrity of religious discourse by making effective use of materials gleaned from the previous chapter, three distinct, though obviously interrelated, steps must be taken. First, the move from the scientific to the religious sphere must be completed. That is, the precise ways in which religious explanations would have to be constructed in order to parallel the explanatory patterns outlined in the third chapter must be specified. The present chapter is devoted largely to this task. Not only will a point by point carryover from the scientific realm be attempted, but close attention also will be given to the ways in which the use of this particular explanatory structure can provide a shield against the critical barbs of skeptics of the theoretical integrity of religious discourse.

Once the carryover from the scientific to the religious sphere is completed, it must be determined whether religious explanations formulated in so strict an analogy with scientific ones can hold any plausibility. After all, while it may be possible to develop religious explanations in conformity with the structure of certain scientific ones, unless there is at least some hope of explanations so structured turning out to be true, there would seem to be little point in continuing in their pursuit. The simple possibility of formulating such explanations along rigorously scientific lines would lose much, if not all, of its interest were it discovered that there is not even the remotest chance that they could prove acceptable to modern, educated people. So, the next two chapters will focus upon the question of the plausibility of religious explanations formulated in conformity with the constraints outlined in the third chapter.

Finally, the Wittgensteinian fear of writers like D. Z. Phillips must be addressed. Phillips and others have argued, under the inspiration of Wittgenstein's reflections upon the nature of religious commitment, that if religious utterances are modeled too closely upon scientific ones, they can lose their distinctively religious character. They may seem to be religious in nature, but they are actually nothing more than the superstitious or self-interested mutterings of believers dazzled by the prestige of the sciences.[1] So, since the conception of religious explanations developed in this present chapter will be in frank imitation of structures used in the sciences, the worry that the uniquely religious element in such scientifically modeled discourse may be lost must be subdued. In recognition of this worry, the final chapter will be reserved for an argument designed to show that the structures of discourse outlined here can be integrated into richly religious contexts without jeopardizing the special role of religion in human life.

A few preliminary points must be stressed before any investigation into the possibility of shaping religious explanations in conformity with scientific ones can begin in earnest. It is of extreme importance, for instance, to bear in mind that the investigation of scientific explanations undertaken in the preceding chapter was devoted exclusively to a consideration of types that rely heavily upon the invocation of explanatory entities for the purpose of accounting for specific ranges of phenomena. So, in the attempt to use the explanatory structures of the third chapter as models for the religious realm, God or other beings to which reference is made in the course of providing religious explanations must be construed as explanatory entities.

This construal of God or other such religiously significant referents[2] as explanatory entities carries a number of rather far-reaching implications. Among the more important of these is the fact that the conception of God as an explanatory entity involves more than the simple realization that he is being invoked to play a particular explanatory role. There are specific ontological implications as well. Since explanatory entities are those which are held responsible for the determination of specific patterns of phenomena, were they supposed to be merely imaginary or fictitious, their invocation would turn out to be explanatorily useless. Fictitious, imaginary, or other nonexistent beings cannot be held responsible for patterns of occurrences. It is only when explanatory entities are supposed to exist and, furthermore, supposed to have certain features that empower them to shape the patterns for which they are held responsible that they can be invoked intelligibly as explanatorily efficacious controlling mechanisms. Hence, any reference to God as an explanatory entity, instead of drawing his existential status into question, necessarily presumes it.

A second point that must be kept vividly in mind is that the course of these present deliberations cannot be taken to imply anything about the actual past, present, or future practices of religious communities. Although it might be interesting to know whether religious explanations of the sort outlined here have ever actually been attempted or whether such explanations form a vibrant part of currently active religious traditions, nothing whatever that might be uncovered through linguistic surveys of various religious communities during assorted periods of history would have any detrimental impact upon the thesis that religious explanations of this sort could be offered. Of course, the actual occurrence of such explanatory patterns obviously would prove their possibility. But the mere dearth of actual examples would leave the issue unresolved. Should it be shown, however, as is the intention of the remainder of this study, that religious explanations in conformity with the structures outlined in the third chapter can be formulated without the loss of whatever features make religious traditions uniquely religious, then enough would have been said to demonstrate the possibility of such religiously significant explanatory types.

The last point that must be emphasized before beginning an investigation into the possibility of molding religious explanations in conformity with the structures of the preceding chapter is that the third chapter was not designed to provide an exhaustive account of the nature of scientific explanations. Only one particular sort of explanatory strategy was discussed and even that strategy was treated only cursorily. More than likely, there are many other sorts of important explanatory types employed in the various sciences. So, should the particular sort of explanation discussed here prove incapable of providing an acceptable model for the religious sphere, it must not be assumed that other scientifically explanatory types also would be destined to failure when pressed into the service of religion. On the other hand, should the specific structure under investigation here succeed, there would be nothing about this one success that necessarily would prohibit explanatory structures of other types from being employed similarly within religious contexts.

With these preliminary comments out of the way, attention finally can be turned to the task at hand. To initiate the application of the results of the preceding chapter to the religious sphere, it should be recalled that the scientist interested in constructing an explanation by making reference to the capacities and activities of explanatory entities must begin by marking out the patterns of phenomena that are to be explained. If this same procedure is to be followed in the religious case, the patterns of phenomena God is expected to explain must be specified clearly.

The first step toward introducing God as an explanatory entity allows the immediate provision of a functional definition for 'God'. Since God is expected to play a particular explanatory role, since he is supposed to account for some specific range of phenomena, 'God' can be defined with respect to the particular function God is supposed to perform as "that entity that is to account for such-and-such a range of phenomena."

Consider, for the sake of illustration, an example in which some theologian, say Fred, hopes to introduce God as an explanatory entity to account for certain regular patterns he has noticed in his own life. In the course of day-to-day living, Fred has noticed that his daily needs always are supplied. No matter what may happen, he always has plenty of food, warm clothes, and proper housing. During periods of employment at the local university, Fred was not surprised that he could buy enough to eat, dress warmly, and rent a comfortable house. But even during those perilous days when he was working on his dissertation and was desperately trying to find his first teaching job, he always seemed to make ends meet. Once in a while, he found a check in the mail from his parents or from a long-forgotten, distant relative. Other times he would manage to mow a few lawns or clean some gutters. Even now, with the budget-cutting ax falling everywhere else, Fred's job seems secure and, when things get tight, he always is able to pick up a night class or find a check in the mail from sales on his books or from reviews he has done for big publishing companies.

It is crucial to distinguish two different, though certainly related, issues here before moving to a consideration of this specific example. The first concerns the possibility of offering an explanation. Is it possible for Fred to construct a religious explanation of his constant succor in conformity with the standards delineated in the preceding chapter? The second matter concerns the plausibility of Fred's explanation. Even if Fred could succeed in offering a religious explanation of the appropriate sort, would it be a plausible one? The latter issue depends heavily upon the theoretical environment in which Fred's explanation is offered. He might be supplying an explanation for a pattern of phenomena that already can be explained by reference to some other set of explanatory entities. That is, Fred might have some doting uncle who keeps a watchful eye on him, sending blank checks through the mail or providing odd jobs when needed. Alternatively, it might be the case that while no explanation of the entire pattern of succor can be offered, an account can be provided for each individual instance of support. So, perhaps this check can be explained by reference to the salary schedule at the university, that odd job can be explained by the need of some invalid neighbor to get the grass cut, and so on. In the most extreme case, it might be that an account of neither the pattern nor the individual instances of support can be explained otherwise. Perhaps Fred has no watchful uncle. Perhaps his neighbor is in perfect health but, for no apparent reason whatever, felt a sudden and quite uncharacteristic urge to ask Fred to cut his grass. With such shifts in theoretical context, assessments of the plausibility of Fred's explanatory invocation of God might alter dramatically.

The question of the plausibility of Fred's explanatory appeal cannot be slighted. It will have to be faced squarely. But it cannot be addressed adequately until the first issue is settled. Is it possible for Fred to offer any religious explanation, even an implausible one, in conformity with the constraints that emerged in discussing the nature of scientific appeals to explanatory entities? Consider, then, Fred's attempt to structure his explanation in conformity with the details of the preceding chapter. Following that explanatory strategy, Fred must begin by systematically marking out the patterns of phenomena he wishes to explain. Roughly summarized, his desire is to invoke God in his explanation of why his needs always are met. So, as a functional definition of 'God', Fred could suggest "that entity that accounts for a constant supply of food, clothing, and shelter."

The importance of this initial definition should not be underestimated. Although it may not be sufficiently precise to determine the exact nature of God, it does provide an initial footing for subsequent research. At this point, Fred is in the same position as scientists on the frontiers of research. In the sciences, the leading edges of research are cluttered with functionally defined entities. Many subatomic particles, for instance, were distinguished initially as "those entities that account for such-and-such images on photographic plates" or "those entities that account for such-and-such vapor trails in cloud chambers." Just as such functionally defined entities in the sciences yield sufficient understanding to guide the detailed organization of research programs designed to evolve various functional definitions into fully articulated accounts of the nature and behavior of explanatorily powerful entities, so Fred is in a position to use his functional definition of 'God' as a guide to further research.

The reason functional definitions are able to guide subsequent research is very simple: they attribute positive capacities to entities. So, in Fred's case, his functional definition of 'God' implies that God is something capable of supplying him with food, clothing, and shelter. This attribution of a specific capacity provides a basis for accepting or rejecting understood mechanisms as relevantly analogous. By knowing that God is that which provides for his needs, Fred can conclude that God is not a rock, a threatening cloud, or a bump in the night on the straightforward grounds that things such as these are incapable of supplying food, clothing, and shelter. Further investigation of the capacities of other sorts of things will lead quickly to their elimination as possible candidates for relevant analogy with God.

It might be tempting to conclude that this initial step of functional definition is nothing more than a disguised form of *via negativa*. By defining 'God' as "that entity that accounts for a constant supply of food, clothing, and shelter," Fred is doing nothing more than conceding that God is not a rock, not a threatening cloud, and so on. Although it may appear that a positive assertion is made in the course of presenting a functional definition, in fact nothing more than a series of denials ensues. So, Fred is in the uncomfortable position imagined by Antony Flew when he noted that someone may "dissipate his assertion completely without noticing that he has done so. A fine brash hypothesis may thus be killed by inches, the death by a thousand qualifications."[3]

This move to the conclusion that functional definitions can provide nothing more than negative characterizations is a bit premature, however. Fred's definition certainly does exclude the possibility of God being a rock or a threatening cloud. But this exclusion of certain things as relevantly analogous to God on the ground that they do not possess the requisite capacities for providing food, clothing, and shelter hardly leaves Fred empty-handed. Quite to the contrary, knowing that God has this particular capacity is enough to allow the focus of attention to shift in the direction of dogs, housekeepers, parents, landlords, and others similarly capacitated. While God's capacity for caring may make him dissimilar to rocks and clouds, it makes him very similar to dogs, housekeepers, parents, and the like. In fact, as will soon become evident, this capacity makes God more than just vaguely similar to such caring beings, it makes him precisely similar to them in certain clearly specifiable respects. In conformity with the findings of the third chapter, it soon will become clear that the positive, functional attribution of a capacity for caring to God amounts to more than the simple recognition of obscure analogies between God and certain other things. It amounts to making certain univocal predications of God and such things as dogs, housekeepers, and parents.

Not only does this initial functional definition of 'God' provide a positive characterization of God sufficient to guide further research, it also provides the beginnings of a set of criteria for individuating and subsequently identifying God. Kai Nielsen, following Flew and Hepburn,[4] has complained:

God is held to be an individual, albeit incorporeal, i.e., purely spiritual, but we have no idea of what counts as an incorporeal thing, a purely spiritual agent, a non-physical agent, an unlimited agent, and the like. The latter putative characteristic would seem to preclude any picking out or identification, but even if we can put aside that consideration and admit the uniqueness of God . . . he must be at least in principle in some way identifiable. . . . But there is no understanding of what it would be like to identify such a putative individual.[5]

Putting to one side, for the moment, whether God must be conceived as a bodiless, spiritual, or unlimited agent, it is clear that a functional definition of 'God' allows the first step toward the individuation and subsequent identification of this divine being. Suppose it be granted that human beings have no way of telling whether they are confronted with bodiless or unlimited agents. Still, recourse can be taken to God's functional definition. If Fred knows that God is that entity that provides his food, clothing, and shelter, then he knows that his front lawn and his brother's pet rock are not God. Of course, at this point, Fred's functional definition may be insufficiently precise to single out God from among other beings, such as his mother or some generous benefactor, who also might be thought to provide for his needs. Nevertheless, Fred is on his way to singling out God and, with a bit of work, may complete the task successfully. By adding more precision to his functional characterization, by appending other capacities to his understanding of God's nature, or by noting that his mother or benefactor were not in the proper position to provide for his needs on various occasions, Fred can narrow the field of possible candidates for God considerably.

It is necessary to pause here in order to thwart a couple of objections to this way of identifying God. Should it be argued that Fred may never have a set of criteria by which he can uniquely identify God, it need only be noted that such a constraint upon him is a bit too stringent. After all, such strongly individuating criteria are rarely, if ever, available for anything. Certainly people do not identify their cars, pens, or boats by such fail-safe criteria. There is always the theoretical possibility that a demon deceiver could manufacture a car just like the one in some parking lot, complete with a properly dented fender, and by making an undetected switch, fool the owner into thinking he was driving the same car home that he drove to work. The fact that there may be no uniquely identifying criteria for God would not put him into some special category. The same problem arises for baseball bats and fishing poles.

It might be retorted that this particular response overlooks a crucial difference between the identification of physical objects and the identification of God. If the only way of identifying physical objects were by reference to uniquely individuating properties, then there might be something to this sort of response. It would be true that there is no fail-safe method for uniquely identifying cars and baseball bats. It always would be possible for a second object to be produced that possessed all the same, supposedly unique properties of the first. But in the case of physical objects, there is another, indexical way of identifying individuals. Instead of identifying a car or baseball bat by reference to certain of its features, it is possible to distinguish it uniquely by reference to some perceptual relation in which it stands to me. This car may be distinguished as the one I am looking at now or the one I am touching now. Since God cannot be perceived, he cannot be uniquely identified in this way.

There are at least two ways in which this retort might be neutralized. By citing familiar examples of perceptual illusion or hallucination, it might be suggested that this form of indexical identification is no more foolproof than identification by reference to supposedly unique features of objects. It is always possible that, although I believe I am seeing some car now, in fact I am not. Thus, the car stands in no uniquely identifying perceptual relation with me. But there are problems with this line of response. First, it quickly leads into difficult issues regarding the nature of veridical perception, the possibility of distinguishing illusory or hallucinatory perceptions, and the exact relation of physical objects to perceptual fields. Second, it is possible to retreat from an indexical identification in terms of a perceptual relation to one in terms of an appearance relation. Instead of identifying the car as the one that I see now, I might identify it as the one that I seem to see now.

While this form of indexical identification is not without its problems, a second line of response can be taken that enables problems in the philosophy of perception to be bypassed altogether. By switching from cars and baseball bats to electrons and protons, the temptation to argue along the lines of what I can see now or can seem to see now loses its attraction. Electrons and protons have never been seen or touched. In fact, it may well be that the very notion of seeing or touching such entities is an incoherent one. Nevertheless, physicists have no difficulty telling electrons from other unseen particles of various sorts. Their identifying procedure is precisely the same as Fred's. By knowing what electrons can and cannot do, physicists are able to determine both the presence and the absence of electrons in terms of the presence or absence of phenomena for which they are typically held responsible.

Before leaving this discussion of the identification of God through the specification of functional definitions, it should be noted that this particular method of individuating God does not in any way depend upon developing some method for picking out bodiless, spiritual, or unlimited agents. Even if there is some necessity to attribute such features to God, they need not be the ones by which he is identified. A favorite cat may be identified by a conspicuous scar on its face. If it becomes known that this particular cat has a unique liver ailment, then one can conclude confidently that finding the cat with the strange scar is finding the one with the liver ailment. No surgery is required. Similarly, if Fred were to find that God not only had certain capacities, but also that God was a bodiless agent, he could conclude confidently that finding the being with the appropriate capacities would be finding a bodiless agent.[6]

Once an initial functional definition of 'God' has been provided, attention can be turned to making it more precise by carefully specifying the exact range of phenomena for which God is expected to account. Alternatively, functional definitions of 'God' can be augmented by adding new patterns of occurrences to God's explanatory range. But the next major step toward understanding God as an explanatory entity would require the search for an analogous range of phenomena for which the controlling mechanism already is understood. Once such a range were found, if the controlling mechanism in the analogous case were understood in any degree of detail at all, the concept of God as an explanatory entity could be enhanced significantly. Beyond the mere functional definition of 'God' as "that entity that accounts for such-and-such a range of phenomena," the nature of God could be fleshed out by making reference to the ways in which the relevantly analogous mechanism determines its own range of phenomena. This elaboration of the nature of God would involve the now familiar process of attempting to attribute to God those features of the relevantly analogous mechanism that are explanatorily efficacious while stripping away irrelevant and detrimental ones.

Return for a moment to Fred, the theologian who was trying to employ God in his explanation of why he always has plenty of food, clothing, and shelter. Fred got to the point of specifying the range of data God was expected to explain. In light of this specified range, he was able to define the term 'God' functionally as "that entity that accounts for a constant supply of food, clothing, and shelter." Fred is now ready to cast about for some relevantly analogous range of phenomena for which the governing mechanism already is known. Suppose he were to discover that the children of his rich neighbors always seem to have plenty of food, clothing, and shelter. Intrigued by this analogy with the range of phenomena he hopes to explain, Fred might investigate more carefully to see if the children are supplied in exactly the way in which he himself is supplied. Suppose, upon thorough investigation, Fred becomes satisfied that the children's case is relevantly analogous. Then he must see whether he can find a controlling mechanism for the children's case that he understands. Suppose that once again Fred is successful. He finds that it is the parents of the children who provide them with food, clothing, and shelter and, furthermore, it is because of their love for their children that those parents provide such doting care.

At this juncture, Fred is in a position to attribute love to God. That is, Fred can argue that God provides food, clothing, and shelter for him out of love in just the way that his rich neighbors lovingly provide for the physical comfort of their children. In making this move, however, several important consequences must be accepted. First, it must be realized that the attribution of love to God on the basis of this particular analogous case carries an arbitrary element with it. Had Fred found another range of relevantly analogous phenomena for which the explanatory features of the operative mechanism were different, he would have been in a position to attribute those features, rather than love, to God. So, the simple discovery of a relevantly analogous case is insufficient to allow the confident conclusion that God is being characterized as he "really" is. Had Fred found that some parent fed and clothed his children out of morbid guilt feelings, he might have afflicted God with morbid guilt rather than blessed him with undying love.

Of course, there might be other considerations that could lead Fred to opt for one relevantly analogous case over another. He might discover some sacred, revelatory text that could help him decide one way rather than the other. He might find that the attribution of one efficacious feature would allow a wider explanatory range or would fit more neatly with the rest of God's character traits than another attribution would. Fred even might discover that the attribution of one feature to God would inhibit God's abilities to play nonexplanatory roles. In this way, Fred might find that attributing morbid guilt to God would make him much less attractive as an object of devout worship than would the attribution of love. But even these and other possible constraints upon Fred's choice would never guarantee that the field of relevantly analogous cases always can be narrowed to one. So, since there will always be a possibility of finding more than one relevantly analogous case that could be used to fill out an understanding of the nature of God, guarantees that God is depicted accurately never can be made. There is always the possibility of error. Therefore, if Cartesian levels of certainty are sought, this is not the path to follow. Insights into God's nature that are gleaned in conformity with the patterns of the preceding chapter can provide no higher degrees of certainty than can be obtained by using similar patterns of investigation in the sciences.

It also should be noted that Fred's attribution of love to God involves a univocal predication of God and his creatures. This is not, of course, a reflection upon the inabilities of Fred. Rather, it is a reflection on the elementary and cursory nature of the developments in the third chapter. It will be recalled that the discussion of the explanatory strategies in that chapter were only of the most rudimentary sort. Explanations derived their force from the fact that mechanisms controlling analogous ranges of phenomena already were understood. In the sea of air example, it was the fact that the way in which the pressure of the Pacific determines the expansion and contraction of rubber balls already was understood that allowed an understanding of the way in which the pressure of the sea of air can determine the sizes of balloons. If the pressure of the sea of air were not thought to be precisely similar to the pressure of the Pacific, there would be no way of guaranteeing the intelligibility of the mode of behavior of the sea of air without ranging beyond the techniques outlined in the course of the discussion of that example. Clearly, there might be other explanatory strategies, supplemental to the ones considered in the preceding chapter, that could permit the carryover of less than precisely similar characteristics in application to newly introduced explanatory entities. There also may be ways of modifying characterizations of entities that were conceived originally by way of univocal predication without thereby destroying their explanatory capacities. In fact, there would appear to be some evidence of such strategies being employed in the development and modification of assorted conceptions of subatomic particles. Probably a careful investigation of the introduction and subsequent alterations of Bohr's conception of the atom would reveal numerous ways of evolving an understanding of explanatory entities without taking recourse to univocal predications. But for the purposes of this study, the more basic strategies outlined in the third chapter will prove sufficient. So, if Fred attributes love to God because it is the love of certain rich parents that accounts for the constant supply of food, clothing, and shelter for their children, then to guarantee the explanatory efficacy of the love he attributes to God without moving beyond the simple patterns of that chapter, Fred must attribute the same love to God as he found in the parents.

It is very important to keep the issues straight here. It is certainly possible that, upon further reflection, Fred might want to retract his original attribution of love to God. He may discover, for instance, that the doting love of his rich neighbors is also responsible for certain patterns of behavior that would be inappropriate if attributed to God. Or, contrary to his original supposition, he might discover that the patterns of the children's supply of food, clothing, and shelter are not really relevantly analogous to his own patterns of succor after all. But all of this is beside the point at issue here. When Fred finally settles on a case that he believes to be relevantly analogous and he finally decides precisely which features of the known mechanism are the efficacious ones, then he must carry exactly those features over in application to God. Otherwise, the parasitic nature of this particular explanatory strategy is lost. Instead of being able to claim that the understanding of the analogous case can be transferred to the religious sphere for the purpose of understanding the operative nature of God, Fred would be forced to make the rather uninformative claim that while such-and-such a feature is responsible for certain phenomena in the known case, God has a quite different feature that accounts for another range of the same kind of phenomena.

It certainly must be admitted that limiting Fred's theological use of explanatory structures to those outlined in the third chapter has some serious disadvantages for those inclined to follow Saint Thomas.[7] If he is to employ this explanatory strategy properly, Fred must be willing to predicate certain features of God and other things univocally. But this limited strategy also has some rather attractive advantages. Obviously, it allows a major step beyond the mere functional definition of 'God' to be taken. By ascribing specific properties to God, his positive characterization can be elucidated more fully. Also, an important step can be taken toward the individuation of God, a step that will allow progress to be made toward fixing the reference of 'God' by providing a wider basis upon which he might be positively identified. Furthermore, Fred has a way to move beyond merely symbolic or analogical talk about God. By using the procedures outlined in the preceding chapter, he is freed from the bonds imagined by writers like Robinson, Tillich, and Copleston.[8]

Finally, it should be noted that by selecting a relevantly analogous mechanism from outside the religious sphere, the meaning of 'God' can be defined without having to rely upon other bits of religious discourse. To see this point, consider Fred's selection of prosperous parents as a source of analogy for attributing love to God. Noting that the love of these parents spurred them to support their children, Fred was able to move to the conclusion that God is characterized by that same love. Since the love of God and that of the parents is the same, should someone ask the meaning of 'is loving' when attributed to God, recourse would not need to be taken to peculiarly religious contexts. Instead, the best way to come to a fuller understanding of the love of God would be to investigate more thoroughly the love of Fred's rich neighbors. That is, an understanding of 'is loving', when applied to God can and should come from an investigation of the social, psychological, and economic roles played by Fred's rich neighbors as they respond to the wants and needs of their children.

The selection of a relevantly analogous case from outside the religious sphere places the burden of intelligibility of at least some predications of God outside the confines of peculiarly religious discourse. This fact has several immediate ramifications. First, objections against the intelligibility of religious discourse that arise from the supposed peculiarities or eccentricities of specifically religious language can be ignored safely. At least those stretches of talk about God that are introduced in accordance with Fred's introduction of 'is loving' derive their meaningfulness from nonreligious contexts and so remain immune from variously imagined debilitations thought to arise from the uniqueness of religious contexts. Second, the use of this particular explanatory structure places a high premium upon the intelligibility of sources of analogous mechanisms. Only insofar as the source of analogy is understood will there be any insight gained into the nature or structure of newly introduced explanatory entities. Were the love of Fred's neighbors completely incomprehensible, love attributed to God would be equally mysterious. Alternatively, were the love of Fred's neighbors fully and clearly grasped, God's love also would be understood extensively. Finally, since in this sort of case the intelligibility of religious contexts relies upon the comprehensibility of nonreligious ones, augmentations in the understanding of God will result from any increase in the understanding of nonreligious sources of analogy. Thus, should God turn out to be difficult to study in a direct fashion, his nature might be investigated more readily by turning to a prolonged scrutiny of analogous cases.

Before moving on to a discussion of the honing process in the religious case, one particular objection that may be raised at this juncture must be faced. According to the strategies outlined in the third chapter, before the religious devotee can move beyond the functional definition of 'God', some relevantly analogous range of phenomena must be found for which the controlling mechanism already is understood. But, it might be claimed, no such range ever can be found. After all, consider Fred's search for cases where food, clothing, and shelter are supplied constantly. He chose to focus upon his rich neighbors and their children. A closer look at this case, however, reveals that it cannot be relevantly analogous. Sometimes such parents are forgetful and so let their children suffer without lunch or dinner. Sometimes they are faced with economic crises and so cannot afford to buy needed clothing. Inevitably, someday, all parents will grow old and sick, leaving their children to fend for themselves. But God never fails Fred. Since he never forgets, never loses on the stock market, and never becomes old and enfeebled, God never will allow Fred to suffer a shortage of food, clothing, or shelter. In short, human parents, in their finitude of love, never can prove relevantly analogous to an infinitely loving and powerful God.

In his discussion of the problem of identifying God, Hick mulls over this difficulty in more general terms. He writes:

God is described in Christian theology in terms of various absolute qualities, such as omnipotence, omnipresence, perfect goodness, infinite love, etc., which cannot as such be observed by us, as can their finite analogues, limited power, local presence, finite goodness, and human love. One can recognize that a being whom one "encounters" has a given finite degree of power, but how does one recognize that he has *un*limited power? How does one observe that an encountered being is *omni*present? How does one perceive that his goodness and love, which one can perhaps see to exceed any human goodness and love, are actually infinite? Such qualities cannot be given in human experience.[9]

Some of Hick's worries do not carry over to the consideration of the case at hand. One of his main concerns is the problem of recognizing an experience as one of an unlimited or infinite characteristic when all human experience is of a limited and restricted scope. Since nothing in the sort of case envisioned here involves experientially encountering God as an unrestricted being, this problem simply can be sidestepped as irrelevant. But, what is relevant about this passage from Hick is his claim that within the realm of human experience, only finite love, power, and so on ever are encountered. Hence, cases of perfect goodness, omnipotence, and the like that could be taken as relevantly analogous for the characterization of God as an explanatory entity never can be found. So, the explanatory strategy discussed here never can be used in the attribution of such "infinite" characteristics to God.

One possible recourse here might be to admit defeat. That is, theologians like Fred simply could refrain from trying to use this particular explanatory structure for attributing traditionally Christian characteristics like perfect goodness or infinite power to God. Either this traditional view of God could be abandoned for a more modest one or some other method of so characterizing God might be sought. But another alternative would be simply to recognize that this objection is nothing more than a sheep in wolf's clothing.

The quickest way to reveal the impotence of this particular objection is to return to the specific example at hand. Fred is concerned to attribute the love of certain rich parents to God. But, so it is objected, the case of the prosperous neighbors is not relevantly analogous because Fred needs to attribute infinite love to God while his neighbors are possessed of only finite love. But what precisely is meant by "infinite" here? Is the difference between God and the parents to be conceived in terms of quantity so that God is imagined to have huge, heaping mounds of love while the parents have only a few grains of the stuff? Hardly.

To restate the problem more precisely as well as more helpfully, Fred is faced with a discrepancy between the range of phenomena for which the parents' love accounts and the range for which God is expected to account. Now the crucial issue is to determine exactly where the source of this discrepancy lies. If Fred were to discover that his neighbors' love *would* account for a range precisely parallel to God's range were it not for the fact that his neighbors periodically lapse into fits of forgetfulness about their responsibilities, capriciously torment their children during rainy weather, and feel the economic pinch of bad days on the stock market, then simply stripping away the explanatorily detrimental features of the human case will bridge the gap between infinite and finite love. In this sort of case, infinite love is nothing other than plain old garden-variety love that is not restricted by the interference of other facets of human personality or blocked by the exigencies of social and economic life. To say that God's love is infinite or perfect, then, is to say nothing more than that his love is not limited by the detrimental features that limit Fred's rich neighbors.

If Fred were to discover that the discrepancy between the range of phenomena for which God is expected to account and the range for which his neighbors' love accounts could not be chalked up to the inhibitive influence of certain personal and environmental factors, then he would be faced with the simple fact that he has not picked a relevantly analogous range of phenomena from which an explanatory model can be drawn. At this point, several courses would be open. Fred might resume his search for a relevantly analogous range in the hope of finding a more promising one. Alternatively, he might alter his explanatory expectations by recharting the explanatory range for which God is expected to account so that it more adequately fits the explanatory range of the rich neighbors. Finally, he might seek a property in his neighbors other than love in the hope of shifting their explanatory range to coincide more adequately with God's. Of course, none of these tactics necessarily would guarantee that Fred's quest would end ultimately in success. But such guarantees are never available, be the quest a religious or a scientific one.

It is extremely important to emphasize that whatever failure Fred might have to face in his explanatory quest, such failure would not be the result of some purported peculiarity that stems from the "infinity" or "perfection" of God's love. Either his failure would be a temporary one, due to the fact that he had not yet stripped away explanatorily detrimental features from the divine case or it would be the result of being unable to find a relevantly analogous range of phenomena for which the governing mechanism is understood. While the first difficulty could be eliminated through the normal honing process, the second is a mundane consequence of the fact that theoretical endeavors are not preplanned melodramas. Not every explanatory quest will end in success. Sometimes relevantly analogous ranges of phenomena for which the governing mechanism is understood cannot be found. In such cases, the theologian must confront the same disappointment faced every day on the frontiers of science.

It must be admitted that when Fred is confronted with a discrepancy between the explanatory range of his neighbors' finite love and that of God's infinite love, he may not be certain how to proceed. He may not know whether this discrepancy is due to the fact that he has not yet stripped away various detrimental features from the human case or whether it is the result of picking a range of phenomena that is not really relevantly analogous to the range for which God's love is expected to account. But his indecision on this matter would not stem from any purported difficulties with terms like 'infinite' or 'perfect'. In fact, it would have nothing at all to do with the religious side of the analogy. Instead, it would stem from a lack of understanding of his neighbors' love. If Fred had full knowledge of his neighbors' case, he would know which, if any, detrimental features prohibit the extension of loving behavior on specified occasions. The more complete his knowledge of the interference of such inhibitive factors, the more complete would be his understanding of how his neighbors' love would operate under counterfactual circumstances. In turn, the fuller his understanding of how his neighbors' love would operate when uninhibited by assorted detrimental factors, the more easily could Fred determine the potential for carrying his neighbors' love, suitably stripped, over in application to the religious case. If, so stripped, it would account for a range of phenomena relevantly analogous to the range chosen for God, then Fred would be in fine shape. If it would not account for such a relevantly analogous range of phenomena, Fred would be forced to begin anew his quest for some relevantly analogous range.

Once the initial positive characterization of God has been made by affirming that he possesses those features that are explanatorily efficacious in the analogous case, the honing process can begin. As was noted above and outlined in the preceding chapter, the first step in this process consists in carrying over explanatorily efficacious features from the known mechanism. Once these features have been attributed to the newly introduced mechanism, explanatorily irrelevant and detrimental properties must be purged. As was noted in the discussion of the scientific case, the purging of irrelevant and detrimental properties is subject to a few constraints. If purgations require some violation of prior logical or theoretical commitments, then some epistemic sacrifice will have to be made. As was seen in the second chapter, the possibility of abandoning various prior logical or theoretical commitments is not entirely out of the question. But, in general, it is less systematically destructive to allow superfluous properties to tag along with explanatorily efficacious ones than it is to sacrifice bits of accepted theory for the sake of sharpening the conception of a newly introduced explanatory entity. With regard to explanatorily detrimental features, the consequences of alternative courses of action must be weighed carefully. If detrimental features can be stripped away with only minor alterations in previously accepted theory, probably a purge of the offending features from the characterization of an explanatory entity will prove to be the most attractive course of action. On the other hand, should the cost of stripping away a detrimental characteristic prove highly disastrous to accepted theory, if the retention of that detrimental feature in the conception of a newly introduced entity would not prove too damaging to its explanatory effectiveness, then that retention probably would be tolerated. Finally, if the retention of some detrimental feature would prove explanatorily disastrous while stripping it away would be costly to accepted theory, then probably a new search for some other explanatorily relevant range of phenomena governed by some different and more easily assimilated mechanism would be initiated.

There is one way in which this sharpening of God's explanatory effectiveness would differ rather sharply from the scientific case. In the interest of theoretical progress, the sciences usually can ignore with impunity the wider social and psychological roles their explanatory posits might be asked to play. As long as the attribution and purgation of various properties does not violate any logical or theoretical commitments, the scientist normally may proceed merrily along. God, however, is expected to perform many nontheoretical functions. In fact, these may be even more important than his theoretical roles. For example, since he is usually expected to be a suitable object of worship, many believers would find a loathsome, unlovable, or disgusting deity to be critically deficient.

Because God's nontheoretical roles are every bit as important, if not more so, than his theoretical ones, the impact of introducing explanatorily efficacious properties or purging superfluous and detrimental ones upon these other spheres of importance must be measured. For instance, if it were found that the introduction of some explanatorily efficacious property would render God morally reprehensible or would prohibit him from becoming a suitable object of worship, that property could be attributed to God only at serious cost to his overall function as a religiously effective entity. But here as elsewhere, the costs must be weighed against the benefits. If no other property could be found that would play the relevant explanatory role more suitably, then the theoretical advantages must be measured against the nonepistemic disadvantages. Perhaps a large gain in explanatory effectiveness would be worth a small sacrifice in the believer's conception of the dignity, moral purity, or venerability of God.

Besides the simple carryover of explanatorily efficacious properties with the attendant purging of superfluous and detrimental ones, increased precision also can be enhanced in other ways. For instance, consider the balloons from the last chapter. If the scientist's sea of air were expected to account for some exact correlation of balloon diameters with various altitudes or were expected to explain various precise rates of change in balloon diameter with rates of change in altitude, then an adequate explanation of such precisely determined ranges of phenomena would have to provide a much finer analysis of the nature and activities of the sea of air than would be required in the explanation of a much more vaguely delimited explanatory range. Similarly, if Fred were to try to show how God's love can be used to explain some precisely defined set of phenomena rather than the vaguely general fact that certain needs always are met, he would be moving toward increased explanatory precision. His move would be in the same direction as the scientist attempting to move from an invocation of a sea of air that can explain only the simple fact that balloons change sizes with changes in altitude to an invocation of a sea of air that can account for exact rates of change and correlations of balloon diameter with altitude.

One way in which the characterization of an entity can be shaped to account for a more carefully specified range of phenomena is through the positing of finer mechanisms. Such posits also can bring increased understanding of the manner in which various explanatorily efficacious properties determine their ranges of phenomena. To note only that the pressure of the sea of air determines the expansion and contraction of balloons in the same way as the Pacific Ocean determines the diameter of rubber balls may be sufficient to explain satisfactorily why balloons change size at varying altitudes. But this elementary comment is distinctly less satisfactory if an explanation is sought for certain precise correlations of changes in altitude with changes in balloon size. A more precise account of exactly how pressure determines balloon size is wanted. To satisfy this thirst for a more fully developed explanation, the scientist may turn to the introduction of finer mechanisms that are drawn from a knowledge of other operative mechanisms. So, it might be suggested that the pressure of the air upon the surface of balloons be conceived in terms of an operative mechanism analogous to popcorn smashing against the lid of a popper. Correlations of balloon size with altitude could then be explained in terms of differences in numbers or speeds of "popcorn-like" impacts of air molecules on rising or falling balloons.

With regard to the religious case, analogies with popcorn makers are limited. More likely, religious theorists will look to persons as promising relevantly analogous mechanisms. So, increased understanding into the nature and functioning of God will result frequently from an increased understanding of human personality. For Fred, explanatory precision would result if he were able not only to note that God's love is the same as that of his rich neighbors, but also to provide some insight into the nature of human parental love. It would appear, then, that psychology, sociology, or any other field of investigation into human behavior would be of intense interest to religious theorists. By yielding a deeper grasp of the mechanisms responsible for human behavior, such fields could prove a fruitful resource in the attempt to articulate more completely the nature and operation of God.

Unfortunately, applying the findings of the human sciences to the articulation of God's nature is not as straightforward as it sounds. There are numerous models of human personality employed in the sciences and not all of them are appropriately carried over into religious contexts. Since the model most frequently used in the characterization of God is one in which human beings are thought of as free agents, distinguished by assorted character traits and consciously motivated by various desires and beliefs, the investigations of someone like B. F. Skinner, particularly as they are encapsulated in a work like *Beyond Freedom and Dignity*,[10] usually would not be of much help to the theologian. Only when a science offers an appropriate conception of humanity or when it provides information that can be refocused successfully to cast illumination upon an appropriate model will the theologian find help in his attempt to develop his conception of God as a person.

With all this interest in the conception of God as shaped by reference to human models, a rather persistent objection against the theological enterprise must be addressed. Kai Nielsen has written:

If God is conceived in anthropomorphic terms, He is, in important respects, Zeus-like. . . . Such a God is indeed a determinate being among beings, though indeed a being of most extraordinary characteristics. With such a conception of God, putatively assertive God-talk is quite verifiable, but what is said . . . is for the most part just plainly false. Nonanthropomorphic conceptions of God, by contrast, are largely characterisable as a denial of the claims of anthropomorphic theism.[11]

Such nonanthropomorphic conceptions, Nielsen goes on to argue, leave God unidentifiable and so 'God' is reduced to unintelligibility.[12]

Three distinct claims are introduced here. First, Nielsen claims that anthropomorphic conceptions of God lead to false assertions about his existence and activities. Second, he says that nonanthropomorphic conceptions of God are essentially negative, leave God unidentifiable, and so give no intelligible meaning to 'God'. Finally, he argues that all conceptions of God must be either anthropomorphic or nonanthropomorphic.

It is difficult to know how to respond to this particular argument. Questions of the truth or falsity of religious assertions can, and will, be put off for subsequent consideration. But with regard to Nielsen's supposed dilemma, it is hard to see where the position under present consideration might fit. After all, while appeal is made to a conception of God as a person, this hardly can be called a form of anthropomorphism. The invocation of human personality as a relevantly analogous mechanism for the characterization of God in no way implies that God is an ordinary being or even a superior, magnified, extraordinary human being. It is certainly true, of course, that the choice of human beings as relevantly analogous to God will lead to the claim that both God and at least some people share certain explanatorily efficacious properties. But there also will be radical differences between God and human beings. The theologian's position is no different from that of the scientist imagined in the preceding chapter. While it is true that a sea of air may be modeled on the Pacific Ocean, the implication that a newly conceived sea of air must be just another ocean filled with fish is preposterous. In similar fashion, the mere fact that God and people share efficacious properties hardly can be taken to imply that God is just another human being of a certain type.

On the other hand, Nielsen's characterization of nonanthropomorphic conceptions of God does not seem to fit the case at hand either. According to Nielsen, such conceptions are formulated by way of denial, leave God unidentifiable, and so result in an unintelligible conception of 'God'. Yet, in the preceding pages, it has been seen that the explanatory strategy under current investigation provides positive functional definitions and the attribution of positive efficacious properties to God. It also allows a way of identifying God and leaves 'God' as intelligible as any term similarly introduced in the sciences. Perhaps the moral to be drawn is that Nielsen has formulated something of a false dilemma.

Before moving away from this general sketch of the ways in which the conception of God as an explanatory entity might be evolved and refined, a few of the advantages of taking this particular approach to the specification of God's nature need to be emphasized. One of the most appealing features of this strategy is that it allows a response to persistently recurrent objections to theological discourse. For example, it provides a way out of the problem suggested by Nielsen's question:

How are we to, or can we understand the putative truth-claim that there exists a reality transcendent to the world which manifests itself in the world while remaining undetectable in space and time? What would it be like for such an utterance to be either true or false? And what would it be like to specify the objective referent for the terms purporting to characterise such a reality.[13]

Nielsen seems to believe that a being that is entirely outside the constraints of spatio-temporal existence, a being that could not be experienced either directly or indirectly within the spatio-temporal world, would have to remain an unintelligible mystery. The nature of such a being never could be specified, even in part. The existence of such a being could never be determined. Indeed, purported truth claims about such a being never could be checked by taking recourse to the spatio-temporal world of human experience.

If the strategies outlined in the preceding pages of this and the third chapter are followed rigorously, then there would seem to be nothing in Nielsen's fears that should cause the theologian to lose any sleep. After all, there are methods other than ostension and its sophisticated variants that can be used to fix the reference of a term like 'God'. It was seen that a functional definition in terms of the range of phenomena for which God is expected to account allows a way of distinguishing God from other possible referents. But the development of such functional definitions nowhere presumes that God is a spatio-temporal being. Similarly, by taking recourse to relevantly analogous mechanisms, something of God's nature can be determined. Again, there is nothing in the process of such a specification of God's nature that requires him to be spatio-temporally locatable. All that is required is that the range of phenomena for which the known mechanism accounts is relevantly analogous to God's range. Then, the efficacious features of the analogous mechanism can be attributed to God. Of course, if those features were temporal or spatial ones, like being fifteen years old or being seven feet tall, then their attribution to a being outside space or time might be problematic. But few theologians find such features to be the ones they wish to apply to God. Love, trustworthiness, and justice prove to be more theologically attractive and none of these is typically spatio-temporal.

Were Nielsen's worries applicable to the theologian, they would have to be of equal concern to the scientist who follows the procedures outlined in the third chapter. But, like theologians, scientists appear to proceed in blithe disregard of Nielsen's constraints. Consider, for instance, the way in which electrons might be introduced to account for certain patterns of phenomena in cloud chambers. Now certainly such phenomena are spatio-temporally located and can be detected by observers within the bounds of the spatio-temporal world. But no scientist worth his salt would concede that electrons themselves could be observed within space and time. Electrons cannot be observed at all. Their presence may be determined by the occurrence of certain phenomena, but electrons are not identical with those phenomena. After all, electrons are not little streaks of bubbles in cloud chambers or little lines on photographic plates. Furthermore, with regard to at least some explanatory entities employed by the sciences, not only can they themselves never be observed within space and time, they do not even seem to be in space and time. At least some of the more radical conceptions of subatomic entities leave one with the suspicion that spatio-temporal categories must be stretched considerably, if not discarded altogether. Along much less exotic lines, consider the explanatory invocation of magnetic fields. Should they be considered to be in space and time? Certainly many of the phenomena they govern are. But if magnetic fields are spatio-temporal entities, and since many iron bars are magnetized, it would seem that two spatio-temporal objects can be in the same place at the same time. This is surely a disconcerting consequence. Perhaps it is not so clear, then, that magnetic fields are in space and time.

But all this chatter about electrons and magnetic fields being inside or outside space and time is really beside the point at issue here. Even if it were shown that every entity invoked by the sciences is uncontroversially spatio-temporal, Nielsen's concerns still would not be validated. The simple fact is that spatio-temporal existence and locatability are bogus constraints. The strategies outlined in the third chapter are nowhere dependent upon either one. So, the theologian following these strategies confidently can join the scientist who continues his explanatory investigations in happy disregard of Nielsen's strictures.

Of course, there is one thorn remaining in Nielsen's flesh. In the passage cited above, he was concerned not only with the fact that a transcendent God would have to be outside the bounds of space and time and so could never be located within a spatio-temporal context. He also was convinced that purported truth claims about such a transcendent being never could be checked. Clearly, this is nothing more than an updated and specific application of Flew's famous challenge. Flew originally wrote, "'What would have to occur or to have occurred to constitute for you a disproof of the love of, or of the existence of, God?'" [14] Nielsen, in recognition of the overly restrictive nature of Flew's original challenge, has liberalized it in the light of the sort of Quinean considerations summarized in the first chapter. Since there would seem to be no statement whatever that can be falsified conclusively in the manner envisioned by Flew, Nielsen tried substituting the weaker constraint that "a putatively factual statement actually has factual significance . . . only if some differential experience is relevant to its truth or falsity." [15] Since he believes that there could be no occurrence or manageably small set of occurrences that would be evidentially relevant in any way to the claim that a transcendent God exists, Nielsen concludes that supposed truth claims about such a being would have to be factually meaningless.

With the materials available from the investigations undertaken in the preceding pages, it should be clear that much can be offered in response to Flew's updated challenge. Whether God be transcendent or not, if he is conceived as an explanatory entity in line with the discussion of the third chapter, then there are ranges of phenomena that will count either for or against his existence. There are even ranges of phenomena that will count for or against truth claims that might be made concerning God's nature and constitution. Although a more detailed discussion of the basis for determining the truth values of religious explanations must be reserved for the next chapter, it is not at all difficult to specify at least some of the ranges of phenomena that would be evidentially relevant to claims about God's existence and nature. All those patterns for which God is expected to account certainly would fall into the category of evidentially relevant data.

Unfortunately, as should be evident from the third chapter, the explanatory ranges of God will not stand in any simple-minded evidential relation to claims made about him. As can be seen from a few examples, the evidential relationships involved are much too complex to allow the easy conclusion that particular stretches of data can verify or falsify explanatory claims in any direct way. Consider, for instance, a theologian who is faced with some stubbornly recalcitrant range of data that seems to be inexplicable by making reference to God. There are any number of ways in which this data might be handled. Obviously, the most drastic course of action would be simply to repudiate the existence of God. But other, less radical alternatives also are available. Instead of rejecting God's existence, the range of phenomena for which God is expected to account could be so circumscribed that unaccountable data fall outside his explanatory range. The sciences certainly offer historical precedent for such a move as this. Consider, as only one example, the recent history of medical biology. With the discovery of microbes, it was tempting to suppose that all diseases were caused by germs. Unhappily, because a survey of the data would not support such an explanatory range for germ theory, a much more restricted range had to be accepted. This restricted explanatory range not only brought germ theory into line with the data, but also guided medical research into areas beyond the microscopic world. Increased understanding of viruses and human nutrition were only two of the many benefits that resulted from this refocus of attention.

Alternatively, the religious devotee could adjust his understanding of the nature and functioning of God in order to account for recalcitrant explanatory ranges. As in the sea of air case, this reconception of God's nature might involve nothing more than a purging of explanatorily detrimental properties. Just as the failure of balloons to deteriorate was taken into account by eliminating the attribution of the corrosive properties of salt water to the sea of air, so the conception of God might be stripped of characterizations that enfeeble his explanatory power. If this strategy should prove inadequate, adjustments of a more complex sort could be introduced. Perhaps a more detailed analysis of the efficacious features currently attributed to God would help. By introducing finer mechanisms into the conception of God's nature, a closer fit between his explanatory capacities and his explanatory range might be achieved.

It might even be necessary to renew the search for analogous mechanisms to allow the substitution of a more adequate conception of God. By reconceiving God along entirely new lines of analogy, it might be possible to find a way of showing how God can account for some particularly difficult range of data. Had the sea of air theorist been faced with a similar crisis in the last chapter, had it been found that there is no way of accounting for some range of data by taking recourse to the activity of the Pacific Ocean, he would have been forced to find some other, more helpful source of analogous mechanism. Although the discovery of some new controlling mechanism would have altered deeply his conception of the ways in which balloon sizes are determined, such systematic rethinking might have been the only way out.

All of these and many other alternative responses to stubborn data can be found exemplified in the sciences. Consider, for instance, the long history of atomic physics. In the days of Democritus, atoms were thought to be indivisible particles of stuff. But as it was discovered that indivisible atoms were unable to account for various chemical, electrical, and physical phenomena, they were purged of their indivisibility and allowed to be conceived as breakable into complexes of protons, neutrons, and electrons. With the need for a more sophisticated understanding of these newly introduced subatomic particles came the utilization of particle accelerators for the purpose of developing finer analyses of the precise natures of each such subatomic entity. Finally, in the wake of yet other data resulting from assorted experiments with light, magnetism, and electricity, pressure recently has begun to mount for a thorough reconception of elementary particles along entirely new lines of analogy. Waves have seemed a particularly attractive alternative, but at present, because no single, ultimately satisfying conception of atoms is currently available, a search for yet other sources of analogy accompanies the continued elaboration of both particle and wave models.

In connection with this brief survey of some of the complexities of the evidential relationships between phenomena and explanatory entities, a few additional comments are in order. The first regards the problem of evil. There seems to be wide agreement with Basil Mitchell who noted that the problem of evil is "the most intractable of theological problems."[16] The reason why this problem is so profoundly difficult becomes very clear upon a bit of reflection concerning the indirect relationships between God as an explanatory entity and the range of phenomena he is invoked to explain. The power of the problem of evil lies in the way it is formulated. Typically, those who construct the problem do not try to show that the occurrence of suffering, unhappiness, or some other evil decisively or directly falsifies some specific claim about God. If they did, their strategy could be dismissed along with Flew's original challenge as unduly simplistic. Instead, the problem of evil is formulated in recognition of the complexity of the evidential relationships between the course of experience and claims about God's existence and his nature. Thus, it is argued, a particular occurrence of evil counts against a larger body of commitments, no one of which is jeopardized, though at least one of which must be repudiated.

The believer is left with several avenues of escape. For instance, he might try to readjust his conception of God's explanatory range, arguing that the evil occurrence in question falls outside God's explanatory scope and into the sphere of responsibility of free human or angelic agents. Alternatively, the believer may try to account for the offending occurrence of evil by adjusting his understanding of the nature of God. Purging his characterization of God by eliminating reference to omnipotence or omniscience probably would do the trick, should this option be chosen. But in a careful formulation of the problem of evil, each possible escape route is anticipated in such a way as to make all of them distasteful to the believer. That is, the problem is so posed as to leave many avenues of escape open to the believer, though each such option requires the sacrifice of some religiously essential commitment. Whether any such careful formulation of the problem of evil actually succeeds at systematically trapping the believer may be uncertain, but because it relies upon a full appreciation of the complex and often indirect evidential relations between data and theoretical commitments, the problem of evil cannot be casually brushed aside as overly simplistic in its assumptions.

The second point to be made is in regard to the relation of verifying data to religious explanations. With all the attention that has been devoted to Flew's falsification challenge, it is easy to overlook the indirect way in which supposedly verifying data impinge upon theoretical commitment. It cannot simply be assumed that data that can be explained by making reference to God straightforwardly confirm his existence. The evidential relations between such data and God are every bit as complex as those which obtain between God and more recalcitrant data.

As just one facet of the complexity to be explored here, consider the fact of explanatory interchangeability. Two sets of entities, each of which can account for the same range of data, are explanatorily interchangeable. For explanatory purposes, one set can serve as well as the other. So, any basis for preference of one over the other will have to be determined with reference to factors beyond the obvious recognition that both sets can account fully for the same explanatory range. While there may be a great number of reasons for preferring one set of entities to another, equally explanatory, set, attention typically settles around two distinct questions. First, it must be determined whether either set of entities can be invoked to explain yet other ranges of phenomena. If one set can explain not only the range in question, but also some additional range for which the other cannot account, then the former will tend to be favored for its more comprehensive explanatory powers. Second, the compatibility of each set of explanatory entities with wider theoretical enterprises must be assessed. If one set can be integrated more easily into a wider body of theory, or employs less controversial efficacious properties, it will tend to be favored. Thus, for the religious theorist, it is not enough that God can be shown to account for some range of phenomena. If it should be discovered that there is some other entity or set of entities that can perform the same explanatory roles as God and yet will fulfill other roles as well or perhaps fit more satisfactorily into some wider framework of theoretical commitment, the existence of God will be placed into considerable doubt. In sum, even though God might account for all the relevant phenomena, his existence would not necessarily be confirmed.

It is this fact of the interchangeability of explanatory entities together with its attendant threat upon existence claims that seems to make current evolutionary theory so frightening to many conservative Christian communities. Advocates of creationism obviously believe that God is able to account for all the relevant geological and biological data. Nevertheless, they appear unable to rest content with this supposition. The problem is that natural selection might also be able to explain the same data. Since the genetic principles behind evolutionary theory seem to be much more easily assimilable into the larger theoretical contexts of chemistry and physics, should both God and natural selection prove equally able to account for all the data, God still would appear to be left explanatorily inferior and so theoretically superfluous. Therefore, since they suspect that reference to God could be invoked legitimately only if natural selection were found to be unable to account for the appropriate explanatory range, creationists feel a peculiar urgency to demonstrate not only that God can account for all the relevant data, but also that evolutionary theory cannot.

To move beyond these general remarks about the application of a scientific model within religious contexts, specific sorts of plausible explanatory ranges for God must be introduced. It is fairly easy to go on and on in a rather sweeping and general way about the sorts of constraints that would have to be imposed were God to be invoked as an explanatory entity. However, without a closer consideration of at least some of the ranges of phenomena for which God plausibly might be expected to account these general reflections will be of minimal practical value. So, while the question of the truth or falsity of particular religious explanations shall remain reserved for discussion in the next two chapters, attention now must be turned toward some preliminary exploration into the possibility of finding plausible explanatory ranges for God.

Even the briefest historical survey of any moderately sophisticated religious tradition will reveal at least three distinct ways in which God or some other religiously significant entity is employed explanatorily.[17] Consider, for the sake of a familiar example, the history of the Judeo-Christian tradition. One of the most common sorts of explanatory appeal to God, particularly among more conservative elements of this tradition, occurs in the course of explaining personal religious behavior. Frequently, when asked why prayers are said at certain times, why unblemished lambs are occasionally sacrificed, why members regularly tithe or attend services, or why unusual clothing is worn, explanations ultimately will end in appeals to the nature or desires of God.

Imagine someone trying to explain why he attends church services on such a regular basis. In an attempt to answer this question, the believer probably will begin by making reference to his own wishes or desires. He might say, for instance, that he wants to prosper in his business affairs, that he wants to get to heaven or, less egoistically, that he wants to please God. Without further elaboration, this explanation will remain essentially incomplete at this point. To anyone ignorant of the complexities of this man's faith, there will appear to be no important connection between regular church attendance and financial prosperity, eternal rewards, or God's bliss. Thus, to complete his explanation, the believer must forge some link between his personal behavior and whatever he believes is accomplished by that behavior. In this particular example, some important connection between faithful attendance at church and riches, eternal life, or divine happiness must be drawn.

In order to forge the link required here, the nature or wants of God must enter into play. The believer must show exactly what it is about God that stimulates him to respond in the desired way to the believer's behavior patterns. Again, with regard to the specific case at hand, the believer must show what feature about God's makeup insures that regular church attendance will result in business success, eternal life, or divine bliss. Perhaps it will be suggested that God will provide financial security or eternal bliss in exchange for such minimal behavior because he is an old softy, easily moved by little gestures of love and respect. Perhaps the believer will explain that God is extraordinarily vain and so gets great pleasure out of watching believers legalistically toe the mark. Out of a less menial conception of God, the devotee might argue that God has promised success or eternal happiness to those who attend church and, since God is both honest and trustworthy, he will honor his promises. Whatever account of God might be offered, the concern of the believer will be to link various forms of behavior with certain anticipated ends by way of an explication of God's nature and behavior.

It must be admitted that little insight into explanations of this sort can be gained by following the strategies outlined in the third chapter. Appeals to relevantly analogous patterns of phenomena with their attendant controlling mechanisms, investigations of the explanatory efficacy of various properties, and all of the rest of the conceptual apparatus drawn out of the consideration of scientific explanations are of almost no avail here. The reason why all of this is of so little value in an understanding of this first sort of explanation is quite simple: in offering an acceptable account of his personal religious behavior, the religious devotee need only refer to his intentions and certain of his beliefs regarding how such intentions can be fulfilled effectively. Since the beliefs that determine individual behavior need not be true, probably true, or even rationally defensible and, furthermore, since such beliefs need not be generated by intellectually respectable processes, any believer can offer a complete explanation of his personal behavior without demonstrating anything whatever with regard to the epistemic strength or integrity of his convictions. Only two things are required in order for an explanation of this first sort to be adequate. First, the believer must be convinced that his characterization of God is an accurate one. Second, he must be convinced that the behavior he is attempting to explain really is determined by his conception of God in just the way he says that it is.

Although not much insight into this first sort of religious explanation can be gained by consulting the investigations of the preceding chapter, gleanings from that chapter can be applied more fruitfully to explanations of a second sort. This second way in which explanations are used in religious contexts is to account for occurrences taken to be miraculous. Events thought to be miraculous may range anywhere from ones of great historical or theological significance, like the resurrection of Jesus or the changing of water into wine at Cana, to those of a more garden variety, such as whispered messages in the night or answers to unpretentious prayers.

This second type of explanation poses some unique problems. Obviously, there is the question of the authenticity of purportedly miraculous occurrences. If Jesus never rose from the dead or water never was changed into wine at the wedding feast of Cana, then there is nothing to explain. Since most miraculous happenings take place in the privacy of believers' homes or are reported by people whose veracity may be open to question, it is usually difficult, if not impossible, to authenticate such occurrences after the fact. Fortunately, this thorny problem lies well outside the concern of our investigations. For the purposes of this study, it simply can be assumed that events of this sort have occurred.

There is a second difficulty that arises at this point that is closely connected with the first. Supposing that the sorts of events in question really have occurred, one is still left with the problem of determining whether they should be taken as truly miraculous. Given that the resurrection of Jesus or quiet whisperings really did happen, should such events be labeled as genuine miracles? Some general criterion by which the miraculous can be singled out and identified as such must be uncovered.

Happily, the needed criterion is fairly easy to come by. In attempting to determine whether an event is a miraculous one, it is important to look for features of that event that cannot be accounted for by taking recourse to the activity of natural mechanisms. With the discovery of some such feature, an event marks itself out from among the ordinary course of things. Consider someone who prays for rent money and, just at the last possible moment, receives the amount required in the mail. Certain features of this case can be explained quite easily by taking recourse to known, natural mechanisms. For instance, delivery through the mail can be attributed to the activities of the postal system. Current banking practices account for the fact that scribblings on the enclosed pieces of paper can be converted into cash. But what about the fact that the check was for exactly the right amount and that it came just in the nick of time? If it were discovered that the person who had needed this money had spoken previously to the donor about his financial problems and, that this particular donor subsequently had sent along the right amount of money at the proper time, an explanation by recourse to a natural mechanism would be available and the event could be judged as charitable, but not miraculous. On the other hand, were it discovered that there was no way in which the donor could have known of this need, then this event might be suspected to be miraculous. If, upon yet further investigation, it were discovered that the donor had had a thoroughly inexplicable and uncharacteristic urge to send along a check that then happened to be of just the right amount, made out to just the right person, and delivered at just the right time, then explanatory recourse to natural mechanisms would fail. At this point, the religious devotee might deem this event a miracle and seek to explain it by taking recourse to God.

A moment must be taken here for some comments about this criterion for determining the occurrence of miracles. First, it should be noted that decisions concerning its applicability are not infallible. There is nothing here that should suggest that mistakes never can be made about the occurrence of miracles. If some sort of Cartesian certainty is sought, it cannot be found here. Mistakes not only can be made, they frequently are. Events once judged to be miraculous may, upon subsequent investigation or upon the discovery of previously unknown natural mechanisms, come to be considered as nothing more than ordinary occurrences. Second, with the expansion of human understanding regarding the mechanisms operative in nature, the range of events thought to be miraculous will tend to narrow. The more natural mechanisms that are discovered and the wider the range of occurrences that can be explained by them, the less chance there will be that some new event will be dubbed a miracle.

Suppose something were found that turned out to be inexplicable by reference to natural mechanisms. There would be one final problem that must be faced before such a supposed miracle could be explained in accordance with the strategies outlined in the third chapter. All of the discussion of explanations thus far has been restricted to a consideration of ones formulated to account for patterns of occurrences, but most miracles are singular events. Jesus rose from the dead only once. He changed water into wine only once. Most people who pray for rent money do not receive it on a monthly basis. Therefore, if miracles are usually uniquely singular events and the explanatory strategies outlined in the preceding chapter are designed for patterns of occurrences, how can the gleanings from that chapter be used to help formulate explanations of miracles?

It is certainly true that most purported miracles are uniquely singular events. It is also true that the explanatory strategies outlined thus far only can be used to account for patterns of phenomena. Hence, if singular miraculous occurrences are to be explained, investigations far beyond the bounds of this study must be undertaken. Either some way of adapting the strategies disclosed in the third chapter to permit their utilization in the account of individual events must be found or some entirely different explanatory structure must be uncovered that can be applied more appropriately in the formulation of explanations for single events. Because neither of these additional kinds of investigations would prove of direct relevance to the issues at stake here, current attention will be devoted exclusively to the explanation of miraculous patterns of occurrence. Though considerably rarer than the citation of specific events, there is an occasional dubbing of some entire pattern of phenomena as miraculous. Sometimes it is argued that no natural mechanism is capable of accounting for some regular arrival of funds or some persistent recurrence of quiet whisperings in the night.

With this continual emphasis upon miracles as events or patterns of events characterized by features that are inexplicable by reference to natural mechanisms, it might be objected that the strategies taken from the third chapter necessarily must fail. After all, explanations of the sort described there must be generated on the basis of finding some relevantly analogous range of phenomena for which the controlling mechanism already is known, but in the identification of something as a miracle, the distinguishing feature is one that cannot be explained by taking recourse to a natural mechanism. Therefore, the theologian is left with a dilemma. Either he can find some analogous range of phenomena for which a natural mechanism is known or he cannot. If he can find such a range, then the distinguishing feature from the supposedly miraculous case also can be explained by taking recourse to the same natural mechanism, in which case, the purportedly miraculous occurrence will not turn out to be a miracle at all. If he cannot find such a relevantly analogous range for which a natural mechanism already is known, than he will not be able to generate an explanation of the occurrence in question at all. So, either the purported miracle will turn out to be explainable, but not miraculous, or may be determined to be miraculous, but remain unexplained.

There are two flaws in this objection. First, the dilemma as stated depends upon the supposition that the theologian only can look for an analogous range of phenomena for which a *natural* mechanism is known. There is no reason why the religious devotee must be restricted so artificially. If his purpose is to allay skeptical fears about the cognitive integrity of religious discourse, then an appeal to ranges of natural phenomena controlled by natural mechanisms probably would be most persuasive. Since the intention of this protracted argument is to undercut the force of such skeptical arguments, current attention obviously will have to be limited to this natural sphere. If the theologian's intention is only to explain some miraculous occurrence, however, there is no reason why his search must be limited so arbitrarily. Perhaps the realm of supernatural phenomena and supernatural mechanisms would provide a fertile field of relevant analogies.

Second, even if the restriction to natural mechanisms were imposed, this objectionable dilemma could not be generated. The criterion by which a pattern of phenomena is identified as miraculous does not require the presence of properties that *never* can be explained by taking recourse to natural mechanisms. It only requires that in the case in question, no such recourse is possible. Consider the regular, fortuitous arrival of needed funds. Many times such patterns of arrival are explicable by reference to natural mechanisms. Generous benefactors regularly send money to the needy. In the purportedly miraculous case, however, the decision to treat the persistent arrival of money as miraculous turns on the fact that, though such arrivals may be explicable by reference to natural mechanisms in certain other cases, in this particular case, such recourse is impossible. There simply is no such natural account available.

With these points in mind, return to the supposed dilemma once more. It was argued that the theologian either may find a relevantly analogous range of phenomena for which a natural mechanism is known or he may not. If he does not, there is no reason why he should not search beyond the natural realm. Of course, there is always the possibility that even here he might be stymied. A relevantly analogous range may never be found anywhere. But this possibility, although an unfortunate one, illustrates nothing more than the rather mundane fact that not all explanatory quests are guaranteed to succeed. In religion as well as in the sciences, research programs occasionally may fail.

Suppose, on the other hand, that a relevantly analogous range for which a natural mechanism is known can be found. It certainly does not follow that this same mechanism can be used to explain the miraculous case as well. It only follows that the same efficacious properties, if attributed to some other mechanism, could do the explanatory job. To bring this point to clarity, consider for one final time the fortuitous arrival of money. In an analogous case, it might be found that the generosity of some conveniently available benefactor accounts for the regular arrival of money in the mail. But that same benefactor cannot necessarily account for the new pattern of fortuitously arriving money. He might be dead, out of the country, or ignorant of this particular needy person. Thus, some other benefactor, in this case God, must be invoked to account for the new case by noting that this new responsible agent, like the analogous one, is also generous.

At this juncture, the way should be clear for miraculous patterns of events to be explained along the lines of the third chapter. Once a pattern of events is identified as miraculous, the search for analogous ranges of phenomena with their attendant controlling mechanisms can be initiated. Upon finding relevantly analogous mechanisms, the familiar honing process subsequently can be carried through.

A third way in which religious communities use their discourse for the provision of explanations is in the attempt to account for patterns of phenomena that they do not consider to be of miraculous origin. It is not difficult to understand why devotees might try to construct religious explanations for patterns of phenomena for which it is impossible to offer a naturalistic account. Nor is it hard to understand why an attempt might be made to explain specific occurrences religiously for which naturalistic explanations are impossible. It is not even too difficult to understand the interest of religious communities in patterns of phenomena that are composed of specific, naturalistically explainable occurrences. In such cases, while the individual occurrence of each instance could not be considered miraculous, if the patterns as wholes could not be explained naturalistically, then those patterns might be thought to be miraculous and so explainable religiously. What is surprising, however, is that anyone would hope to offer a plausible religious explanation for patterns that already can be explained by reference to the determinative activities of natural mechanisms. Religious theorists not only try to do this, they also occasionally try to explain patterns of phenomena for which there is a naturalistic explanation of their occurrence as patterns as well as a naturalistic explanation for each of the individual occurrences out of which they are composed.

Putting questions regarding the plausibility of religious explanations of this third sort to one side for the moment, it should be noted that such religiously explained patterns vary drastically in their scope. Sometimes, along very modest lines, believers try to explain why certain patterns of tribulation or blessing occur. Looking at the course of their own personal histories, histories that might be explained quite easily along naturalistic lines, such believers still feel pressed to give a religious account of why they have suffered lives of trouble or enjoyed recurring patterns of comfort. Typically, reference to God's justice, his love, or some other aspect of his nature are made in the course of supplying explanations of this restricted kind.

Broader sweeps of historical pattern that stretch far beyond the bounds of individual lives to encompass whole nations or even the entire world also might be explained by making similar references to God's nature or activities. Patterns of rise and fall among empires that might be perfectly explainable along historical, political, or sociological lines also might receive a religious account in terms of God's favor or anger. Even wider patterns, stretching beyond the personal and social lives of human beings also might be subjected to this same explanatory attempt. Patterns of biological dependency that rest upon ever-wider patterns of regularity in the laws of physiology or biochemistry, while fully explainable from a scientific standpoint, still can trigger attempts at explanation by way of an invocation of God's wisdom or power. Often such accounts as these are pushed beyond the limits of their explanatory functions and reshaped into attempts to prove the existence of a divine designer.

This third sort of explanation, whether modestly or grandly employed, whether ultimately plausible or implausible, conforms well to the requirements outlined in the third chapter. First, the religious theorist, like the scientist, must begin by mapping out the range of phenomena he hopes to explain. If this range of phenomena can be specified in nonreligious terminology, then no particular problems arise. The theologian simply notes the range for which God is expected to account.

However, suppose the theologian should desire to account for some range of phenomena that is marked out by using specifically religious terms. Suppose, for instance, that he did not want to explain why he always has enough to eat or why he never has to go barefoot in the snow. Instead, he wants to explain why he is the recipient of showers of blessing. There are only two possibilities here. It might be possible to recharacterize the range of phenomena the theologian hopes to explain in less controversial, more topic-neutral terminology. So, instead of talking about showers of blessing, he might specify the range of phenomena he wishes to explain by talking about having plenty of food, proper clothing, and fancy houses. Such rephrasing will serve to undermine the claims of skeptics who are anxious to condemn religious phraseology as cognitively meaningless. If the religious theorist can specify his range of phenomena in nonreligious terminology, then he can functionally define 'God' in that same nonreligious terminology. Furthermore, if he can find an analogous mechanism from outside the religious sphere, he can begin to provide a positive characterization of God's nature without any recourse whatever to peculiarly religious terminology.

There may be occasions when the theologian will not be able to employ this rephrasing tactic. Nothing that has been shown about the nature of scientific explanations or about religious explanations modeled on scientific ones precludes the possibility of ranges of phenomena capable only of characterization in controversial phraseology. There may turn out to be ranges of phenomena that can be described only in terms that are peculiar to religious contexts. If there should be such a range, and should some religious devotee desire to explain it, then two additional comments are in order. First of all, there is no reason to suppose that phenomena that can be described only by using uniquely religious terminology must be excluded from the sorts of explanatory strategies under current consideration. So long as the phenomena in question can be clearly marked out, no matter what the method of demarcation might be, the theorist will be able to proceed in accordance with the methods detailed in the preceding chapter. He will be able to begin his search for relevantly analogous ranges of phenomena from which the efficacious features of known mechanisms may be drawn. Second, it must be noted that while there would seem to be nothing to prohibit a religious theorist from attempting to explain religiously characterized phenomena along the lines of the third chapter, such attempts at explanation fall outside the interests of this particular study. As will be recalled, the original intention of the present study was to show that at least certain stretches of religious discourse are as cognitively respectable as parts of the most rigorous of the sciences. Although theologians who are not bothered by skeptical attacks upon their discourse may proceed to investigate the possibility of using reference to explanatory entities in their account of uniquely religious phenomena, cases of this sort will prove less than ideal for use in the attempt to provide a persuasive argument for the cognitive integrity of talk about God.

Of course, the mere fact that some specific attempt at religious explanation does not provide the best persuasive example for proving some epistemological point is no reason for theologians to dismiss it as lacking real explanatory potential. While no further mention of such cases as these will be made here, it should not be thought that this silence on the subject implies some sort of condemnation of such explanations. Rather, it should be concluded only that such explanations do not prove very useful for the particular purposes at hand.

Once a range of phenomena that can be characterized in nonreligious terminology has been selected, a relevantly analogous range has been found, and the efficacious features from the known mechanism have been attributed to God, the theologian may proceed toward honing his conception of God along lines now quite familiar. As has been emphasized already, because God must be able to fulfill various nontheoretical roles as well as theoretical or specifically explanatory ones, the theologian always must make sure that his attribution of efficacious properties to God as well as his stripping away of explanatorily superfluous and detrimental ones does not inhibit God's capacity to function in this variegated array of religiously important ways. Since there is no reason why God would be incapable of explaining several distinct ranges of phenomena, once the theologian has honed his conception of God to account for one range, he might wish to further develop his understanding of God by showing how some new range of data might be explained by God as well. So long as he operates within the constraints outlined here, there is no reason why the theologian cannot proceed in this task of enlarging his conception of God's nature.

With the introduction of this third sort of range of data for which a religious theorist might attempt to formulate an explanation, a range that includes patterns of phenomena for which there are already perfectly adequate naturalistic explanations, the question of the plausibility of religious explanations becomes acute. While it may be fully possible to structure religious accounts along the lines of scientific ones, is it ever possible to so formulate plausible ones? Is there even the remotest of chances that such explanations might be true?

Before turning to an extended consideration of these matters, one final comment about the construction of religious explanations on the model of the third chapter must be stressed. As was briefly noted in connection with the discussion of the last sort of range of data for which religious explanations might be offered, the examples used here must be recognized as extraordinarily oversimplified. Normally, religious theorists are not interested in the explanation of single, isolated patterns of phenomena. Instead, their concern is to account for complicated, overlapping ranges while, at the same time, attempting to retain various complex, nontheoretical roles for God. Nevertheless, though the detailed tracing of these more complicated explanatory strategies might prove to be significantly more taxing, only the details would differ from the simpler kinds of cases considered here.

V

The Plausibility of
Religious Explanations

—

In "The Status of Religious Beliefs," Frank B. Dilley wrote:

> It should be quite evident that religious belief-systems cannot be grounded by scientific tests for factuality as interpreted by empiricists. The options, given empiricist readings of scientific method, are to justify any hypothesis in terms of direct appeal to sense experience or to justify an hypothesis about unobservables in terms of a prediction of observable events which cannot be predicted on any alternative hypothesis.
>
> Plainly beliefs in supernatural beings cannot be justified in either of these ways, given the kind of world that we inhabit . . . hence religious belief-claims cannot be established by scientific criteria.[1]

This provides an abbreviated example of the skeptical strategy employed by Huxley, Freud, Lenin, and the rest of the thinkers discussed in the first chapter. Dilley, like his predecessors, argues that both a true appreciation of recent scientific progress and a clear understanding of the nature of scientific theory construction yield the conclusion that religious belief is incapable of competing in the theoretical arena of the sciences. In his own particular implementation of this time-honored strategy, Dilley advances in two distinct stages. First, he roughly outlines a set of criteria by which the plausibility of scientific claims must be assessed. Then, he argues that religious belief claims cannot meet his specified standards for the sciences.

The burden of the last four chapters has been to provide a protracted reply to just this sort of skeptical challenge. By assuming that any explanation offered and accepted within uncontroversial branches of the physical sciences is cognitively meaningful, attention has been shifted away from the unprofitable pursuit of an adequate characterization of cognitive meaningfulness. Instead, concern has been focused on the nature and structure of scientifically acceptable explanations. In the third chapter, one particular form of scientific explanation was delineated and, in the fourth chapter, it was argued that religious explanations can be modeled on this same scientific pattern.

To leave this response to the skeptical challenge of Dilley and others at this point would be to leave it seriously incomplete. If the argument to this juncture has been correct, it has been demonstrated that religious explanations can be formulated in conformity with the same standards employed in the most rigorous of the sciences. Unfortunately, the skeptical attack taken by Dilley still has not been blocked. It still may be argued that even if religious arguments can be formulated legitimately, they are nevertheless wildly implausible. There is not one shred of reason why such explanations should be taken seriously by contemporary, even moderately educated human beings. Therefore, to complete the present response to the skeptical challenge, it must be shown that religious explanations of the sort envisioned in the fourth chapter are not all obviously implausible. At least some of them demand serious attention.

The first task that must be undertaken in trying to finish out this protracted defense of the epistemic integrity of religious discourse is to find some set of acceptable criteria by which to judge the plausibility of religious explanations patterned after the scientific model presented in the third chapter. Clearly, it is of utmost importance to complete this first task properly. After all, as is painfully obvious from a perusal of the passage quoted from Dilley's work, very little of lasting value is accomplished by showing that some particular range of religious explanations or truth claims meets, or perhaps fails to meet, a bogus standard for plausibility in the sciences. If the empiricist standard suggested by Dilley were applicable in the sciences, using it might have some bearing upon the determination of the merit of assorted religious claims. But, as is much more likely, if his standard were found to be inadequate even for the sciences,[2] the simple fact that religious truth claims cannot meet it would show nothing whatever with regard to their cognitive integrity. Therefore, every precaution must be taken to find a genuine standard by which to judge the plausibility of religious explanations.

Ideally, it would be nice to be able to decide whether specific religious explanations of the sort under consideration here were actually true or false. It would be extraordinarily convenient to have some standard of truth whereby such decisions confidently could be ground out. Unfortunately, there seem to be a number of reasons for believing that this ideal never can be reached. Probably the most important of these reasons for pessimism rests upon the fact that, in general, there appears to be no straightforward method for singling out specific truth claims for isolated testing. As Quine has so influentially put it:

Any statement can be held true come what may, if we make drastic enough adjustments elsewhere in the system. Even a statement very close to the periphery can be held true in the face of recalcitrant experience by pleading hallucination or by amending certain statements of the kind called logical laws. Conversely, by the same token, no statement is immune to revision.[3]

Taking the ways in which assertions in the physical sciences are assessed as support for his position, Quine concludes in this same paper that

total science is like a field of force whose boundary conditions are experience. A conflict with experience at the periphery occasions readjustments in the interior of the field. Truth values have to be redistributed over some of our statements. Reëvaluation of some statements entails reëvaluation of others. . . . But the total field is so underdetermined by its boundary conditions, experience, that there is much latitude of choice as to what statements to reëvaluate in the light of any single contrary experience.[4]

Whether the drastic conclusions that Quine subsequently has teased out of this vision of the evidential relations between the course of experience and scientific truth claims must be drawn has turned out to be a highly controversial question.[5] Regardless of the proper answer to this question, his comments here are most germane to the subject at hand. As was glimpsed in the last chapter, religious explanations modeled in conformity with the patterns of the third chapter do not stand in any straightforward evidential relation to the course of experience.[6] It was seen, for example, that disconfirming occurrences do not decisively disconfirm since it is almost always possible to introduce ad hoc adjustments or make minor alterations in order to salvage endangered claims. If the worst should happen, inspiration can be taken from the kind of dodge often exemplified in the history of science. As Kuhn has noticed, when particularly stubborn data seem to resist all attempts at reconciliation with some accepted theory, "Scientists may conclude that no solution will be forthcoming in the present state of their field. The problem is labelled and set aside for a future generation with more developed tools."[7]

Just as disconfirming instances were found to fail at conclusive disconfirmation, so it was discovered also in the last chapter that confirming ones could not decisively confirm. It was seen that even though an explanatory entity might be able to account for the entirety of some particular explanatory range, it would not necessarily be accepted. If another entity were found that could not only account for that explanatory range, but also could explain some wider range or, perhaps, could be assimilated more easily into some larger body of accepted theory, then the latter entity normally would be preferred to the former in spite of the fact that the former could account for all of its explanatory range. In short, it was found that religious explanations, just like scientific claims, do not face the tribunal of experience alone. Instead, they face it in concert with a whole host of other theoretical commitments.

This simple observation that religious explanations can never be assessed in isolation from other theoretical commitments is sufficient to dash any hope of deciding, with any degree of probability whatever, whether any specific one taken alone is actually true or false. Such a determination could be made only if it were known already which of an almost endless number of other commitments, both religious and nonreligious, were actually true and which false. Unfortunately, given the nature as well as the current state of human knowledge, there can be little confidence in the possibility of marking out any such set of clearly and uncontroversially known truths. Indeed, as has been seen, even the classical laws of logic do not stand above question.[8]

While the conclusive determination of the truth value, or probable truth value, of assorted religious explanations must remain an unrealized and unrealizable goal, it should not be concluded that any further investigation into the plausibility of religious explanations must prove ultimately fruitless. There are at least two important benefits that can be reaped from additional investigation. In the first place, insofar as the conceptual links between religious explanations and other theoretical commitments can be traced and insofar as the exact ways in which religious explanations must face the tribunal of experience in concert with larger bodies of commitment can be disclosed, it will be possible to move beyond the correct, but extraordinarily unhelpful, claim that religious explanations are never tested in isolation. It also will be possible, at least in part, both to determine precisely how religious explanations are assessed and to discover the implications of the acceptance or rejection of particular religious explanations for other areas of theoretical commitment.

In the second place, once a clearer understanding of the ways in which religious explanations are assessed has been obtained, a basis will be provided for allowing the determination of the plausibility of such claims in light of currently entrenched commitments in the sciences. It would be the height of epistemological foolishness to presume that some specific stretch of currently accepted scientific theory is known to be certainly and uncontroversially true. On the other hand, it would be naive in the extreme to maintain that current scientific commitments may be abandoned easily. In fact, a large number of the claims of contemporary science are among the most thoroughly entrenched and deeply held of human beliefs. So, given the tenacity and importance of current scientific commitments, it would be extremely valuable to know whether any religious explanations can plausibly be accepted relative to modern scientific doctrine.

In pursuing a fuller understanding of the bases upon which religious explanations of the sort under consideration here are to be evaluated, it is necessary to bear in mind that explanations of this type are devised to account for certain patterns of phenomena. Furthermore, it should be remembered that such explanations are constructed in a very specific fashion. Once an explanatory range has been chosen, the religious theorist must find a relevantly analogous range for which the controlling mechanism is understood. Then the explanatorily efficacious properties of that understood mechanism must be carried over to the characterization of a newly introduced explanatory entity of religious significance.

Once it is recognized that religious explanations of this sort must be generated in this fashion, it becomes fairly easy to enumerate at least some of the most basic conditions that must be met if they are to gain even initial plausibility. For instance, if some religious explanation patterned after the model of the third chapter is to receive anything more than the most cursory consideration, it must have an explanatory range that really exists. After all, if it were discovered that God, or some other religiously important entity, had been introduced to account for some pattern of occurrences that does not actually exist, there would seem to be little reason to pursue the question of explanatory plausibility any farther. The fact that there is nothing to be explained in this case would appear to be sufficient to cancel any plans for additional investigation.

In connection with this fundamental condition for explanatory plausibility — that the patterns of phenomena to be explained must actually exist — a few supplementary points must be stressed. In general, the existence of the requisite patterns can be determined in the same kinds of ways as existence questions are settled in the scientific sphere for the simple reason that the ranges of phenomena to be explained religiously can be marked out without making any special appeal to peculiarly religious criteria for individuation. By characterizing the range of phenomena in nonreligious terminology, the normal procedures that are used for checking on the existence of occurrences so characterized outside the religious realm can be brought to bear in the religious case as well. So, for example, if the religious devotee were to offer an explanation of why money always shows up just in time to pay the rent, the claim that money really does so appear could be checked in the same ways as it might be checked outside the sphere of religious concern. Since no special investigative techniques beyond those normally found outside religious contexts need be employed in cases where ranges of phenomena to be explained religiously can be specified in nonreligious terminology, there should be no foothold here for the skeptic of the cognitive integrity of religious discourse.

Unfortunately, the religious devotee may not always be willing to limit his explanatory attempts to ranges of phenomena that can be so uncontroversially specified and checked. He might hope to explain some pattern that can be characterized only in specifically religious terms. That is, instead of trying to explain why money always shows up in the nick of time, he might hope to explain why spiritual blessing always results from the moving of the Spirit of God in the heart of the believer. If a pattern like this really cannot be characterized in less controversial terminology from outside the peculiar realm of religious discourse, then the skeptic of the intelligibility of language taken from religious contexts will be back on familiar ground. A basis will be provided for him to retreat to old, but influential, arguments against the meaningfulness of religious terminology and to accuse the religious theorist of introducing patterns of phenomena the existence of which could never be verified or falsified.

It is extremely important to understand the precise significance of the fact that religious theorists may try to explain ranges of phenomena that can be specified only by using terminology peculiar to religious contexts. In the first place, it must be continually stressed that not all religious explanations are devised to account for such controversial patterns of occurrence. As was noted above, many patterns that are to be explained religiously can be described in thoroughly uncontroversial terms and their existence checked by ordinary, even mundane, means. So, even though the skeptic may find promising ground for criticism against controversially specified patterns, his accusations could never be taken as universally applicable to all of the religious theorist's explanatory activities. Second, even in the case of controversial patterns, there is no reason why the religious theorist should cower in submission to the skeptic. Obviously, for the argumentative purposes of this present extended attempt at showing the cognitive integrity of religious discourse, there is not much to be gained by putting stress upon the ability of religious explanations to account for such controversial ranges. Rehabilitative purposes are much better served by focusing attention on the religious explanation of more uncontroversially specified ranges of phenomena. Nevertheless, the typical religious theorist is not worried about the sophisticated attacks of the skeptic. So, unless it can be shown that whatever terminology may be necessary for specifying some explanatory range really is meaningless, the religious theorist can proceed happily in his explanatory quest. In similar fashion, the practicing religious theorist also may ignore skeptical qualms about the existence of controversial ranges of phenomena. There is no obligation upon the part of the devotee to convince the skeptic that his cherished patterns exist. So long as the theorist and perhaps others within his religious community have reason to believe that the patterns in question exist, the quest for a religious explanation may be undertaken legitimately.

In short, it is important to distinguish between what the religious believer may be free to undertake and what is required to salvage effectively the cognitive respectability of religious discourse in the face of powerful skeptical objections. The latter project dictates a prudent evasion of problematic areas when a course of smoother sailing is open. The former entails no responsibility to prove conclusively the existence of anything to the skeptic. Of course, were the theologian able to prove the existence of some range of controversial phenomena to the skeptical challenger, this fact would be of considerable apologetic interest. But such conclusive proof to outsiders is of no more urgency to the practicing theologian than it is to the practicing physicist. Like the physicist, the theologian needs only to convince the membership of his own community in order to proceed toward an attempt at plausible explanation.

There is only one other peculiarity about the confirmation of the existence of ranges of phenomena to be explained religiously that must be addressed here. As was noted in the fourth chapter, religious theorists frequently hope to use the explanatory strategies outlined in the third chapter for the purpose of explaining miraculous patterns of occurrence. As was argued in the last chapter, the confirmation of a miraculous pattern of phenomena must proceed in two stages. First it must be determined whether the pattern dubbed as miraculous actually has occurred. Second, if the pattern in question really did happen, it must be decided whether it was indeed a miracle.

With regard to the issue of deciding whether some particular supposedly miraculous pattern really took place, the problems to be faced are precisely those just discussed in connection with the confirmation of any pattern of phenomena. But at the second stage of confirmation, when it must be determined whether the pattern in question was really a miraculous one, it must be remembered that the evidence to be amassed is essentially negative in structure. It must be shown that no natural explanatory mechanism can account adequately for the pattern under consideration. Once again, as was noted in the previous chapter, conclusive proof will never be forthcoming. Because the sciences have not yet uncovered all of the mechanisms responsible for patterns of occurrence in nature, the theologian can never be sure that he has exhausted all the possibilities whereby his supposedly miraculous pattern might be naturally generated. There is always the possibility that some hitherto undiscovered natural mechanism is responsible for the event in question. Here again, as elsewhere, conclusive proof is not required. Insofar as the religious theorist has reason to believe that his pattern has occurred and that its occurrence cannot be attributed to the operation of natural mechanisms, the search for a religious explanation can be justified. Furthermore, in his quest for a confirmation that his chosen pattern is indeed miraculous, it is clear that no epistemic hurdle unique to religious contexts must be overcome. In fact, in the course of his determination, the religious theorist never consults any fund of religious understanding at all. Instead, he concentrates upon a survey of the gleanings of the sciences in order to decide whether his pattern might be explained naturalistically.

Once it has been determined that some pattern of phenomena really exists, a second fundamental condition for explanatory plausibility must be met. The range of phenomena chosen by the religious theorist as relevantly analogous to the range he wishes to explain must actually be relevantly analogous. That is, the mechanism that is thought to be responsible for determining the range of phenomena chosen as relevantly analogous really must be understood and it really must be responsible for the same features in the supposedly analogous case as those for which the religious theorist seeks an explanation in his new case. So, to provide a concrete illustration, if the theologian were to hope to explain his unfailing supply of food, clothing, and shelter, he would have to choose some analogous range of phenomena that is not only an exemplification of the persistent supply of food, clothing, and shelter, but for which the responsible mechanism already is understood.

Finally, once it has been determined that the range of phenomena chosen as relevantly analogous really is relevantly analogous to the religious range, one last fundamental condition for explanatory plausibility must be met. It must be determined whether the theologian has isolated the proper features from the known mechanism in his characterization of his newly hypothesized explanatory entity. That is, the properties that the theologian attributes to his newly conceived mechanism as responsible for the features of the range he hopes to explain must be the very same ones as are responsible for those same features in the relevantly analogous case. Furthermore, the theologian must be certain that his carryover of the relevantly analogous features in attribution to his newly introduced entity does not imply the repudiation of more deeply entrenched logical or theoretical commitments. If it is parental love that accounts for a constant supply of material goods to certain children in a relevantly analogous case, then that same parental love must be attributed to God in such a way as to preserve more entrenched commitments if that same constancy of supply is to be explained adequately in the religious case.

The fundamental plausibility considerations discussed thus far can be summed up simply and quickly. If a religious explanation formulated in accordance with the strategies outlined in the third chapter is to gain even initial consideration, it must be constructed properly. An extant explanatory range must be chosen. A relevantly analogous range of phenomena also must be chosen and the proper explanatorily efficacious properties from an already understood mechanism must be attributed to the newly posited entity without undue epistemic sacrifice.

Put in this brief way, these fundamental plausibility considerations appear almost too obvious and uncontroversial to merit explicit stating. Nevertheless, their importance should not be underestimated. Failure to properly meet any of these conditions will cast a religious explanation immediately into serious question. Indeed, in most cases, the discovery of such a basic failure would result in the straightforward dismissal of an explanatory hypothesis as improperly constructed. On the other hand, by meeting these conditions, a religious explanation moves beyond the level of mere curiosity. The recognition that a particular religious explanation has been formulated in conformity with the same strategies as are used in the most uncontroversial branches of the physical sciences raises its status to a level of initial plausibility sufficient to demand a more probing and serious investigation of its epistemic merits.

Once a religious explanation has passed these initial tests of plausibility and been found to be of sound construction, it must move into competition with other extant explanations of the same range of phenomena. It is very possible, indeed commonplace, for impeccably formulated explanations to be driven from the field by their competitive superiors. Furthermore, there is a wide array of ways in which the competition may be found superior. If there is another explanation available that not only accounts for the same range of phenomena, but also can be used to explain some broader range as well, a properly formulated explanatory hypothesis may be rejected for its relative impotence. Being unable to account for such a sweeping range of data, it usually will be forgotten in the enthusiasm to adopt its more powerful competitor. In similar fashion, an explanation may fall into disrepute because there is another explanatory hypothesis that can be integrated more easily and thoroughly into some larger whole of human understanding. In a case like this, the competitor that is less compatible with wider fields of accepted theory may be dismissed for one of two reasons. Either its adoption will be inconsistent with other, already entrenched theoretical commitments or it will simply fail to cohere with them. If the problem is with consistency, any competitor that remains consistent with previously accepted theory will tend to be favored in the interests of epistemic conservation. The adoption of an explanatory hypothesis that is inconsistent with other convictions requires either the abandonment of those other commitments or a repudiation of the law of noncontradiction. Normally, both of these alternatives will be resisted if they can be avoided by opting for a more consistent competitor. The case in which an explanation fails to cohere with the rest of human understanding is not quite so serious. But even here, if there is some competitor that does cohere more fully with a wider body of accepted theory, it will tend to be preferred in the hope of achieving a greater unity among the fragments of an increasingly diversified and compartmentalized corpus of human knowledge.

Along somewhat different lines, a properly formulated explanation may succumb to its competitors because of a relative deficiency in explanatory precision. Of two alternative explanations, both of which explain the same breadth of data and both of which are equally compatible with other bits of accepted theory, the explanation that is more precise will tend to prevail. That is, the explanation that can account successfully for a more detailed characterization of the explanatory range usually will be preferred. So, if one hypothesis can explain not only why balloons expand when they ascend and contract when they descend, but also why they expand and contract at exactly the rates they do, it will tend to prevail on grounds of explanatory precision over an hypothesis that can be used only to explain simple expansion and contraction behavior.

It is even possible for hypotheses to compete on grounds of intelligibility. Consider two hypotheses that are equally acceptable on all criteria discussed to this point. If one has been modeled on a known mechanism that is understood more thoroughly than the mechanism used to fashion the understanding of its competitor, the former will tend to be accepted as more fully explanatory. After all, the source of analogy from which it draws its explanatory power is grasped in much more intricate detail than is the mechanism from which its competitor is drawn. In much the same way, if one hypothesized mechanism is envisioned as operating in accordance with more firmly entrenched principles than those by which its competitor is imagined to be governed, the former wil tend to be viewed in a less controversial light than the latter. Again, an explanatory posit whose understanding has been modeled on mechanisms taken from some highly regarded field of human inquiry will tend to benefit from the prestige of that discipline. For this reason, were physics generally regarded as epistemically superior to Freudian psychology, conceptions of explanatory entities fashioned after the pattern of Freudian mechanisms would find themselves at a serious disadvantage to competitors carrying the coveted badge of the queen of the natural sciences.

It would be nice to be able to pause at this juncture in order to provide a scheme for ranking the above criteria according to their importance. Unfortunately, no simple ranking seems possible. The relative importance of these criteria appears to shift from context to context. Sometimes a broader explanatory scope is sacrificed for greater explanatory precision. On other occasions, just the reverse seems to be the case. Similarly, each of the above criteria seems to rise to prominence at certain times and to sink into relative insignificance at others. Perhaps with a much more extended investigation, some of the underlying principles that determine the rise and fall of criterial importance could be uncovered. Probably such an investigation would lead to the discovery of many additional criteria not mentioned here. But since an investigation of this scope would extend far beyond the more modest purposes of this particular inquiry, this quick glimpse into some of the criteria by which competitors are judged will have to suffice.

Leaving the discussion of the nature of competition among rival alternative explanatory accounts in this rather unsettled state, cases in which explanations face no competitors must be explored. It is certainly possible for a theorist to formulate an explanation for some pattern or patterns of phenomena that have hitherto remained unexplained. It is also possible to offer an explanation of a range of phenomena that already has been explained, but to focus explanatory attention upon some aspect of that range that falls outside of the domain explained by any extant account. That is, the theorist might find that certain aspects of some pattern of occurrences already have been explained but other aspects have not and so may try to explain those yet unexplained ones.

In either case, whether an explanation is offered for some new range of data or it is suggested to account for some hitherto unexplained feature of a range that already has been explained in other regards, there is no competition whatever to be faced. On the rather innocuous sounding principle that any explanation is better than none, it would be tempting to conclude that, if properly formulated, an explanation that faces no competition must necessarily win the day. Such an explanation must be embraced as the most plausible hypothesis simply because it is the only one available.

It probably would be a mistake to draw this conclusion. Strange as it may sound, there seem to be times when having no explanation is better than having one. In fact, to throw an additional complication into the preceding discussion about competition among rival hypotheses, not only does it appear that occasionally having no hypothesis is better than having one, it also would appear that there are cases where choosing an explanatorily inferior hypothesis is to be preferred over the adoption of some more adequate competitor. In *The Structure of Scientific Revolutions*, Thomas Kuhn tried to shed some light on these rather startling facts about the way in which hypotheses gain favor. He wrote:

Usually the opponents of a new paradigm can legitimately claim that even in the area of crisis it is little superior to its traditional rival. Of course, it handles some problems better, has disclosed some new regularities. But the older paradigm can presumably be articulated to meet these challenges as it has met others before. . . . In addition, the defenders of traditional theory and procedure can almost always point to problems that its new rival has not solved but that for their view are no problems at all. . . . Even in the area of crisis, the balance of argument and counterargument can sometimes be very close indeed. And outside that area the balance will often decisively favor the tradition.[9]

According to Kuhn, there are times when a new theory can win the day over its more powerful opponent. Even though it may have less explanatory depth, be less precise, or be riddled with more problems, a newcomer still can attract many adherents away from an established, entrenched theory. Finding a great deal of historical evidence for this startling fact from his perusal of the history of science,[10] Kuhn willingly concluded that the

man who embraces a new paradigm at an early stage must often do so in defiance of the evidence provided by problem-solving. He must, that is, have faith that the new paradigm will succeed with the many large problems that confront it, knowing only that the older paradigm has failed with a few.[11]

It would seem, then, that if Kuhn's historical research into the development of the physical sciences can be trusted, there are many times when a new paradigm will attract adherents away from its epistemologically stronger competitors. Often, Kuhn went on to argue, the attractiveness of a weaker paradigm is rooted in its promise for future development. Impatient with the persistent failures of accepted theory, researchers will turn to undeveloped alternatives in the hope that one of them might blossom into a more fully elaborated and viable position with a little nurturing attention.[12]

Larry Laudan has found Kuhn's analysis of the pursuit of new and undeveloped theories somewhat unsatisfying. His reasons for dissatisfaction are basically two. In the first place, Laudan believes that Kuhn's assessment of the history of science is inaccurate at certain points. Second, he finds Kuhn's discussion to be lacking in precision.[13] By taking his own close look at the history of science, Laudan has evolved what he believes to be a clearer understanding of the perplexing fact that lesser competitors frequently are given preferential treatment. With the intention of purging this fact of its air of mysterious irrationality, Laudan distinguished between two distinct bases upon which decisions among alternatives may be made. On the one hand, he argued, there can be appraisals of adequacy. Describing this first basis for deciding among alternatives, Laudan wrote, "We may, to begin with, ask about the (momentary) *adequacy* of a research tradition. We are essentially asking here how effective the *latest* theories within the research tradition are at solving problems."[14] According to this passage, then, appraisals of adequacy amount to the determination of the current problem-solving capacities of the latest theoretical formulations to be found within existing research traditions.

On the other hand, Laudan claimed, additional determinations beyond mere assessments of current adequacy can be made. The progressiveness of particular traditions also can be measured. In Laudan's view, such assessments of progressiveness are made along two, not necessarily complementary, lines and so a distinction must be maintained between

1. *the general progress of a research tradition*—this is determined by comparing the adequacy of the sets of theories which constitute the oldest and those which constitute the most recent versions of the research tradition[15]

and

2. *the rate of progress of a research tradition*—here, the changes in the momentary adequacy of the research tradition during any specified time span are identified.[16]

In harmony with this distinction, Laudan has argued that one may decide either the general progress or the rate of progress of a research tradition. General progress amounts to a determination of the difference in theoretical adequacy between the earliest and latest versions of some bit of theory while the rate of progress is simply a measurement of the speed at which theories are increasing in their theoretical adequacy. Unfortunately, Laudan offered little advice about how to make precise assessments of either.

Before the position of Kuhn can be contrasted sharply with that of Laudan, one final distinction offered in *Progress and its Problems* must be reviewed. Laudan wrote, "It is clear that scientists often choose *to accept* one among a group of competing theories and research traditions, i.e., *to treat it as if it were true*."[17] But it is not always necessary for a scientist to accept a theory in order to work on it. Quite to the contrary, according to Laudan, "*scientists can have good reasons for working on theories that they would not accept*."[18] Among the good reasons for pursuing a theory that is not accepted might be included the judgment of future promise or theoretical fertility. Employing his new distinction between accepting and pursuing theories, Laudan went on to conclude:

> To *accept* a budding research tradition merely because it has had a high rate of progress would, of course, be a mistake; but it would be equally mistaken to refuse to pursue it if it has exhibited a capacity to solve some problems (empirical *or* conceptual) which its older, and generally more acceptable, rivals have failed to solve.[19]

Is there any way to specify the conditions under which it is rational either to accept or pursue a research tradition? Laudan answered in the affirmative. Believing that the general conditions under which the rationality of both pursuing and accepting research traditions could be fairly simply stated, he wrote, "*It is always rational to pursue any research tradition which has a higher rate of progress than its rivals*."[20] With regard to the rational acceptance of theories, Laudan advised, "'*Choose the theory (or research tradition) with the highest problem-solving adequacy*.'"[21]

At this point, it is not difficult to understand Laudan's quarrel with Kuhn. In Laudan's view, Kuhn has failed to make enough distinctions. By overlooking the difference between pursuing and accepting research traditions, Kuhn has been led to the confused conclusion that the acceptance of a weaker competitor is not only possible, but actually an essential element in any healthy and prospering scientific environment. After all, as Kuhn has argued, if there were never anyone to adopt and champion the cause of the underdog, new alternatives filled with promise would die of neglect rather than mature into strong, viable paradigms.[22]

To leave the difference between Laudan and Kuhn on this level, however, would be to neglect a much more profound disagreement between them. While it is certainly true that Laudan emphasizes a distinction between the pursuit and the acceptance of theories while Kuhn does not, Kuhn believes he has powerful reasons for refusing to follow Laudan in this distinction. Laudan is convinced that it is possible and even desirable to accept one theory while pursuing another.[23] In fact, he claimed that it is a "historical fact that *a scientist can often be working alternately in two different, and even mutually inconsistent research traditions.*"[24] For Kuhn, the opportunity of accepting one paradigm while pursuing another simply never arises. According to *The Structure of Scientific Revolutions:*

Successive paradigms tell us different things about the population of the universe and about that population's behavior. . . . But paradigms differ in more than substance, for they are directed not only to nature but also back upon the science that produced them. They are the source of the methods, problem-field, and standards of solution accepted by any mature scientific community at any given time.[25]

Because Kuhn believes that diverse paradigms differ not only in their referents, but also in methodological canons, scope of problems to be solved, and standards by which proposed solutions may be judged, he concluded, "The normal-scientific tradition that emerges from a scientific revolution is not only incompatible but often actually incommensurable with that which has gone before."[26] To push his incommensurability claim even farther, Kuhn called upon certain gleanings from psychological research[27] that led him to argue, "Surveying the rich experimental literature . . . makes one suspect that something like a paradigm is prerequisite to perception itself."[28] Convinced that paradigm commitment plays an essential role in determining the content of human observation, Kuhn finally contended:

Paradigm changes do cause scientists to see the world of their research-engagement differently. In so far as their only recourse to that world is through what they see and do, we may want to say that after a revolution scientists are responding to a different world.[29]

Because of these rather drastic consequences of moving from one paradigm to another, Kuhn is convinced that shifting among paradigms is difficult at best. In fact, the move from one paradigm to another can be accomplished through nothing short of a conversion experience. He says, "The transfer of allegiance from paradigm to paradigm is a conversion experience that cannot be forced."[30] Or, as he notes in greater detail:

At the start a new candidate for paradigm may have few supporters, and on occasion the supporters' motives may be suspect. Nevertheless, if they are competent, they will improve it, explore its possibilities, and show what it would be like to belong to the community guided by it. And as that goes on, if the paradigm is one destined to win its fight, the number and strength of the persuasive arguments in its favor will increase. More scientists will then be converted, and the exploration of the new paradigm will go on. Gradually the number of experiments, instruments, articles, and books based upon the paradigm will multiply. Still more men, convinced of the new view's fruitfulness, will adopt the new mode of practicing normal science, until at last only a few elderly hold-outs remain. And even they, we cannot say, are wrong. Though the historian can always find men—Priestly, for instance— who were unreasonable to resist for as long as they did, he will not find a point at which resistance becomes illogical or unscientific. At most he may wish to say that the man who continues to resist after his whole profession has been converted has *ipso facto* ceased to be a scientist.[31]

As this passage vividly illustrates, in Kuhn's view, the only ones who continue to pursue work within a particular paradigm are those who have adopted it.

With his extreme commitment to the diversity of referents, methodologies, problems, standards, and even perceptual worlds that are introduced by differing paradigms, it would seem to be an obvious step to the conclusion that it is impossible for a theorist to entertain more than one paradigm at a time. While Kuhn did conclude that "the decision to reject one paradigm is always simultaneously the decision to accept another"[32] he stopped short of the more radical conclusion that researchers are incapable of simultaneously entertaining alternative commitments. To the contrary, he appeared to indicate that such simultaneous consideration is possible when he went on to argue:

The act of judgment that leads scientists to reject a previously accepted theory is always based upon more than a comparison of that theory with the world. The decision to reject one paradigm is always simultaneously the decision to accept another, and the judgment leading to that decision involves the comparison of both paradigms with nature *and* with each other.[33]

Nevertheless, while it may be possible to entertain more than one view at a time and while it may even be possible to accept one paradigm while pursuing another, Kuhn is firm in his conviction that no one ever does pursue a paradigm that he does not accept and, furthermore, it is not at all desirable to do so. As he remarked on this point:

So long as the tools a paradigm supplies continue to prove capable of solving the problems it defines, science moves fastest and penetrates most deeply through confident employment of those tools. The reason is clear. As in manufacture so in science—retooling is an extravagance to be reserved for the occasion that demands it. The significance of crises is the indication they provide that an occasion for retooling has arrived.[34]

In sum, then, according to Kuhn, a theorist may convert to a new, currently weaker alternative. By a commitment of faith, such a theorist may devote his energies to showing that the promise latent in his new choice can be realized. Only the subsequent history of the development of this new choice in comparison with the history of the development of the older, abandoned paradigm can reveal whether this particular theorist's conversion from an established to a newer position was a good idea. In contrast with Kuhn, Laudan believes that the adoption of a currently weaker alternative is never proper, though it may be a good idea to pursue a weaker theory while continuing to accept its stronger rival.

Any attempt to determine whether Kuhn, Laudan, or some other yet unmentioned thinker is correct on these issues would involve a lengthy deliberation far beyond the scope of this investigation of the plausibility of religious explanations. Although no final resolution of these matters can be reached here, it is still possible to set a more modest goal. By assuming the validity of Kuhn's analyses, something of the plausibility of religious explanations from his perspective can be ascertained. In the same way, by assuming the perspective of Laudan, an assessment of the plausibility of religious explanations relative to his views is possible. Since both Kuhn and Laudan are among the most important theorists who have taken a position with regard to the evaluation of the plausibility of rival theories, an assessment of the plausibility of religious explanations relative to their positions certainly would prove valuable, although it might be less impressive than an assessment in light of the known truth on these matters.

In pursuit of the question concerning the plausibility of religious explanations from the perspectives of Kuhn and Laudan, two different sorts of cases must be distinguished. According to some religious communities, religious truth claims of any sort, including religious explanations, can and often do enter into rivalry with scientific ones. Typically, this sort of "rivalist" attitude is expressed by the more conservative elements of any developed religious tradition. For instance, Christian Fundamentalists are usually convinced that their biblical account of creation comes into conflict with the teachings of currently accepted biological theory. But according to other religious communities, it is impossible for the claims and explanations offered from a religious perspective ever to conflict with the findings of the natural or social sciences. This "nonrivalist" stance often is taken by more liberal branches of religious traditions and is maintained for any of a number of diverse reasons. Langdon Gilkey, for example, has suggested that biblical accounts of the origins of humanity cannot conflict with biological ones because biblical explanations are of a different type from those offered in the sciences.[35]

It is important to keep the question of the plausibility of religious explanations offered by rivalist communities clearly distinct from plausibility considerations regarding explanations offered by nonrivalist communities. Of course, if an explanation modeled on the pattern of the third chapter is offered by either rivalist or nonrivalist communities, it must be properly formulated in order to reach the stage of initial plausibility. Once properly structured in accordance with the strategies outlined in that chapter, the work of Kuhn and Laudan can be brought to bear. Since the consideration of the rivalist position is much simpler than that of the nonrivalist, it will be tackled first.

Obviously, from the rivalist perspective, though a religious explanation may be forced into competition with scientific ones, it may be fortunate enough to be faced with no extant scientific alternative. To begin with, consider the case where a religious account is offered for a range of phenomena that cannot be explained by any other currently available one. In Laudan's view, it would appear to be irrational to reject such a religious explanation since, to be rational, one always must accept the research tradition that has the greatest current problem-solving capacity. Since an explanation that can account for a range of phenomena is able to solve at least one problem, it would seem that it should be preferred to the total lack of an explanation. After all, a nonexistent explanation cannot solve even one problem.

However, things are a bit messier here than they first appear. According to Laudan, it is research traditions that are to be accepted or rejected on the basis of problem-solving adequacy, not individual explanatory hypotheses. Given Laudan's cursory comments on the precise nature of research traditions, it is a bit difficult to individuate them clearly.[36] But if anything within a rivalist religious community would count as a research tradition, it would probably not be particular bits or pieces of theological doctrine. Rather, the network of evolving doctrines that has served to distinguish and unify that community over its historical development would provide a more likely candidate. Though markedly different in some ways from scientific research traditions, historically developed theological traditions do bear a resemblance to their scientific counterparts. Theologians are specially trained professionals committed to certain methodological practices. As they work toward solutions for commonly shared theoretical problems, their proposals are subjected to the critical scrutiny of their peers and subsequently abandoned or modified in the light of such criticisms.

From this perspective, the place of a religious explanation faced by no scientific competitors takes on a new cast. While a theological tradition may offer an explanation of a certain range of phenomena for which current scientific traditions cannot offer any account, the decision to embrace or reject such a religious explanation must be based upon the rationality of accepting the theological tradition from which that explanation springs in light of competitive alternative traditions. Of course, if the theological tradition in question were not in competition with current scientific or other religious or non-religious traditions, it would probably be safe to assume that the adoption of that tradition together with its explanation of the specific range of phenomena at stake would be rational because the solution of even some problems by an extant tradition is better than the solution of none by a nonexistent tradition. On the other hand, in the case of a rivalist religious tradition that finds itself in competition with other research programs, that tradition currently must be more adequate at problem solving than any of its rivals if it is to be rational to accept it together with its attendant explanation of the data in question.

Even were it discovered that some particular religious tradition must be currently rejected in favor of some other, more adequate tradition, it still might be rational to pursue it. According to Laudan, it is always rational to pursue a tradition that has a higher rate of progress than its rivals. So, if some theological tradition were able to offer an account of a range of data that could not be explained from within the context of some currently accepted tradition, then it would be able to solve a problem that could not be solved by its more adequate rival. Should other solutions to problems emerge on a regular basis, the rate at which that theological tradition was progressing might be sufficiently rapid to justify its continued pursuit. In fact, should such problem solving continue, it might be possible for a currently unacceptable religious research tradition to replace its more powerful rival by eventually proving superior in overall problem-solving ability.

From Laudan's perspective, the case in which some religious explanation is in competition with a more adequate rival account is just as complicated. If it should turn out that not only is the rival explanation more adequate than the religious one, but also the research tradition from which that rival springs is superior to the religious tradition in question, then it would seem that both the rival research tradition together with its attendant explanation of the data at stake must be accepted. Of course, should the progress of the weaker religious tradition be sufficiently rapid, it still might be rational to pursue it.

Consider the case where a particular religious explanation is weaker than its rival even though the religious tradition from which that explanation springs is more adequate than the tradition from which the rival springs. In this sort of case, it would be rational to accept the religious tradition while rejecting the rival one. Since the more adequate rival explanation comes out of a research tradition that cannot be accepted, it would appear that Laudan's position demands the acceptance of the religious explanation over its rival even though it provides a weaker explanatory account of the particular range of data in question.

The case in which a religious explanatory account is in competition with a weaker rival would be treated by Laudan in accordance with the same bases for plausibility utilized in the above cases where religious explanations were faced with more powerful explanatory opponents. In all of these cases, Laudan's primary concern is with the problem-solving adequacy of research traditions from which explanations spring rather than with the adequacy of specific explanations taken in isolation. Should both religious explanations and the research traditions from which they spring prove to be epistemically stronger than rival explanations with their competitive research traditions, then the religious explanations would appear to be worthy of uncontroversial selection. After all, not only would they be able to beat their competitors in terms of explanatory adequacy, but the traditions out of which they arise would be more fully adequate than the traditions from which their competitors spring.

Were it to be discovered that some particular religious explanation is explanatorily superior to its rival, while the rival were found to spring from a more acceptable research tradition, the religious account would appear to be at a serious disadvantage. Arising out of a weaker tradition, it could not be accepted rationally. Of course, if it were discovered that the religious research tradition in question were progressing at a rate sufficient to merit additional pursuit, there might come a time when that tradition could be evolved into a more adequate competitor and so could be accepted rationally together with its attendant explanatory account.

It is not possible to be so decisive when taking Kuhn's point of view in the evaluation of the plausibility of explanations offered by rivalist religious communities. Consider the case where a religious explanation is offered for a range of phenomena for which there is no alternative account available. Should the paradigm from which this religious explanation springs be embraced? Obviously, if that paradigm should turn out to be the currently entrenched one and should there be no crisis at hand, Kuhn would have to conclude that there is no reason to give it up. Only in the case of crisis, when faith in a hitherto entrenched paradigm seems no longer possible, should theorists contemplate alternatives.

Suppose the paradigm from which the religious explanation springs were not currently entrenched. Should it be embraced under these conditions? The answer to this question varies with changes in the intellectual environment. Should the adoption of the religious paradigm require the repudiation of some other paradigm commitment, then, according to Kuhn, only the subsequent history of paradigm development can tell. Were researchers to adopt some orphaned paradigm and subsequently turn it into an option sufficiently powerful to overthrow its entrenched rival, those who had adopted it would prove to be intellectual heroes. But were their adopted child to wither and die, their faith in such an ill-fated program would be shown very little sympathy. On the other hand, should the adoption of a religious paradigm be compatible with the acceptance of all other currently entrenched paradigms, then there would seem to be every reason to embrace that religious perspective. After all, according to Kuhn, paradigm-governed research always is to be preferred to the extraordinary inefficiency of preparadigm investigation.[37]

Any case where a religious explanation is offered in competition with either a stronger or a weaker explanatory rival would be treated by Kuhn along very similar lines.[38] As with the perspective of Laudan, Kuhn is convinced that what is of ultimate importance is not the relative strength of alternative explanations. Instead, what must be considered is the power of the paradigms from which rivals spring. Unless some crisis has been precipitated, both weaker and stronger explanations springing from entrenched paradigms are certainly worthy of acceptance in Kuhn's view. With regard to the value of opting for explanations that spring from paradigms that are not currently favored, as was noted above, only time will tell. The future course of paradigm development must decide the value of accepting or rejecting alternatives to the mainstream.

Explanations offered by nonrivalist religious communities are an entirely different kettle of fish, one to which the reflections of Laudan and Kuhn regarding the competition among rival research traditions or paradigms do not apply so neatly. There are a number of different reasons why religious communities might be convinced that their explanatory attempts cannot enter into competition with those offered by the sciences. For instance, it might be thought that the explanatory interests of religious believers are necessarily different from those of the scientific world. Thus, there never can be any overlap of scientific explanatory ranges with religious ones and so the possibility of competing explanations for the same explanatory range never can arise. Alternatively, it might be argued that religious explanations are of a different sort from scientific ones. Hence, even were the explanatory ranges of the two to overlap at some point, any religious explanation that might be offered would be of a very different type from that of the sciences and therefore the acceptance of a religious explanation would be perfectly compatible with the simultaneous acceptance of a scientific one. It might even be claimed that religious explanations never can be incompatible with scientific ones for the simple reason that there is no such thing as a religious explanation. Only the sciences can explain. Thus, since it is never possible to offer a religious explanation for any range of phenomena, it is obviously impossible to have a conflict between religious and scientific explanations.

Due to the nature of the particular type of religious explanation being considered here, none of these reasons for the necessary compatibility between religious and scientific explanations will work. As was seen in the course of the discussion in the fourth chapter, the explanatory scope of a religious explanation of this sort might very well overlap with the scope of a scientific explanation. The believer might want to explain his constant supply of food, clothing, and shelter. But assorted branches of sociology or, more likely, economics or political science might hope to explain these same patterns of supply. Along slightly different lines, the believer might want to explain various patterns of visionary appearances or sequences of quiet whisperings in the night that also might be of interest to the psychologist or neurophysiologist. It also is impossible to opt for the suggestion that religious and scientific explanations are of fundamentally different and therefore noncompetitive types. The sort of religious explanation under consideration here is of precisely the same structure as certain scientific explanations. In fact, great pains have been taken to carefully model such religious explanations on rigidly scientific patterns. Finally, the claim that religious explanations are impossible must be rejected. If the argument completed to this point has been correct, religious explanations must be considered possible. Indeed, some of them might even turn out to be plausible.

Even though none of these reasons for the necessary compatibility between religious and scientific explanations can be accepted, it is still possible to give a reason why religious explanations of this particular sort might turn out to be incapable of entering into rivalry with scientific ones. Inspiration can be taken from the relatively frequent phenomenon of explanatory overdetermination. Consider the face of a clock. Suppose someone were to offer a suggestion as to why the hands on the face of his clock move in the patterns that they do. Specifying the specific pattern for which he hoped to provide an account, this theorist might proceed to look for an analogous range of phenomena. Suppose he were to find an analogous range for which the known determinative mechanism was a system of ropes and pulleys. Taking this case as relevantly analogous, he might argue that behind the face of his own clock there is a similar system of ropes and pulleys. Now suppose that the sister of this theorist were to decide to explain this same pattern of phenomena by using the same explanatory strategy. But instead of using a system of ropes and pulleys as an analogous mechanism, suppose she were to make reference to a system of interlocking gears. Finally, imagine that the back of the clock in question eventually was opened to reveal not only a system of operative ropes and pulleys, but also a system of grinding gears. Upon subsequent investigation, suppose that it were found that either this system of ropes and pulleys or the system of interlocking gears could determine the movements of the hands on the clock without any aid whatsoever from the other mechanism.

Several conclusions would have to be drawn from this sort of case. First, the brother's explanation of the movement of his clock's hands is a sufficient one. But, of course, so is his sister's account. Furthermore, neither account is reducible to the other since each makes explanatory reference to entities that are not invoked by the other account. Should one or the other be rejected as unnecessary? Clearly, for the purpose of providing an adequate explanation of the movements of the hands on the clock, one is enough. Nevertheless, it would be extremely foolish to repudiate one of the two on some short-sighted simplicity consideration. While there may be no purely explanatory reason for keeping both, there are certainly powerful nonexplanatory reasons for doing so. When the back of the clock finally was opened, both operative mechanisms were observed. So, unless extremely elaborate modifications in currently entrenched perceptual or optical theory are to be introduced, the coexistence of these two explanatory accounts must be tolerated.

If nonrivalist religious communities are to take creative inspiration from this kind of example, they must begin by providing some reason to believe that God's operative activity never will conflict with the functioning of natural mechanisms. It might be suggested, for example, that only a capricious God would consider interrupting the smooth operation of his universe and, since God certainly is not capricious, he can be trusted never to interfere with the functioning of natural mechanisms. Obviously, the plausibility of such suggested "noninterference" principles will have to be weighed on an individual basis.

It is not necessary, of course, for a nonrivalist religious community to claim that every pattern of occurrence is codetermined by natural and supernatural mechanisms. In specific cases where the activities of God are explanatorily invoked in addition to the presentation of a scientific reference to natural mechanisms, plausibility constraints will be of a rather different sort from those employed for rivalist explanations. Obviously, the question of scientific explanatory competitors, either superior or inferior, will have to be excluded from the outset. Nevertheless, it is still important that nonrivalist religious explanations modeled on the structure of the third chapter meet the initial plausibility conditions outlined near the beginning of the present chapter. If such explanations are not formulated properly, either because their explanatory range does not actually exist or because their invocation of God as explanatorily efficacious has been constructed incorrectly, then they must be repudiated immediately as defective. If such nonrivalist explanations pass these initial tests of construction, then additional reasons why they should be embraced must be given.

These additional reasons obviously cannot be directly explanatory since in this kind of case a reference to natural mechanisms alone will prove to be explanatorily sufficient. But there are all sorts of nonexplanatory reasons that might be cited. Some of these could be epistemic in nature. Unlike those of the clock case, arguments drawn from the gleanings of perception probably would not prove to be central ones. Still, there are other theoretical constraints beyond simple perceptual ones. Other reasons that might be given could be of a nonepistemic nature. Perhaps peculiarly religious, pragmatic, or existential reasons for accepting a religious explanation might be offered. It might be argued, for instance, that the belief that God controls certain patterns of phenomena makes it easier for people to revere him or makes the drudgery of everyday existence more bearable or makes human beings feel more "at home" in this cold and foreign world. Due to the vast diversity of epistemic or nonepistemic reasons that conceivably could be given for introducing reference to God's determinative activity in this sort of case, it would be necessary to assess the plausibility of any such proffered reasons on a case by case basis.

Throughout this entire process of evaluation, two distinct issues must be kept separate. The cognitive or theoretical intelligibility of a nonrivalist religious explanation depends solely upon its proper formulation. If correctly constructed, it will be as intelligible as any similarly constructed scientific explanation. The plausibility of such an explanation, however, depends upon the strength of the reasons that can be found for introducing such a religious explanatory account above and beyond any already available scientific one. Since such reasons need not be of a specifically theoretical sort, the plausibility of such religious explanations ultimately may rest upon pragmatic or other nonepistemic considerations.

There is another way in which it might be thought that nonrivalist religious communities could introduce explanations patterned after those of the third chapter. This way depends upon a distinction between two sorts of ways in which explanatory entities might be invoked. On the one hand, explanatorily efficacious mechanisms may be introduced to account for certain patterns of phenomena. But it is also possible to make explanatory reference to a second level of responsible mechanisms, mechanisms that are thought to determine the regular patterns of behavior found in explanatory entities of the first sort. Thus, it might be suggested that the sciences are devoted exclusively to the invocation of explanatory entities for the purpose of explaining specific patterns of phenomena. Religious communities, however, may introduce God in order to explain why the explanatory entities invoked by the sciences persist in their regular patterns of determinative behavior.

While this strategy might appear initially to be a promising one, it soon founders on the hard rock of scientific reality. The fact of the matter is that the sciences do not limit themselves to invocations of the first sort. While it is true that scientific explanations are given for patterns of phenomena, they also are offered to account for the regular patterns of behavior manifested by previously introduced explanatory entities. As just one example, consider the recent history of germ theory. Microbes were introduced originally to account for certain symptomatic regularities in human disease. Patterns of symptoms were explained by reference to the behavior of certain microscopic organisms found in the human body. However, microbiologists were not content to let matters rest at this level. They were concerned to discover why such microbes always acted in such regular patterns. Upon further investigation, answers were given in terms of yet finer mechanisms, mechanisms found within the cellular structure of microbes that were responsible for the regular behavior of those little beasts. Even this did not ultimately prove to be satisfying to those engaged in medical research. They sought for yet finer mechanisms that could account for such regular cellular behavior. At least some of these finer mechanisms have been disclosed through biochemical research. Should an explanation of the regularity of the behavior of chemical mechanisms be desired, reference could be taken to the activities of explanatory entities familiar to the atomic physicist. In short, because the sciences do not seem willing to rest content at any particular level of explanatory invocation, this particular strategy cannot guarantee that scientific explanations never will come into competition with religious ones. Thus, nonrivalist religious communities would do well to steer clear of the claim that while scientific explanatory entities can explain the regularity of patterns of phenomena, only God can be used in the explanation of the regular behavior of scientifically explanatory entities.

Up to this point, only a rough outline of the bases upon which the plausibility of religious explanations can be determined has been offered. It has been argued that before any explanation, rivalist or nonrivalist, can be considered seriously, it must be formulated properly in accordance with the patterns sketched in the third chapter. But a properly formulated rivalist explanation may have to be abandoned if it proves unable to beat its competitive rivals. Something of the ways in which properly formulated rivalist explanations are to be judged in relation to both their explanatory inferiors and superiors as well as the ways in which they must be assessed when they face no competition whatever have been traced. An outline also has been offered of the markedly different ways in which properly formulated nonrivalist explanations are to be evaluated. Although the present discussion of the plausibility considerations applicable in the evaluation of religious explanations is by no means comprehensive or complete, enough has been said to allow the profitable exploration of the explanatory adequacy of a few particular religious accounts. Such exploration is the burden of the next chapter.

VI

Plausible
Religious Explanations

—

IN THE PRECEDING CHAPTER, criteria were developed by which the
plausibility of one kind of religious explanation can be assessed.
Because such explanations are patterned after a very specific scientific
model, they must be constructed along rigidly determined lines. To
begin with, they should be offered only for extant ranges of
phenomena. Once an explanatory range has been chosen, a relevantly
analogous range of phenomena for which the governing mechanism
already is understood needs to be found. Finally, the explanatorily
efficacious features of that known mechanism must be carried over
properly into the religious sphere and attributed to God[1] without
undue epistemic or religious sacrifice.

After a religious explanation has met these initial plausibility
conditions, the direction that further plausibility assessments will
take depends upon whether the explanation in question is offered
from a rivalist or nonrivalist religious perspective. Since rivalist explanations are expected to compete with alternative accounts, they
must be evaluated by comparing their virtues with those of their
competitors. According to Larry Laudan, however, rivalist religious
explanations must not be compared directly with their competitive
alternatives. Instead, attention should be turned to the traditions
from which such explanations spring. In his view, it is rational to
accept only those explanations, religious or otherwise, that spring
from research traditions that are currently more adequate at problem
solving than the traditions from which their competitors arise. But
even if a particular explanation proves to be unworthy of current
acceptance, it need not be dropped altogether. It may turn out to be

worthy of pursuit. For Laudan, it is always rational to pursue a research tradition that shows a higher rate of progress than its competitors. Thus, explanations that spring from rapidly developing traditions may deserve considerable attention while failing to merit assent. Thomas Kuhn differs from Laudan with regard to the criteria by which rivalist explanations should be assessed. For Kuhn, the orderly discipline of paradigm-governed research always is to be preferred to the aimless wandering characteristic of preparadigm investigation. For this reason, if a religious paradigm gives rise to an explanation for a range of phenomena that falls outside the purview of other extant paradigms, it should be accepted. But in cases where a religious explanation is offered for a pattern of phenomena that already falls within the explanatory scope of an entrenched paradigm, the choice is not so clear. Of course, it is always rational to accept an entrenched paradigm that is not in a state of crisis. But one need not spurn explanations that spring from less favored paradigms. Only the future course of paradigm development will determine the value of accepting or rejecting alternatives to the mainstream.

When it comes to criteria for evaluating the plausibility of non-rivalist religious explanations, Laudan and Kuhn offer little insight. Once nonrivalist explanations have passed the tests of initial plausibility and it is known that they are formulated properly, further assessment must proceed along different lines. Typically, nonrivalist religious explanations will be offered for ranges of phenomena that already have been explained adequately in other ways. In cases of this sort, the addition of religious accounts cannot be justified on explanatory grounds. Rather, their introduction must be legitimated by appeal to nonexplanatory exigencies. Even in those few cases where nonrivalist religious explanations are offered for ranges of phenomena that have not been explained in other ways, the possibility that an alternative explanation may emerge in the future cannot be precluded. For this reason, even nonrivalist religious explanations that currently face no explanatory alternatives should not be justified on explanatory grounds alone. Other epistemic and nonepistemic reasons for accepting them should be offered as well.

Using this outline of plausibility criteria for both rivalist and nonrivalist religious explanations as a guide, attention can be turned to evaluating the adequacy of a few promising candidates. But in this turn to specific cases, special care must be taken to avoid resurrecting the spirit of positivism. As was noted in the second and third chapters, even those sympathetic with the attempt to rehabilitate the cognitive integrity of religious discourse have fallen prey to the insidious tendencies of this philosophical movement. For instance, Basil Mitchell falsely assumed that all scientific hypotheses are related deductively to the course of experience. He also thought that such hypotheses could be confirmed or disconfirmed by experimental data in a relatively straightforward way. For these reasons, he felt compelled to conclude that religious explanations cannot measure up to rigorously scientific standards.[2] Frederick Ferré mistakenly thought that all scientific explanations must involve the subsumption of the phenomena to be explained under lawlike regularities. Since religious explanations cannot meet this condition, Ferré joined Mitchell in reducing such explanations to a secondary epistemic status.[3] Ian Ramsey never shook himself free of any of the main positivist doctrines. He too conceived of science as a search for lawlike regularities. From these regularities, he believed that the scientist should be able to deduce instances that will permit the empirical verification or falsification of hypotheses. Failing to realize that even the most rigorous of the sciences cannot live up to this vision of theoretical integrity, Ramsey grudgingly concluded that religious discourse cannot be structured scientifically.[4]

Since explanations patterned after the scientific model described in the third chapter are not structured along positivist lines, no deductive relation between explanations of this sort and the course of experience should be expected. Therefore, in assessing the plausibility of religious explanations patterned after the model offered in the third chapter, the positivist myth of deductivism must be eschewed. Similarly, since no explanations of this sort stand in simple evidential relations with the course of experience, the myth of verificationism must be repudiated as well. Explanations are linked evidentially to experience, of course, but no single event or even manageably small series of events will confirm or disconfirm them conclusively.

Unfortunately, in beginning a search for plausible religious explanations, it must be admitted that the field of possibilities is restricted immediately by the nature of the explanatory strategy under current investigation. The structure of scientific explanation that was described in the third chapter is of a very specific sort. It can be used only to construct explanations for patterns of phenomena and so is incapable of providing a way of formulating accounts for individual occurrences. For this reason, religious explanations for unique events cannot be constructed by using this model as a guide. Thus, if the Christ events are taken as unique, it will be impossible to explain them by employing the strategies under consideration here. Similarly, religious explanations of the origin of the world cannot be formulated along these explanatory lines. In fact, since most phenomena that are thought to be miraculous are unique events rather than persistent patterns of occurrence, the vast majority of purported miracles also will remain inexplicable by these means.

This limitation of scope still leaves a wide spectrum of diverse phenomena that can be treated effectively. While accounts for individual occurrences cannot be generated, widely different patterns of phenomena may be explained by believers from radically divergent religious traditions. Indeed, the explanatory structure under consideration here is surprisingly neutral theologically. Charismatic groups, possessed by the significance of ecstatic speech patterns, may use this strategy to devise religious explanations for regularities in their linguistic behavior. Fundamentalists may use it to develop creationist accounts as rivals for evolutionary explanations. Nonrivalists may be tempted to construct explanations of anything from broad historical patterns to more modest patterns of personal succor. Rivalists and nonrivalists alike may try to explain patterns of mystical encounter.

Clearly, not all religious explanations from this bewildering array will be equally plausible. Quite to the contrary, though properly formulated, many will turn out to be absurd. The tantalizing question is, of course, whether any religious explanations can be constructed that are of sufficient plausibility to merit more than passing attention. Since there can be no hope of considering every imaginable candidate, it is necessary to settle for a representative sampling of some of the more promising ones instead.

In choosing this sampling, examples from three popular categories should be considered. Rivalists and nonrivalists alike have been tempted to try to construct religious explanations for the broadest patterns of natural phenomena. Among such broad patterns can be counted those that have been uncovered by the physical as well as the life sciences. Since religious explanations of the sort under consideration here can be formulated to account for such sweeping natural patterns, one or two from this category will be considered. Along more restricted lines, rivalists or nonrivalists often attempt to provide explanations for certain pervasive historical patterns. Because religious accounts for such historical patterns also can be structured in conformity with the model of the third chapter, an example or two from this category will be investigated as well. Finally, both rivalists and nonrivalists frequently take an interest in explaining personal patterns like the regular recurrence of mystical encounter, spiritual rejuvenation, or profound peace. Samplings from this third category should not be neglected either, since it is possible to construct accounts for such personal ranges along the lines being considered here.

In a search for possibly plausible religious explanations of the first category, explanations for the broadest of natural patterns, a good start can be taken by turning to design arguments. Over the centuries, believers from many different traditions have been impressed with patterns of apparent design in the universe and have attempted to account for these orderly patterns by making reference to the creative and controlling activity of God. Some have found such patterns of apparent design so compelling as to force them beyond mere explanations of design to the formulation of design arguments, arguments intended to be of sufficient power to prove the existence of God. In *Dialogues Concerning Natural Religion*, David Hume captured the spirit of such design proofs. He wrote:

Look round the world: Contemplate the whole and every part of it: You will find it to be nothing but one great machine, subdivided into an infinite number of lesser machines. . . . All these various machines, and even their most minute parts, are adjusted to each other with an accuracy which ravishes into admiration all men who have ever contemplated them. The curious adapting of means to end, throughout all nature, resembles exactly, though it much exceeds, the productions of human contrivance—of human design, thought, wisdom, and intelligence. Since therefore the effects resemble each other, we are led to infer, by all the rules of analogy, that the causes also resemble, and that the Author of Nature is somewhat similar to the mind of man. . . . By this argument . . . do we prove at once the existence of a Deity and his similarity to human mind and intelligence.[5]

This particular design proof rests heavily upon a mechanistic analogy. Interacting elements in nature are judged to be closely similar to the interactions among parts of humanly designed machines. With the powerful impact of the writings of Charles Darwin, attention has tended to shift away from purely mechanistic patterns to more organic and ecological ones. Hume anticipated this shift of emphasis toward biological patterns in his later characterization of design proofs. He noted:

It is with pleasure I hear Galen reason concerning the structure of the human body. The anatomy of a man . . . discovers above 600 different muscles; and whoever duly considers these will find that, in each of them, nature must have adjusted at least ten different circumstances in order to attain the end which she proposed. . . . The bones he calculates to be 284; the distinct purposes aimed at in the structure of each, above forty. . . . But if we consider the skin, ligaments, vessels, glandules, humors, the several limbs and members of the body, how must our astonishment rise upon us, in proportion to the number and intricacy of the parts so artificially adjusted! . . . To what pitch of pertinacious obstinacy must a philosopher in this age have attained who can now doubt of a Supreme Intelligence![6]

Given the current intensity of interest in Darwinian theories, particularly with respect to their relation to traditional theistic doctrines of creation, it is probably best to focus upon the possibility of formulating plausible religious explanations for biological, rather than for more purely physical or chemical patterns of phenomena. In this turn to the biological world, the first question that must be asked is whether there are any extant patterns of phenomena for which a religious explanation might be constructed. Whether rivalist or nonrivalist, a religious explanation modeled after the scientific pattern of the third chapter cannot be considered to be even initially plausible unless it is developed to account for some actually existing range of phenomena.

In his critique of design proofs, Hume seriously questioned whether there is anything at all to explain. He wrote, "We have no *data* to establish any system of cosmogony. Our experience, so imperfect in itself and so limited both in extent and duration, can afford us no probable conjecture concerning the whole of things."[7] Hume made these comments, of course, before the massive compilations of Darwin. But even Darwin's studies are seriously incomplete. Though he amassed volumes of detail regarding the interdependencies among species as well as individuals, Darwin offered no data regarding extraterrestrial biology. What reason is there to believe that life forms elsewhere must display the same features of apparent design found here on earth? While apparent design on earth may point in the direction of a designer, the occurrence of chaotic phenomena elsewhere would point in the opposite direction. So, without knowing whether such counterevidence exists elsewhere, it would be a mistake to conclude that the appearance of design on earth indicates that there must have been an intelligent creator. Perhaps it would be better to remain agnostic on the matter. After all, it may be that the appearance of biological order on earth is just a fluke, the result of a fortuitous concatenation of chance happenings. Perhaps the conclusion to be drawn is that "the universe goes on for many ages in a continued succession of chaos and disorder. But is it not possible that it may settle at last . . . so as to preserve a uniformity of appearance, amidst the continual motion and fluctuation of its parts?"[8]

There are two distinct points that must be made in reply to this line of objection. In the first place, it must be remembered that Hume's attack was directed against design *proofs* rather than design *explanations*. Plausibility constraints upon proofs are very different from those imposed upon explanations. So, while the possibility of chaotic biological data elsewhere in the universe might weaken seriously the force of any attempt to prove the existence of a divine designer, it is of no relevance whatever when it comes to matters of divine explanation. Explanations are offered for precisely delineated ranges of phenomena. All that is required of a plausible explanation is that it explain the range it is expected to explain. Thus, it does not matter in the slightest that such an explanation, religious or otherwise, may be inadequate for ranges of data that fall outside its explanatory scope.

The second point to be made is in connection with Hume's suggestion that the quest for explanations in terms of governing mechanisms may be an illusory one. Perhaps the appearance of biological order is nothing more than the result of chance coincidence. Given enough time, a chaotic universe may fall into an appearance of orderly assemblage. For this reason, there is no guarantee that any governing mechanism at all lies behind the face of patterned appearances.

This particular line of objection forms but one part of Hume's famous attack upon the cognitive integrity of the sciences.[9] As such, it is as much a threat to Darwinian attempts at biological explanation as it is to religious ones. If Hume is correct at this point, then any attempt whatever to explain patterns of phenomena by reference to governing mechanisms must be abandoned. Scientific explanations are in as much trouble as religious accounts. Since the religious skepticism under consideration in this present study depends directly upon a deep faith in the cognitive integrity of the physical sciences, Hume's attack upon the sciences need not be discussed. If Hume is correct, then the sort of religious skepticism traced in the first chapter must collapse. On the other hand, should Hume prove incorrect, then it is necessary to try to rehabilitate the cognitive integrity of religious discourse in the ways being developed here.[10]

Given the assumption of the writers discussed in the first chapter—the assumption that the physical sciences are epistemically above reproach—it is beyond doubt that Darwin has identified an extant range of phenomena suitable for scientific explanation. So, the problem of finding an extant range for the religious believer to explain can be handled in a straightforward way: so long as a religious account is offered either for Darwin's entire range or for some part of that range, the believer can be confident that the range he hopes to explain actually exists.

Once a range of existing phenomena has been chosen, an analogous range for which the governing mechanism already is understood must be found. In design explanations, the analogous range is that of human artifacts and the responsible mechanism is some human creator. Since human intelligence is responsible for the patterns of interactions among parts of clocks, cars, and boats, God is characterized as the intelligent agent responsible for the patterns of interactions found among parts of animals or parts of ecosystems.

Hume would not be impressed with the legitimacy of this second step in the construction of a religious explanation. In disputing the move to human creativity as a model for characterizing the mechanism responsible for natural patterns of interaction, he observed: "The world, say I, resembles an animal; therefore it is an animal, therefore it arose from generation. . . . The Brahmins assert that the world arose from an infinite spider, who spun this whole complicated mass from his bowels."[11] While Hume did not deny that human intelligence is responsible for the patterns of orderliness found in artifacts, he could see no reason for choosing human minds as a model for shaping a conception of God. Spiders generate patterns of orderliness. Why not conceive of the universe as a cosmic web? If a generative source for complicated patterns of interaction is sought, what better source of analogy than animal reproduction? By reproductive means animals produce complex living organisms far more intricately interrelated than the most elaborate of human artifactual creations. Why not conclude that the universe, or certain intricate parts of it, are offspring of some cosmic animal? For that matter, even a tree is more complicated in its interactive details than the most intricate of cars or computers. Why not opt for vegetative generation? Even if human minds must be chosen as the proper source of analogy for shaping a conception of God, "What shadow of an argument . . . can you produce from your hypothesis to prove the unity of the Deity? A great number of men join in building a house or ship, in rearing a city, in framing a commonwealth; why may not several deities combine in contriving and framing a world?" [12]

In short, Hume was convinced that all sorts of relevantly analogous ranges of phenomena exist that are governed by vastly different responsible mechanisms. Why choose one such mechanism as a model for shaping a characterization of God rather than another? Since there is no explanatory reason for shaping a conception of God along human lines rather than along animal or plant lines, Hume concluded that the choice must be arbitrary. Or, if not arbitrary, then egotistical. "By representing the Deity as so intelligible and comprehensible, and so similar to a human mind, we are guilty of the grossest and most narrow partiality, and make ourselves the model of the whole universe." [13]

Once again, it must be remembered that Hume's concern was to attack the possibility of constructing design proofs rather than to undermine the plausibility of design explanations. If design proofs are intended to lead inevitably to the conclusion that a single, theistically characterized God must exist, then legitimate analogues from the plant or animal world pose a serious problem. From patterns of apparent design, it is not necessary to conclude that there is an intelligent, personal creator. Instead, one might conclude that such design is the result of animal or vegetative activity.

However, the impact of alternative analogues upon the plausibility of design explanations is not so straightforward. The simple fact that animals, plants, or human committees may provide fertile sources of analogy for the construction of competing explanations does not undermine the initial plausibility of an explanation in terms of God as a single, intelligent creator. To be initially plausible, all that is required is that an explanation be formulated properly. It is not necessary that it be the best explanation available. So, with regard to the initial plausibility of conceiving God as a single, intelligent creator in an attempt to account for patterns of apparent design, the possibility of formulating alternative explanations is simply beside the point. Of course, when it comes to deciding whether a specific explanation should be accepted or whether it is the best one available, the merits of alternative accounts will have to be considered, but at this stage, such considerations are premature. If a conception of God as an intelligent creator can be constructed properly without undue epistemic or religious sacrifice, then it can be offered as an initially plausible account of patterns of apparent design.

As might be expected, Hume was prepared to leap into the breach with additional arguments against the claim that a conception of God's creative activity can be modeled properly upon the intellectual capacities of human beings. Most of these further objections are familiar ones. He suggested that since humans are embodied, any carryover to the religious case will have to involve the attribution of corporeality to God.[14] He also argued that since human beings are finite and imperfect, it is impossible to use them as proper analogues for constructing a conception of an infinite and perfect God.[15] Finally, he was troubled by the problem of purgation. There are many disanalogies between the way in which God is expected to behave and the ways in which humans act. So, in moving from the human to the divine case, how will it be possible to avoid carrying over bad as well as good human qualities in a characterization of God?[16] All of these objections have been treated in detail in previous chapters and so need not be reviewed again here.[17]

In the course of offering these familiar objections, however, Hume managed to throw in a few new ones. For example, he argued:

A mind whose acts and sentiments and ideas are not distinct and successive, one that is wholly simple and totally immutable, is a mind which has no thought, no reason, no will, no sentiment, no love, no hatred; or, in a word, is no mind at all. It is an abuse of terms to give it that appellation.[18]

That is, the attribution of humanlike intellectual activities to God is incompatible with his divine simplicity and immutability. Whether this suggested incompatibility is a genuine one has been debated for centuries. For the purposes of this study, it is sufficient to note that numerous thinkers have been willing to concede this incompatibility while resisting the temptation to reject the existence of God. Instead, they have sought to evolve a religiously adequate conception of God without attributing either immutability or simplicity to him.[19] Thus, even if Hume's point be granted, it only shows that formulating a conception of God in conformity with certain human models may require a more flexible stance with regard to specific traditional, and perhaps superfluous, divine characteristics.

Although this particular problem may be avoided with a bit of careful theological maneuvering, Hume hinted at a more serious difficulty when he said:

It is a palpable and egregious partiality to confine our view entirely to that principle by which our own minds operate. Were this principle more intelligible on that account, such a partiality might be somewhat excusable; but reason, in its internal fabric and structure, is really as little known to us as instinct or vegetation.[20]

Patterns of biological interdependence are supposed to be explained religiously by appeal to God's intellectual activity. But the understanding of God's creative activities is parasitic upon the intelligibility of human creative endeavor. Now how can there be any hope of explaining biological design by appeal to human creativity if the way in which human creativity leads to design in artifacts is not understood in clear detail?

The difficulty felt by Hume at this point comes from an easy confusion. When the believer offers his religious explanation of biological patterns, he is attempting only to explain why there are such patterns. His answer lies in the claim that God is an intelligent creator. In this explanatory attempt, the believer need not be concerned to explain exactly how God went about creating such patterns. While it might be possible to explain this as well, it is crucial to recognize that such an account would be offered in response to a new, and quite distinct, explanatory question. Explaining why there are biological patterns is quite different from specifying the exact procedure by which God could manage to create such patterns.

To see this point more clearly, return to the explanation of the expansion and contraction of balloons by reference to a sea of air. In trying to explain why balloons change in size with variations in altitude, the scientist had only to recognize that it is the pressure of the Pacific that is responsible for the size of rubber balls. Once he had identified this explanatorily efficacious feature in the rubber ball case, he was in a position to explain why his balloons expanded and contracted in the ways that they did. It is the pressure of a sea of air that determines balloon size. Of course, if he knew exactly how the pressure of the Pacific determines the size of rubber balls, the scientist could try to go beyond the mere account of why his balloons change in size to explain exactly how air pressure does its work. But if he were ignorant of the way in which sea pressure operates, he could rest content with the observation that however the pressure of the Pacific operates to effect changes in rubber ball size, the pressure of the sea of air operates in a similar way to determine the expansion and contraction of balloons. In the face of ignorance about the details of sea pressure, the scientist could remain satisfied that he has explained variations in balloon size even though he has been unable to explain how sea pressure operates.

By drawing this distinction between explaining patterns of phenomena and explaining the mechanisms that determine such patterns, it is possible to understand how patterns of phenomena can be explained by making reference to mechanisms that are not themselves fully understood. For instance, it is possible to see why the common practice of appealing to the ingenuity of watchmakers causes no problems in giving an account of why there are watches. The reason why there are intricately patterned watches is not at all mysterious, even though the inner workings of the human mind and the nature of human creativity may remain a mystery forever. Similarly, the religious devotee might argue properly that the reason why there are patterns of biological interdependence can be brought to light by reference to God's intelligence, even though the details of God's intellectual activity remain darkly obscure.

As a final attempt to block the formulation of a religious explanation for biological interdependencies, Hume's comments about the problem of evil must be taken into account. "Were a stranger to drop on a sudden into this world, I would show him, as a specimen of its ills, a hospital full of diseases, a prison crowded with malefactors and debtors, . . . a nation languishing under tyranny, famine or pestilence."[21] Put in more Darwinian terms, how can the religious believer expect to explain ecological interdependencies in terms of a just and good God when one species survives and even prospers from the suffering and desolation of others? Are not the patterns to be explained too brutal, vicious, and bloody?

Quite surprisingly, it is not at all difficult to salvage both a religious explanation for patterns of biological design and a conception of God as loving and righteous. One way of doing this relies upon the fact that explanations always are offered for closely circumscribed ranges of phenomena. Thus, it is possible to avoid involving God in the explanation of troublesome ranges of biological phenomena by cautiously delimiting his explanatory range. By the simple expedient of pushing problematic patterns outside God's explanatory scope, the religious believer can avoid the embarrassment of having to admit that God is responsible for the darker side of biology. Such dark patterns might be left unexplained. More typically, however, the believer might try to explain evil patterns by reference to the activities of other religiously significant entities. For example, in his consideration of the problem of evil, Alvin Plantinga has suggested that believers might want to invoke the activities of Satan in accounting for the evil in the world.[22]

By this time, it should be quite clear that forming initially plausible religious explanations for biological interdependencies is not at all difficult. This should not come as any surprise, considering the nature of the criteria for initial plausibility. To begin, all that is required is an extant explanatory range. Darwin's will do nicely. Since explanatory ranges may be gerrymandered unmercifully, the believer need exercise only a modicum of caution to avoid including inappropriate patterns of data in God's explanatory range. In the selection of a relevantly analogous range of phenomena, the criteria for initial plausibility do not dictate that the best alternative be chosen. Any genuinely analogous range of phenomena for which the governing mechanism is known will do. Thus, the believer is free to shape his conception of God in conformity with the fact that individual, intelligent human beings are responsible for the patterns of design that are found in artifacts.

Matters become considerably more serious when claims beyond mere initial plausibility are made, however. Once properly formulated, a religious explanation is initially plausible. But whether such an initially plausible explanation is worthy of acceptance or is even sufficiently plausible to merit serious consideration depends heavily upon whether it is offered by rivalists or nonrivalists.

Consider first those religious explanations of biological interdependence offered as rivals to current evolutionary theory. Darwin himself faced rivalist accounts from such prominent biologists as Sir Richard Owen and Louis Agassiz.[23] Currently, this rivalist tradition is kept alive by certain highly visible Protestant Fundamentalists and by various small, specialized organizations.[24] The intention of such individuals and groups is to offer explanations of patterns of biological phenomena that can compete with evolutionary accounts.

If contemporary creationists were to structure their explanations of biological interdependence along the lines suggested here, they would find no problem in reaching the level of initial plausibility. But as rivalists, they would be pressed into competition with the most sophisticated of current biological theories and, given the plausibility criteria of either Laudan or Kuhn, would not find themselves in an enviable position. In the attempt to move their accounts beyond the level of initial plausibility, creationists who offer religious explanations as rivals to evolutionary ones face serious obstacles. With regard to sheer explanatory power, current evolutionary explanations are able to cover an extraordinary diversity of phenomena. Patterns of animal coloration, skeletal structure, mating behavior, sizes of beaks, shapes of claws, and kinds of teeth as well as countless other patterns can be explained in minute detail.

Officially, of course, creationists can cover the same explanatory territory. The same patterns of coloration, skeletal structure, and the rest can be explained by noting that God is a wise creator who, in his wisdom, has chosen to create the biological patterns found in nature. The game is given away, however, when it is asked why God was so wise in giving animals the colors they have, fish the skeletons they have, or various birds their thick beaks. The answer is simple: God was wise in providing such features because those features help these beasts compete for survival. Cardinals, for example, would starve without heavy beaks because they would not be able to crack the hard shells of assorted seeds. For the account of creationists to succeed, then, it must rely upon evolutionary themes. Since evolutionists have no problem accounting for such patterns without reference to God, it would seem that they have the edge on grounds of simplicity alone.

Not only would simplicity considerations militate against the acceptance of creationist explanations, evolutionary accounts would appear to win out on the basis of intelligibility as well. It is at this point that Hume's comment about the obscurity of appeals to intellectual mechanisms steps in with a vengeance. As Hume noted, "Were this principle more intelligible . . . such a partiality might be somewhat excusable; but reason, in its internal fabric and structure, is really as little known to us as instinct or vegetation."[25] Evolutionary mechanisms are understood with great precision. The way in which competition determines which individuals survive has been studied thoroughly. Huge strides have been made toward the understanding of genetic variations and mutations. By grounding genetics in molecular biology, it has become possible to mobilize the vast resources of chemical theory in the attempt to delineate the mechanisms responsible for genetic transmission and species variation. Not only has this focus upon the mechanisms of biochemistry enhanced the understanding of evolutionary mechanisms, it also has pushed evolutionary biology into much closer integration with chemistry and microphysics.

Creationists, on the other hand, have not been able to capitalize upon great strides made in other sciences. Given their interest in personalistic models, creationists might turn naturally to the findings of psychology. The psychological theory of human intelligent and creative activity, however, is still in its infancy. So, creationists cannot count upon psychological studies to generate a fuller understanding of the working of the mind of God. In comparison to the current understanding of evolutionary mechanisms, then, creationists are forced to admit that their divine explanatory entity is relatively unintelligible.

Furthermore, there is little hope of integrating the creationists' personalistic explanation into any wider scientific explanatory enterprise. Even if human psychology were to continue to move in the direction of neurophysiology, the integration of psychological theory into the wider scope of chemical or physical theory would not prove helpful to the creationist. Physicalist models of God's creative activity are not what they want. On the other hand, with the increasing integration of biochemistry with chemical theory and the close ties of chemistry to microphysics, the genetic mechanisms at the heart of current evolutionary theory show great promise of meshing beautifully with a wide variety of current scientific theoretical activity.

It would seem, then, that creationist accounts do not fare well in any direct confrontation with evolutionary explanations. Evolutionary models are simpler, more thoroughly intelligible, and more easily integrated into the wider scientific enterprise. But, if Laudan is correct, all of this is insufficient to dictate the acceptance of evolutionary accounts over creationist ones. What is needed is a comparison of research traditions. Explanations should be accepted only if they spring from the best research tradition and one should always "*choose the theory (or research tradition) with the highest problem-solving adequacy.*"[26]

There is no solace here for the creationist, however. The biological tradition from which current evolutionary explanations spring has been extraordinarily successful. Great strides have been taken toward understanding the mysteries of life: genetic replication, repro-duction, digestion, disease, and health. Indeed, the list of advances that can be credited to modern biological studies is too long to admit of any genuine summary at all. Unfortunately, the religious traditions from which creationist accounts spring can claim no such catalog of achievements. In fact, their record of problem solving is so poor that it is not even possible to muster a list of achievements sufficiently impressive to merit further pursuit along creationist lines. For Laudan, *"it is always rational to pursue any research tradition which has a higher rate of progress than its rivals."*[27] The rate of progress man-ifested by current biological research is nothing short of spectacular. It hardly bears mentioning that creationists have not demonstrated anything approaching such a rate of progress, much less a better one.

From the perspective of Kuhn, the position of creationists is not much better. The evolutionary paradigm is entrenched currently and is certainly not in a state of crisis. Since Kuhn believes that it is always rational to accept any entrenched paradigm that is not in a crisis state, there is no reason to switch to a creationist perspective. Of course, only the future unfolding of paradigm development can deter-mine whether those few mavericks who opt for a creationist underdog will triumph in the end. But given the meteoric rise of the evolutionary paradigm and the fact that it is not only prospering at the present time, but is coming closer to full integration with the thoroughly entrenched paradigms of chemistry and physics, there is not much room for optimism concerning the prospects of creationist alternatives.

The glaring problem for rivalists who are interested in offering a religious explanation for broad patterns of biological phenomena is the incredible power, scope, and fertility of their opposition. Non-rivalists face no such opposition, however. Capitalizing upon the possibility of explanatory overdetermination, nonrivalists can admit the full grandeur of evolutionary explanations without any qualms whatsoever. If the hands of a clock were governed both by a system of gears and by a set of ropes and pulleys, then the explanation of the movements on the face of that clock would be fully explainable by reference to the gear mechanism without jeopardizing in the slightest the possibility of offering an explanation for those same movements in terms of ropes and pulleys. Similarly, nonrivalist be-lievers can admit that biological patterns are fully explainable by reference to evolutionary mechanisms without thereby jeopardizing the possibility of offering religious accounts as well.

If nonrivalist religious explanations of biological phenomena are to press beyond the stage of initial plausibility, nonexplanatory reasons why they should be accepted must be generated. Obviously, in most cases, nonrivalist explanations cannot be justified on explanatory grounds alone. Evolutionary accounts are normally sufficient for explanatory purposes and so religious ones introduced for purely explanatory reasons would have to be judged superfluous. However, there may be many other reasons for accepting nonrivalist religious explanations for ranges of phenomena that already are explained along evolutionary lines. Some of these reasons might be epistemic in nature. For instance, if it could be shown that the Old Testament is a generally trustworthy witness, then the Genesis account of creation might provide some evidence in support of the contention that God is responsible for biological patterns even though such patterns can be explained already by reference to evolutionary themes. In a case of this sort, the epistemic principle that one should trust the testimony of generally reliable witnesses might be brought in support of the contention that an explanation that is not directly justifiable on explanatory grounds might nevertheless prove worthy of acceptance for reasons of an epistemic sort.

It is of crucial importance to be clear about what is being claimed here. It is not being suggested that the Old Testament is a reliable witness. Nor is it being suggested that trusting generally reliable witnesses is epistemically defensible. What is being suggested is that it may be possible for believers to generate valid, nonexplanatory epistemic reasons for accepting certain religious explanations. In fact, believers often try to do this. They begin by offering a series of reasons why a certain doctrine, sacred text, or religious teacher must be taken seriously. Then they argue that this reliable source of information provides some reason for concluding that reference to God will explain some range of data that may be explainable already in nonreligious ways. Now if it were to turn out that some such group of believers were able to carry out this strategy successfully, then there would be some epistemic, though nonexplanatory, reason for accepting their religious explanation.

For those who do not hold out much hope for finding trustworthy religious doctrines, texts, or teachers, probably the most interesting reasons for accepting nonrivalist religious explanations are the nonepistemic ones. Curiously enough, the field of human psychology may provide one of the more fertile sources for generating such nonepistemic reasons for accepting explanatorily superfluous religious explanations. It is often argued, of course, that gleanings from inquiries into the psychological implications of religious belief tend to cast a deep shadow of suspicion upon the cognitive integrity of such belief. As was indicated in the first chapter, Freud's *The Future of an Illusion* helped to encourage this kind of skeptical argument. If the belief that God is in control of the world were found to be psychologically useful, providing believers with a sense of security, giving them a more accepting attitude toward the disappointments in life, or allowing them some sort of personal peace, it would seem both natural and easy to conclude that religious belief must be nothing more than a powerful psychological crutch.

But this easy conclusion must be resisted. There is no such simple, inverse relation between the psychological or existential benefits of accepting religious explanations and their cognitive value. In fact, if the nonrivalist could establish that accepting some particular religious explanation really would have deep psychological or existential value, then he might be in a position to provide a potent, nonepistemic reason for embracing that explanation even though its acceptance could not be justified on explanatory grounds alone. It is important to recognize, however, that it is the actual results of psychological studies that will determine how useful they are to the nonrivalist. Should it be found, for instance, that the acceptance of religious explanations for patterns of biological phenomena is of negative psychological value, then the nonrivalist may have important nonepistemic reasons for rejecting rather than for accepting particular religious accounts. If, on the other hand, the findings of someone like Gordon Allport[28] were validated and it were found that religious belief is of great positive value, leading to greater maturity, tolerance, or independence, then the nonrivalist could use such evidence to bolster his claim that certain religious explanations should be accepted even though they cannot be justified in any directly explanatory way. While evolutionary explanations may be sufficient for explanatory purposes, the nonrivalist could use that psychological data to argue that there are important nonepistemic, nonexplanatory reasons for accepting religious explanations as well.

To this point, it has been possible to be decisive about the plausibility of rivalist religious explanations offered in competition with evolutionary accounts. While rivalists may be able to generate properly formulated religious explanations of various patterns of biological phenomena, such explanations cannot be viewed as even remotely plausible on the criteria of Laudan or Kuhn. Nonrivalist explanations, on the other hand, do not come into direct competition with evolutionary accounts. It has been seen that such explanations can be formulated properly to reach the level of initial plausibility. It also has been seen that such explanations can avoid all of the criticisms leveled by David Hume against traditional design arguments. Finally, a couple of examples of the kinds of epistemic and nonepistemic reasons that might be assembled in support of the contention that even explanatorily superfluous nonrivalist religious explanations might be worthy of acceptance have been sketched in order to provide some indication of how the plausibility of such accounts should be determined.

Unfortunately, the assessment of the plausibility of nonrivalist religious explanations for broad, biological patterns must be left in this somewhat unsettled state. Given the welter of assorted epistemic and nonepistemic reasons that could be offered for accepting nonrivalist accounts, it must be conceded that there is no quick way of providing a final assessment of their merits. Each candidate would have to be considered on an individual basis with special care being taken to evaluate the list of particular reasons that might be brought in support of its candidacy. Such a prolonged investigation falls more naturally under the province of theological apologetics and so lies well outside the scope of this study. Nevertheless, the results of this brief investigation should not be minimized. It must be emphasized that no good scientific or philosophical reason has been found for rejecting nonrivalist explanations of certain pervasive biological patterns. If the argument to this point has been correct, then current evolutionary theory poses no threat to the integrity of nonrivalist religious accounts of patterns of biological interdependence. Furthermore, such accounts cannot be rejected for philosophical reasons. Even Hume's classic catalog of objections against design arguments proved impotent against properly formulated nonrivalist accounts. It would appear, then, that such explanations deserve more than passing attention. Indeed, it is difficult to see on what grounds they might be resisted should a religious community assemble significant epistemic or nonepistemic reasons for their acceptance.

Religious accounts for broad natural patterns, biological or otherwise, have received much philosophical attention for the simple reason that they have a tendency to evolve into design proofs. But believers also have sought to offer religious accounts for more restricted, historical patterns. Augustine's *City of God* provides a detailed example of an attempt to understand a range of historical patterns in religious terms. While few believers ever could hope to match Augustine's comprehensive grasp of historical detail, more limited visions have not always proven to be incapacitating in the struggle to construct religious explanations for historical patterns. Old Testament writers, for example, were fond of suggesting religious accounts for narrowly circumscribed patterns in the history of Israel. The book of Judges offers an excellent example of this. In Judges 2:11–13, the author specifies the pattern to be explained. He notes again and again that the people of God incessantly turned to the worship of foreign gods only to find themselves subjected to persecution at the hands of their enemies. In the midst of their oppression, the people would repent and, subsequently, judges would rise up to deliver them from their suffering. This recurring pattern of idolatry, subjection to enemies, and repentance followed by salvation is documented repeatedly throughout the remainder of the book. The explanation offered for this recurring pattern is in terms of the chastening and forgiving activities of God. In full awareness of such explanations as this one, early Jewish converts to Christianity sought to account for their own patterns of affliction and blessing in terms of their new faith. One of these new converts, Stephen, offered a passionate speech just before his death in which he tried to demonstrate that certain patterns in the history of Israel could be explained in terms of God's interactions with his chosen people. In Stephen's opinion, the hostile reaction of Jewish leaders to the coming of Christ was yet another case where God's people insisted on struggling against his messengers.[29]

To a large extent, the procedures involved in assessing the plausibility of religious explanations for historical patterns follow closely those that are involved in the proper assessment of explanations for natural occurrences. Because of this, certain issues treated in detail during the consideration of the plausibility of religious explanations offered for natural phenomena need not be reconsidered here. Hume's objections against the integrity of design proofs, for instance, are no more forceful when reshaped as objections against the initial plausibility of explanations for historical patterns than they were when brought against religious accounts for natural phenomena. Therefore, in order to avoid tiresome repetition, attention will be focused upon the ways in which plausibility assessments for historical patterns differ from those involved in the evaluation of explanations for natural phenomena.

The first problem to be confronted in assessing the plausibility of religious explanations for historical patterns arises in connection with the verification of the existence of historical explanatory ranges. As has been noted, the first step in demonstrating the initial plausibility of explanations structured after the model of the third chapter is to show that the ranges of phenomena to be explained actually exist. Historical patterns can be notoriously difficult to confirm. If no evidence can be generated to support the contention that a particular historical sequence occurred, it will be impossible to argue that any explanation of such a range is even initially plausible. So, if an account were offered for the regular appearance of manna in the wilderness or for the guidance of a cloud by day and a pillar of fire by night, the prospects of that explanation reaching even initial plausibility would be extraordinarily bleak. There is probably no hope whatever of confirming the existence of such occurrences. Without having some reason to believe in the occurrence of such phenomena, there would be little motivation to try to devise proper explanations for them.

It should not be concluded from the fact that it is impossible to offer confirmation of the existence of certain historical patterns that the confirmation of all such patterns is problematic. Some patterns in history are surprisingly easy to confirm. If one were to seek an explanation of the fact that, time and again, a remnant of the Jewish people has managed to hang on in the face of intense persecution, then the mere fact that there are Jews living today is nearly sufficient. Probably all that is needed by way of supplementation is a little documentation of the narrow escapes of these people over recent decades. Given the course of the last hundred years, such documentation should not be hard to obtain.

Roughly speaking, the less specific and the more recent the pattern to be explained, the easier it will be to document. So, while it cannot be denied that historical patterns are usually more difficult to confirm than natural ones, there is no reason to suppose that verifying their existence is necessarily impossible. If religious explanations for relatively accessible historical patterns are offered, meeting this first condition of initial plausibility should not prove too difficult.

Once an extant range of historical phenomena has been found and its existence confirmed, the proper formulation of an explanation by reference to a relevantly analogous range of phenomena should pose no special problems. For the sake of simplicity, suppose someone were to attempt a religious explanation of the persistence of the Jews. To insure that there will be no difficulty in showing that there is an extant pattern of phenomena to be explained, the explanatory range could be restricted to the last hundred years. Thus, what is to be explained is a particular pattern of recent survival. Over the last hundred years, the Jews have managed to hold on against repeated assault.

Relevantly analogous ranges of phenomena abound. There are many cases of individuals or groups that have been protected in their struggle against prolonged persecution. Parents often protect their young children from bullies. Governmental leaders shield their vulnerable subordinates in time of trial. Soldiers come to the aid of their weaker comrades in the thick of battle. By taking any such relevantly analogous range for which the governing mechanism is known, a conception of God as responsible for the persistence of the Jews could be fashioned along standard lines. As in the case of religious explanations for patterns of natural phenomena, it is relatively easy to reach the level of initial plausibility.

The real problem comes in assessing the plausibility of such explanations beyond this initial level. Is there any reason to think that an initially plausible religious account of certain historical patterns is worthy of acceptance or even worthy of further pursuit? As with the assessment of the plausibility of accounts for natural phenomena, much depends upon whether explanations for historical patterns are offered by rivalists or nonrivalists.

Rivalist accounts for historical patterns are in a little better shape than rivalist explanations for natural phenomena. In the first place, their competition is not so stiff. Normally, rivals for religious explanations of historical patterns would have to come from disciplines that have not achieved the explanatory prestige of the natural sciences. Psychological or sociological explanations might be offered as competitors. Economic or sociopolitical alternatives might be suggested. But none of these nonreligious alternatives enjoys the sheer explanatory success of the natural sciences. Therefore, until psychological, sociological, or other naturalistic explanations improve significantly, the religious rivalist can count as his strength the relative weakness of the competition.

This relative strength enjoyed by the rivalist should not be overemphasized, however. It is true that social scientific explanations are typically less successful than explanations offered in the natural or life sciences and, therefore, rivalist religious accounts stand a better chance of competing when it comes to the explanation of historical patterns than they have when faced with explanations from physics, chemistry, or biology. Nevertheless, even in this arena rivalists may lose, since standing a better chance of competing successfully certainly is not to be confused with winning. Furthermore, even if rivalists should be able to win out over their current competitors, this success, though genuine, would be extremely tenuous. Should such fields as psychology or sociology continue to advance, rivalist religious explanations quickly might lose their competitive edge.

It may appear that because of the current status of psychological or other alternatives, rivalist religious explanations stack up pretty well against their opposition. Nonreligious explanations for historical patterns typically appeal to mechanisms shaped along personalistic lines. Since religious rivalists normally form their conceptions of God along the same lines, explanations that make reference to the activities of God would not seem to suffer from the problem of relative unintelligibility. Personalistic models are not rendered more intelligible by the fact that they are used by historians, sociologists, or political scientists rather than by theologians. Furthermore, insofar as religious rivalists employ the same sorts of models in shaping their conceptions of God as are used by psychologists, sociologists, or historians, it would seem that they do not need to worry about matters of integration. Personalistic explanations do not integrate well into the wider spectrum of scientific activity, of course, but as long as his competitors use the same sorts of models in shaping their explanations, the religious rivalist would appear to be on safe ground. His competitors should have no more success at wider integration than he does.

Unfortunately, this semblance of parity with regard to matters of intelligibility and integration may be nothing more than appearance. If psychology continues to benefit from advances in neurophysiology and biochemistry, then it may be able to achieve a level of intelligibility and integration not attainable by rivalist believers. The integration of psychology with biology or chemistry certainly would lead to a much fuller understanding of psychological mechanisms. While such understanding might increase the intelligibility of psychological, sociological, or other naturalistic explanations that rely upon psychological models, the religious believer would be left behind. Neurophysiological or biochemical insights into human personality would not be of much value in the quest for a sharper understanding of the activities of God.

Of course, as was noted in the discussion of rivalist explanations for patterns of natural phenomena, Laudan would insist that it is the comparative merits of alternative research traditions rather than the strength of specific explanations that is of paramount importance. In this regard, psychological, sociological, economic, or even historical explanatory traditions would seem to win out over religious ones. Each of these disciplines can show some success at problem solving that, though limited, appears to be superior to that of religious explanatory enterprises. Furthermore, the rate at which such disciplines are solving problems seems to be increasing fairly rapidly. For this reason, not only would explanations that spring from more static, rivalist religious traditions appear unworthy of current acceptance, they would seem to be unworthy of current pursuit as well.

From the perspective of Kuhn, matters are not quite so bleak for the religious rivalist. Obviously, it must be acknowledged that psychological, sociological, historical, and economic paradigms are entrenched and there is no reason why such entrenched paradigms should be abandoned. Not one of them is in an obvious state of crisis. Nevertheless, it is difficult to maintain much confidence that crisis can be kept permanently at bay. In most of these fields, there are few thoroughly settled paradigms. Alternatives tend to proliferate. Even in psychology, one of the more stable of these disciplines, factions have not disappeared. Freudians still battle Skinnerians who, in turn, press their case against Jungians. Because unifying, stable paradigms are hard to find in any of these fields, there is the real possibility that crises may precipitate at any time.

While the rivalist may take some comfort from this unsettled state of the social sciences, there is still plenty of risk involved in siding with the religious underdog. The disarray of the social sciences should not be exaggerated. Although there is a certain rivalry among alternative factions, there is surprising agreement about many basic goals and methods. Also, a great deal of effort is being devoted to the evolution of more comprehensive paradigms, paradigms that can demand the sort of widespread allegiance manifested in chemistry or biology. Furthermore, it must be borne in mind that even though alternative paradigms may tend to proliferate in the social sciences at the present time, many of these paradigms are quite powerful, capable of handling a number of diverse theoretical problems. Finally, it should be emphasized that while the social sciences cannot be integrated fully into the wider sphere of scientific endeavor at the present time, they do show some promise of future integration. With its recent emphasis upon neurophysiological and biophysical explanations, even psychology has begun to move toward actually fulfilling its promise of integration. In short, with the extraordinary amount of effort going into improving the theoretical adequacy of the various social sciences, religious rivalists stand little chance of keeping pace, much less prevailing. But, as Kuhn would cheerfully remark, only the future course of paradigm development can tell who will be the winners and who the losers.

Nonrivalist religious explanations for historical patterns are in exactly the same position as nonrivalist explanations for natural patterns. Initial plausibility is not much of a problem. As long as the nonrivalist avoids selecting obscure patterns of historical phenomena, he should face no insurmountable difficulties in documenting the existence of the ranges he hopes to explain. A little care in the proper formulation of his explanations by reference to relevantly analogous ranges of phenomena should insure that his accounts reach the level of initial plausibility. From this point, the plausibility of his explanations must be assessed in terms of the epistemic and nonepistemic reasons that can be marshaled in their support. As with nonrivalist explanations for natural patterns, these reasons may be of widely diverse sorts and so the evaluation of particular nonrivalist accounts for historical patterns must proceed on a case-by-case basis.

The last category of religious explanation to be considered here includes those accounts given for quite personal patterns of occurrence. Patterns of individual tranformation, renewal, succor, peace, and mystical experience would fall under this heading. Obviously, this category will include some of the most controversial of religious explanations. Strangely enough, it also includes some of the most plausible rivalist candidates.

Since rivalist accounts for both natural and historical patterns of phenomena were found to be incapable of moving beyond the level of initial plausibility, the possibility of assembling much more plausible rivalist accounts for personal patterns of occurrence is an interesting one. It becomes even more intriguing in light of the surprising fact that some of the most radically fundamentalist explanations for personal patterns may be capable of reaching fairly high levels of plausibility. In order to see why this is so, it is necessary to give careful attention to one such account.

For the sake of example, suppose that someone were to notice that needed funds always seem to arrive in the mail at just the right times. An explanation of this regular arrival of money might be attempted by making reference to the love of God. Initial plausibility, of course, would depend upon proper formulation. Clearly, the existence of the range of phenomena to be explained could be confirmed in a rather mundane way by opening mail, peering into envelopes, tracking down deposit slips, and the like. Once it were shown that such funds regularly arrived, it could be determined whether the religious explanation of this pattern had been constructed properly. Relevantly analogous ranges are commonplace. Loving parents frequently send money to their needy children. Doting aunts and uncles often do the same. So, there should not be much problem in showing that an explanation of the particular pattern in question could be constructed by using some such relevantly analogous case for modeling a conception of a loving God.

Up to this point, this particular rivalist explanation is in no better shape than rivalist accounts for broad patterns of natural or historical phenomena. To be sure, it has reached the level of initial plausibility, but the true test comes in comparing this explanation with its rivals. Can it prevail against the competition? There are three possible cases that must be considered. First, the religious account being offered may face a superior rival. In most contexts, this superior rival will be able to beat the religious explanation on all counts. Typically, because a naturalistic rival will not require the invocation of supernatural beings, it will be more easily assimilable into wider bodies of human understanding. In this particular case, a superior, naturalistic explanation probably would involve a discussion of the normal functioning of the postal system and make reference to the beneficence of certain rich relatives. Furthermore, taking the perspective of Laudan, it should be noted that the general sociological or political research tradition from which a nonreligious explanation like this one would spring typically would manifest a better problem-solving record than the particular religious tradition from which the religious account springs.

Considered from the point of view of Kuhn, the position of the religious rivalist would be no more enviable. Since the rivalist's religious paradigm would not be as deeply entrenched as its sociological or political competitor, it would take a great deal of faith to embrace it. It also would take an incredible amount of work to bring that religious paradigm into serious contention with more fully developed and explanatorily powerful social scientific competitors. In tacit recognition of their weak position, rivalist believers probably would feel compelled to retract their religious accounts when shown that their chosen ranges of phenomena could be explained without taking recourse to supernatural entities or activities.

The second possibility that might be faced by the rivalist involves competition with a weaker explanatory alternative. In spite of the fact that the rivalist's explanation may be stronger than its opposition, there will be little reason to accept it. Of course, when faced with a weaker competitor, the rivalist's account must be more precise, more intelligible, or in some other way explanatorily superior. Nevertheless, it is his research tradition that causes problems. Given the rapid progress and current explanatory power of the social sciences and the relative impotence of their religious rivals, religious research traditions must be greeted with suspicion. On the criteria used by Laudan, few show sufficiently rapid development to merit pursuit and none are sophisticated enough to merit acceptance. Without a strong research tradition to back them, even the most potent rivalist explanations must be repudiated. Though Kuhn might offer a feeble word of encouragement to those who are willing to commit themselves to weak religious paradigms, he could not offer much hope that such underdogs ever could begin to meet the pace of their competitors.

Due to the power of their competitors, rivalist religious explanations for personal patterns of phenomena have the best chance for acceptance when they are offered for ranges of phenomena for which there are no other extant accounts. Consider, then, this final possibility. Suppose that a rivalist religious account is offered for the regular arrival of funds and that this pattern of arriving monies cannot be explained in any other way. There are any number of reasons why such a pattern might remain inexplicable by reference to natural mechanisms. For instance, it might be that checks are sent through the mail in the normal manner, but when donors are interviewed, they honestly admit that there is no good reason why they sent just that amount of money at just that time. Perhaps they felt uncharacteristic urges of selfless giving. Maybe they picked a name from the telephone book and selected an amount from the score of a local football game. By sheerest coincidence, they might say, their impulsive selections resulted in just the right amount being sent to just the right person at just the right time.

In a case of this sort, where there is no available alternative to the religious account, two distinct possibilities arise. In conformity with the first possibility, it may turn out that some other explanatory enterprise, such as sociology, psychology, or even political science, counts the range of phenomena in question under its own explanatory purview but has been unable to generate a completely satisfactory explanation of this particular range. That is, sociologists, psychologists, or others might count the timely arrival of funds within their explanatory domain but may have to admit that up to the present moment, they have been unsuccessful in accounting for the specific series of timely arrivals in question. In this sort of situation, the rivalist's religious explanation would not be permitted to stand on its own merits. Instead, the religious tradition or paradigm from which it springs would be measured against the current prestige or power of whatever research tradition or paradigm claimed to have explanatory domain over the range of phenomena in question. As in the above cases, the rivalist's religious tradition or paradigm probably would come out the loser. The explanation offered under the authority of that religious perspective typically would be rejected in favor of a "wait and see" attitude toward the currently preferred naturalistic paradigm or research tradition. Again, as in the above cases, Kuhnian encouragement to the underdog or Laudan's willingness to sanction pursuit rather than acceptance might provide a small morsel of comfort to the faithful within the spurned religious community.

Up to this point, rivalist religious explanations for personal patterns of phenomena are in no better position than were rivalist accounts for natural or historical patterns. It is with the second possibility, however, a possibility that is not normally open in the case of natural or historical explanations, where the rivalist may move beyond the level of merely initial plausibility. In this sort of case, while there is no explanatory opponent to the religious account, neither is there any preferable research tradition or paradigm that claims explanatory dominion over the range of phenomena at stake. Under these circumstances, if his explanation were formulated properly in accordance with the strategies outlined in the third chapter then, in Laudan's view, the explanation of the religious rivalist would appear worthy of acceptance. Acceptance in this case would seem to be dictated by the simple fact that the proposed religious explanation solves a problem that is neither solved more adequately by some alternative account nor even on the agenda for solution by any other, more acceptable research tradition. Similarly, due to the wide range of advantages of paradigm commitment listed by Kuhn,[30] the opportunity of embracing a religious explanation under its relevant paradigm should be seized in preference to the aimless drifting attendant upon the complete lack of paradigm governance.

It would appear that this last sort of situation is one that actually does confront religious rivalists upon occasion. Sometimes believers are interested in explaining a range of phenomena or some aspect of an already explained pattern of occurrences for which there is not only a dearth of alternative extant explanatory accounts, but for which there is also a complete lack of explanatory interest taken by other disciplines. While the sociologist, psychologist, political scientist, or historian might be interested in explaining regular mail delivery, such theorists are almost never tempted to explain those features of regular mail delivery that are of most interest to religious devotees. Usually, they will find nothing of theoretical concern in the timely arrival of needed funds. In fact, there is typically so little enticement to explain such occurrences that theorists from these or related fields will rarely even trouble themselves enough to confirm or disconfirm reports of assorted timely arrivals. Furthermore, when confronted with undeniable confirmation of such patterns, their standard response amounts to nothing more than a series of disinterested shrugs accompanied by mutterings about flukes or coincidence. Responses like these, of course, simply are disguised admissions of the lack of interest in any additional pursuit of reasonable explanations.

Here at last the religious rivalist would appear to be able to move beyond the level of initial plausibility. When it comes to providing accounts for patterns of natural phenomena, the believer is confronted with powerful naturalistic disciplines that are sweepingly comprehensive in their explanatory scope. Although physics, chemistry, and the life sciences cannot explain all natural patterns, they typically do appear to be all-encompassing in their intentions. Ultimately, scientists hope to provide naturalistic accounts for any and all naturalistic patterns. Because of this, rivalist religious believers find their own accounts of natural phenomena, arising as they do from relatively weak religious research traditions or paradigms, to be overshadowed by the intimidating research traditions and deeply entrenched paradigms of their naturalistic opponents. Since the explanatory intentions of the social sciences are just as ambitious as those of the physical and life sciences, religious rivalists find themselves in the same predicament when it comes to the explanation of historical patterns. Psychologists, sociologists, and the rest cannot explain all broad historical patterns at the present time. But since they normally include all such patterns within their explanatory purview, religious rivalists almost always are forced into direct competition with the powerful research traditions and paradigms of the social sciences.

At the present time, however, there does not seem to be any naturalistic research tradition or paradigm that intends to account for the sorts of personal patterns that are of the most interest to religious rivalists. Thus, if they properly formulate their religious accounts, rivalists can press their explanations of such ranges of phenomena beyond the level of initial plausibility. According to Laudan, any research tradition that solves at least one problem is better than no research tradition at all. Similarly, for Kuhn, the orderliness of paradigm-governed research is preferable to the chaos of preparadigm groping. Hence, for both Laudan and Kuhn, there would seem to be strong reasons for accepting even the weakest of religious research traditions or paradigms if they are able to offer explanations for ranges of phenomena that fall outside the explanatory scope of any other discipline.

Before turning to a consideration of nonrivalist religious explanations for personal patterns of phenomena, two additional comments should be made about the status of rivalist explanations for patterns that do not fall under the explanatory scope of competitive disciplines. In the first place, while Laudan or Kuhn may not be able to offer scientific or philosophical reasons for rejecting such rivalist religious accounts, there may be religious reasons for repudiating them. Suppose there were religious reasons for rejecting a rivalist explanation for the timely arrival of funds. For instance, it might be argued that it is inappropriate to attribute such patterns of petty indulgence to God or it might be claimed that the religious tradition from which such an explanation springs is itself religiously unacceptable.[31] In a case of this sort, it would appear that there would be some reason to refrain from embracing a rivalist explanation in spite of the fact that it is the only one available. Its explanatory value might be outweighed by its religious disadvantages.

Second, even if both the rivalist account and the research tradition or paradigm from which it springs were religiously impeccable, it must be emphasized that the explanatory acceptability of that rivalist explanation would be directly dependent upon the simple fact that no other competitive discipline happens to be interested in the same explanatory range. This lack of interest on the part of alternative disciplines easily could change. Were sociologists, psychologists, or others to become concerned about such patterns, the rivalist would be thrown back immediately into competition with those significantly more powerful naturalistic research enterprises. In the face of such competition, both Laudan and Kuhn would find considerable difficulty in continuing to tolerate rivalist religious accounts.

With the completion of this extended consideration of rivalist explanations for personal patterns, attention can be turned to nonrivalist accounts. As was noted with respect to nonrivalist religious explanations for natural and historical patterns, all that is required for nonrivalist accounts of personal patterns to reach the level of initial plausibility is proper formulation. Beyond this level, such explanations must be considered on a case-by-case basis. The epistemic and nonepistemic reasons that might be marshaled in support of such explanations are so diverse that they resist systematic characterization. Thus, as with nonrivalist accounts for natural and historical patterns, the plausibility of nonrivalist explanations for more personal patterns cannot be assessed in any general way.

In the consideration of nonrivalist religious explanations for patterns of natural phenomena, it was possible to offer a bit of detail regarding a few of the basic issues involved in making specific assessments beyond the level of initial plausibility. At this point, a brief glance at an example of a nonrivalist account for a personal pattern will afford a convenient opportunity to press a little farther along these same lines. Consider, then, a case where a certain pattern of personal succor is explained by making reference to the loving activity of God. To avoid needless repetition of now familiar themes, suppose this explanation were formulated properly and so could be considered initially plausible. Being nonrivalist, this account would not enter into competitive opposition with alternative, naturalistic accounts. Still, there are two basic sorts of situations that it might confront.

Under the first possibility, the suggestion that God's loving activity is explanatorily efficacious might be introduced in the course of providing an account for a specific pattern of personal succor for which there is no plausible alternative nonreligious explanation.[32] This lack of a naturalistic explanation might be due to the fact that such an account never could be offered for the range of phenomena under consideration. If this were true—if, for whatever reason, a naturalistic explanation for the range in question never could be given—then it would seem that the religious account would be judged as plausible on explanatory grounds alone. As long as it were formulated properly it would offer an account for a range of phenomena for which no alternative nonreligious explanation can, or ever could, be offered.

It might turn out, however, that the lack of a naturalistic explanation was due to the fact that, although such an account may be possible, to date no such plausible explanation has emerged. In this sort of situation, as long as a plausible nonreligious explanation remained elusive, the religious one could be accepted for purely explanatory reasons. It would provide an account for a range of data for which there might be, but currently was not, a plausible alternative account. Should a plausible naturalistic explanation eventually emerge, of course, it no longer would be possible to accept a properly formulated religious account solely on the basis of explanatory need. While not in competitive conflict with the nonrivalist religious explanation, any recently emerged nonreligious explanation would itself be entirely sufficient for explanatory purposes. Thus, any religious explanation under these conditions would be forced into the second fundamental category.

The second sort of situation that might arise for a nonrivalist religious explanation for personal patterns is one in which an adequate nonreligious explanation is already available. Under this possibility, the invocation of God's loving behavior to account for a specific pattern of succor would be explanatorily superfluous. Thus, the fate of such a religious account would depend upon the strength of any other theoretical or nontheoretical reasons that might be given in support of its retention. Without being reduced to a case-by-case evaluation of such additional reasons, there are a couple of germane observations that can be made about the explanatorily superfluous introduction of God in any nonrivalist account of personal succor. First, as should be clear by now, the intelligibility or cognitive meaningfulness of such an explanation would not be at stake. If it were formulated properly, the only question to be answered would be that of its plausibility.

Second, while any number of reasons in support of its retention might be suggested, given the proclivities of religious believers, certain sorts of reasons are more likely to be offered than others. For example, pragmatic reasons are especially popular in justifying religious accounts for personal patterns. As was noted in the case of nonrivalist explanations for natural patterns, it is claimed frequently that religious belief has certain important psychological or sociological benefits. If it could be shown that the acceptance of a nonrivalist explanation of personal succor really would result in psychological or sociological advantages that were unavailable to those who accepted only a naturalistic account, then some pragmatic reason for introducing such a properly formulated though explanatorily superfluous explanation would have been produced. Furthermore, it should be stressed that this reason, if produced, would be peculiarly nonreligious in character. It would have been generated directly from the findings of psychology or sociology.

Along similar lines, existential reasons for accepting an explanation of regular succor in terms of God's love might be offered. Again, if it could be shown that the acceptance of this particular religious explanation really would result in a less alienated attitude toward the world or would provide deeper feelings of unity or personal harmony than would the acceptance of a naturalistic explanation alone, then a properly formulated but explanatorily superfluous account might be retained on existential grounds. As with the introduction of pragmatic reasons, the production and defense of such existential reasons would be nonreligious in character. Such reasons would be generated from certain kinds of psychological, sociological, or even philosophical studies.

The religious theorist would not have to confine himself to nonepistemic reasons for retaining explanatorily superfluous nonrivalist explanations, however. There are certain epistemic, though nonexplanatory, reasons that might be offered as well. Suppose there were some other fragment of theological theory that, if true, would give reason to believe that God is active in the personal lives of believers. Then, whatever reason there might be for believing this relevant fragment of theory to be true also would supply at least some indirect support for the retention of any superfluous explanation of personal patterns of succor. To be a bit more specific, suppose there were some reason to believe that God is like a father insofar as he always tries to look after the emotional needs of his children. Whatever reason there might be to believe this claim would seem to provide a modicum of support for the retention of an explanatorily unnecessary religious account of regular succor in terms of God's loving activity. Though such a pattern of emotional support might be explainable naturalistically, since there would be some reason to believe that God is fatherly, there would be some reason to believe that he is responsible for patterns of succor. In this sort of case, then, there would be some nonexplanatory reason for believing that the explanatorily superfluous religious account in question is true.

As is evident from this example, the degree of support that such nonexplanatory reasons might offer for the retention of superfluous religious explanations would depend directly upon the strength of the evidence available for believing the relevant fragment of theological theory to be true as well as the intimacy of the tie between that relevant fragment and the superfluous explanation under consideration. It also should be noted that since it is at least conceivable that nontheological bits of theory as well as theological ones might be linked evidentially to religious explanations in this same kind of way, nonexplanatory epistemic reasons for the retention of superfluous religious explanations could be of either a religious or a nonreligious kind.

It is even possible to generate explanatory epistemic reasons in support of the contention that an explanatorily superfluous religious account should be retained. Suppose, for example, that a nonrivalist religious tradition already had offered an explanation of some other pattern of succor by making reference to God's loving activity. Furthermore, suppose no naturalistic account of that other pattern could be given. In a case like this, there would be explanatory reasons for accepting the religious explanation of that other range of succor. Now, suppose a new range were found that could be explained by making reference to God's loving activity, but that this new range also could be explained naturalistically. If there were some conceptual link between the truth of the earlier, explanatorily necessary religious account and the truth of this new, explanatorily superfluous one, then the explanatory reasons for accepting that earlier explanation of succor would supply indirect support for the contention that the new explanation, though explanatorily superfluous, nevertheless should be retained. As in the preceding kind of case, since it is conceivable that there could be conceptual links between needed nonreligious explanations and superfluous religious ones, it might be possible to offer nonreligious explanatory reasons as well as religious ones in indirect support of the claim that certain explanatorily superfluous religious explanations should be retained.

In drawing together the results of this investigation of possibly plausible religious explanations, it should be emphasized that once the initial tests of proper construction have been passed by rivalist explanatory accounts, the greatest threat against their acceptability comes from the epistemic power of nonreligious disciplines. Given the recent development of the natural and social sciences, it is pretty difficult for any rivalist explanation that springs from a religious context to gain much credence. Unless rivalist religious traditions or paradigms can heighten their prestige by demonstrating epistemic superiority over alternative perspectives, there seems to be only one way in which their explanations can move beyond the level of initial plausibility. Under present circumstances, only properly formulated rivalist explanations that are offered to account for ranges of data outside the explanatory domain of other theoretical enterprises can be considered worthy of either pursuit or acceptance.

Even though such rivalist religious accounts are the only ones that deserve much serious attention, it must be admitted that there is a rather large collection of these offered currently by rivalist believers. Even without assessing the epistemic merits of assorted rivalist traditions or paradigms in relation to the problem-solving adequacy of alternative disciplines, it is easy to see that a wide range of religious accounts has been given for personal patterns of phenomena. Given the plausibility criteria of either Laudan or Kuhn, this range of accounts must be given closer and more respectful scrutiny than it has hitherto enjoyed. Because religious devotees frequently offer explanations for personal ranges of phenomena that lie well outside the explanatory interests of other disciplines, were it discovered that such explanatory ranges actually existed and that the religious explanations of those ranges already were formulated properly or, with a bit of work, could be recast into proper formulations, then from the perspectives of both Laudan and Kuhn, there would be at least some rivalist religious explanations that could move well beyond the level of initial plausibility.

Properly formulated nonrivalist religious explanations are subject to somewhat different plausibility considerations. They must be formulated properly, of course. But if properly formulated nonrivalist accounts were found that were offered for explanatory ranges that either do not happen to be, or cannot be, explained on any alternative nonreligious account, then such nonrivalist explanations would move beyond the level of initial plausibility on explanatory grounds alone. Those offered in explanation of ranges that already are explainable naturalistically or scientifically could not be retained or even pursued for purely explanatory reasons. But there are many other reasons why explanatorily superfluous nonrivalist explanations might turn out to be worthy of retention or pursuit.

Since nonrivalists, like their rivalist counterparts, offer a number of explanations for ranges of phenomena not otherwise explained, should the explanatory ranges for these accounts be found really to exist and should the explanatory accounts themselves be discovered to be either properly formulated or capable of proper formulation, then such nonrivalist religious explanations would appear to merit serious consideration. Explanatorily superfluous nonrivalist accounts are a bit trickier to handle but, if properly formulated, they certainly would deserve a painstaking evaluation of the assorted epistemic and nonepistemic reasons that might be offered in their behalf.

Before moving on to the topics of the final chapter, it is necessary to stress a few points about the conclusions that have been reached here. Although these comments should not be taken as a temperance of any of the conclusions drawn in the course of this study, they should help to douse flickers of religious arrogance that, though tempting to many, are certainly not justified. First, it must be cautioned that to affirm the current plausibility or even acceptability of certain religious explanations is not to affirm their truth. Many explanations in the history of science and elsewhere have been legitimately accepted as plausible and then subsequently discovered to be false. There is no reason why the same thing cannot happen here. Second, there is no guarantee that certain currently plausible religious explanations must remain so for any extended period of time. As is evident from the preceding summary, the acceptability of many religious explanations rests heavily upon the fact that alternative disciplines take no explanatory interest in assorted religiously significant ranges of phenomena. Should the explanatory interests of nonreligious disciplines shift in the future, a religious explanation that is now deemed plausible could quickly lose its badge of acceptability. Third, it must be emphasized that a serious burden of responsibility rests upon the proper formulation of religious explanations. Among other things, it should be remembered that proper formulation implies that the construction of an understanding of a religiously significant explanatory entity can be completed without the repudiation of more deeply entrenched theoretical commitments from either inside or outside the religious sphere. Therefore, should it be discovered that the adoption of some particular religious explanation requires the acceptance of various disreputable religious doctrines or the rejection of assorted deeply entrenched scientific ones, there would appear to be no alternative but to reject that explanatory account on the grounds of improper formulation.

If the argument to this point has been correct, then it must be admitted that certain sorts of religious explanations are hopelessly inadequate. Most rivalist accounts for natural and broadly historical patterns fall into this category. Surprisingly, certain rivalist explanations, such as those for assorted personal patterns, may deserve more serious attention than they commonly receive. However, it is nonrivalist religious accounts that seem to be on the safest ground. Standard philosophical objections, like those that can be extracted from Hume's famous collection of arguments against design proofs, are impotent against properly formulated nonrivalist religious explanations. Due to the possibility of explanatory overdetermination, the existence of explanatorily adequate scientific accounts poses no problems for the nonrivalist either. With both philosophical and scientific obstacles cleared away, the nonrivalist is freed to search for reasons why his explanations ought to be accepted, or at least pursued.

VII

Explanations
and Religious Life

—

IN *Lectures and Conversations on Aesthetics, Psychology and Religious Belief*, Ludwig Wittgenstein offered a number of fragmentary remarks about the nature of religious commitment that not only have proven to be extraordinarily influential, but that also can be construed as a direct attack upon the sort of position that has been developed over the last few chapters.[1] One of his mildest comments about religious belief was made in connection with the Christian belief in a Last Judgment. He wrote, "What we call believing in a Judgment Day or not believing in a Judgment Day—The expression of belief may play an absolutely minor role."[2] Taking this claim in isolation, it does not seem to be very troublesome. It appears to be perfectly compatible with the conviction that religious explanations can be modeled in conformity with scientific ones. Wittgenstein seems only to be suggesting that there is a great deal more to the religious life than the simple expression of beliefs. Quite certainly this is true, almost trivially so. Believers obviously do more than just express their beliefs. They tithe, sacrifice, worship, and generally try to live up to their convictions.

But taking this passage in such strict isolation leads to a serious distortion of Wittgenstein's position. In other comments, he goes far beyond the gentle reminder that religious belief involves something more than the proffering of truth claims. Two pages prior to the passage cited above, he notes, "Suppose that someone believed in the Last Judgment, and I don't, does this mean that I believe the opposite to him, just that there won't be such a thing? I would say: 'not at all, or not always.'"[3] This suggestion is a good deal more startling than the previous one. Here Wittgenstein appears to be subjecting the time-honored logical laws of noncontradiction or, perhaps, excluded middle to critical attack. He seems to be arguing that when it comes to the Last Judgment, logical constraints do not apply.

As those familiar with the writings of this author have come to expect, Wittgenstein has something up his sleeve here. His apparent attack upon the laws of logic is really nothing of the sort. Instead, a bit of additional probing quickly reveals that he is concerned with quite another matter. To give further clarification, he discusses his relationship with someone who believes in the Last Judgment by remarking, "It isn't a question of my being anywhere near him, but on an entirely different plane, which you could express by saying: 'You mean something altogether different, Wittgenstein.'"⁴ So, what Wittgenstein has in mind when he says that affirming the Last Judgment is not inconsistent with failing to affirm it is that the believer who accepts that Judgment is doing something entirely different from anyone who does not embrace his commitment. The believer is not simply affirming certain truth claims that are denied by others. Thus, the difference between the believer and the nonbeliever cannot be captured properly by noting that the religious devotee affirms something that those outside his community deny. Rather, the Last Judgment

obviously plays much more this role: suppose we said that a certain picture might play the role of constantly admonishing me, or I always think of it. Here, an enormous difference would be between those people for whom the picture is constantly in the foreground, and the others who just didn't use it at all.⁵

With this comment, it would appear that, according to Wittgenstein, belief in the Last Judgment is not assent to a truth claim at all. Instead, it is a kind of subjugation to a picture that plays a regulative role for human behavior. Ultimately, then, the difference between the religious devotee and the nonbeliever might be expressed in terms of regulative commitments. The believer's activities are dominated and controlled by a vision that is not shared by the nonbeliever.

Pressing his distinction between assenting to truth claims and being regulated by pictures, Wittgenstein argues that the believer

has what you might call an unshakeable belief. It will show, not by reasoning or by appeal to ordinary grounds for belief, but rather by regulating for in all his life.

This is a very much stronger fact—foregoing pleasures, always appealing to this picture. This in one sense must be called the firmest of all beliefs, because the man risks things on account of it which he would not do on things which are by far better established for him.[6] In Wittgenstein's view, the unshakability of the believer's commitment to a Last Judgment is a clear indication that this is no mere assent to a truth claim. The religious devotee clings to his belief with a passion that bears no reasonable relation to the amount of evidence that could be mustered in support of the claim that there will someday be some such event. It turns out, according to Wittgenstein, that this unshakability of commitment is only the initial sign that a religious believer's conviction on this matter is of an unusual and special sort. There are also other strong disanalogies between belief in a Last Judgment and more ordinary assents to truth claims. In his survey of the epistemic behavior of religious devotees, Wittgenstein goes on to argue that controversies over a Last Judgment "look quite different from any normal controversies. Reasons look entirely different from normal reasons."[7] Even with these more potent remarks, however, it is difficult to see why Wittgenstein's thought might be considered to be incompatible with the theses of this present study. After all, after raising a series of skeptical objections against the epistemological respectability of religious discourse, an argument was offered in support only of the contention that at least *some* stretches of religious linguistic activity are able to withstand the tests of intellectual integrity applied to theoretical claims in the most uncontroversial branches of the physical sciences. Upon outlining the structure of certain sorts of scientific explanations in the third chapter, an attempt was made in the fourth and fifth chapters to demonstrate only that *certain* religious explanations can be formulated along similar lines. In the sixth chapter, it was argued merely that a *few* religious explanations might be constructible in epistemically impeccable ways and so be worthy of serious scrutiny, if not outright adoption.

This brief recapitulation of previous chapters stresses the extremely restricted nature of the argumentation to this point. No claim ever was made that religious discourse must be exclusively of the sort described in these pages. Quite to the contrary, it is fully possible and even rather likely that there are all types of other linguistic structures employed by believers in the course of praying, worshiping, confessing, and the like. Therefore, Wittgenstein's statement that belief in a Last Judgment is to be interpreted as regulative rather than assertive appears to be in perfect accord with all that has been said here. In concert with the presentation in the six preceding chapters, it easily can be admitted, indeed urged, that religious explanations modeled on scientific ones play only a small part in the overall life of any vibrantly religious community. In concession to Wittgenstein's work, it even might be argued that his discussion of belief in a Last Judgment helps to emphasize the peculiarities of other, nonexplanatory facets of religious activity.

Unfortunately, attention thus far has been focused entirely upon the weakest of Wittgenstein's claims. Much more ominously, when discussing religious discourse in all of its diverse forms, he wrote,

> We don't talk about hypothesis, or about high probability. Nor about knowing.
>
> In a religious discourse we use such expressions as: 'I believe that so and so will happen,' and use them differently to the way in which we use them in science.[8]

This passage discloses the first real hint of incompatibility between Wittgenstein's position and the one espoused here. With regard to any religious utterance whatever, Wittgenstein seems to be suggesting that questions of probability, evidence, and knowledge simply do not arise as they do in the sciences. In contrast with his position, it was argued in the previous pages that religious explanations can be modeled on scientific ones in such a way as to allow questions of a theoretical nature. Evidence both for and against such religiously explanatory hypotheses might be gathered in much the same ways as they are assembled in physics. Some of these explanations might be found to be probably true while others may emerge as probably false. Although completely certain knowledge of the truth or falsity of any specific religious explanation might be precluded by the fact that actual courses of events never may conclusively confirm or disconfirm any hypothesis as it stands in isolation from other theoretical commitments, it nevertheless cannot be denied that the actual course of events does remain in important evidential relation to religious hypotheses of the sort discussed here.

With one last fragment from Wittgenstein, this flicker of incompatibility flames into something considerably more. Regarding the use of evidence to bolster religious commitment, Wittgenstein argued, "If there were evidence, this would in fact destroy the whole business."[9] It would appear from this passage that the oddity of religious belief must not be restricted to a few special cases. All religious beliefs are strange to the scientific eye. Furthermore, if they were to lose this strangeness by coming into closer conformity with more normal, scientific beliefs, their uniquely religious character actually would be destroyed.[10]

A number of writers have fastened onto this strong theme in the work of Wittgenstein with the intention of offering some argumentative support for it. The types of arguments that have been used to support the contention that it is impossible to model religious linguistic activities on scientific patterns tend to fall into any one of three basic categories. In the first place, there are arguments generated from a consideration of the actual linguistic practice of believers. Embracing this strategy, Peter Winch has argued:

> God's reality is certainly independent of what any man may care to think, but what that reality amounts to can only be seen from the religious tradition in which the concept of God is used, and this use is very unlike the use of scientific concepts, say of theoretical entities.[11]

Along parallel lines, D. Z. Phillips has defended his own appeal to the linguistic practice of believers by writing:

> 'But *who says* that religion is a distinct and separable field, etc., etc.?' I find this question extremely odd. It is not a matter of anyone *saying* that there are differences between modes of discourse, but *looking* to see whether there are any such differences, and if there are, *showing* their character.[12]

A large portion of the second chapter of this book was devoted to showing that appeals to the actual linguistic practices of religious communities are fundamentally impotent. Of course, the demonstration that a certain practice is actually extant clearly would prove its possibility, but the mere dearth of actual practice may show nothing more than indolence on the part of believers. Even the demonstration of the conceptual or logical impossibility of a specific practice need not be taken as devastating. There are ways of overcoming these hurdles as well.[13]

Even were the arguments from the second chapter unavailable, it is clear from the writings of D. Z. Phillips that gleanings from the actual linguistic practice of religious devotees are not to be taken at face value. John Hick and Kai Nielsen repeatedly have tried to point out cases where religious communities are functioning quite well and even prospering in spite of the fact that they fail to manifest any of the specific traits cited by Wittgenstein, Winch, or Phillips as essential.

But all of the behavioral evidence that these two have managed to dredge up has been perfunctorily dismissed as irrelevant. Discussing a bit of evidence offered by Hick, Phillips replied in very typical fashion: "I do not deny, then, that there are people whose conception of God is similar to that outlined by Hick. There are some people the truth of whose religion depends on the way things go in their lives."[14] With regard to the philosophical implications of a case of this sort, Phillips went on to say, "I do not find it impressive religiously. Indeed, I should want to go further and say that it has little to do with religion, being much closer to superstition."[15] So, the only religious practice that counts for anything is that of the right sort of believers. Since believers of the right sort cannot be distinguished from those of the wrong sort by any straightforward investigation of extant linguistic practices, it is impossible for convincing arguments to be generated solely from any simple amassing of linguistic data.

The second category of argumentative support for the contention that it is impossible to model religious linguistic activities on scientific ones is marked by the claim that the importation of scientific standards into religious contexts renders religious affirmations either obviously false or meaningless. Giving a general form of this categorical type, Rush Rhees wrote:

The prevalence of science affects the way we think of things, or look at things, besides the special matters which it investigates. It may affect the way in which we understand questions in religion. . . . If anyone were to speak about religious doctrines now in the way in which he might have spoken in the thirteenth century, we should hardly listen. . . . Consider the 'evidence' that was supposed to be afforded by miracles. The difficulty is not because science has shown that there can be no miracles. (How could it show that?) Our difficulty is partly in understanding what a miracle would *be*; and this is a result of our scientific ideas—a result of the mass of preconceptions from which we start and which we cannot escape, regarding how things should be viewed.[16]

More specifically, with regard to the problem of the existence of God and related matters of finding criteria for individuating and identifying him, Rhees argued:

We use 'it exists' chiefly in connexion with physical objects, and anyway we use it where we can ask whether it exists or not. This goes with the sense of *finding out* whether it exists. Now the 'it', whatever it is, is something that we could identify in such an investigation—by, for example, the methods by which we commonly identify a particular physical object. . . . the question whether we mean the same by 'God', I have said, is not a question whether we are referring to the same object. The question whether we are still talking about God now . . . cannot be settled by referring to any object. And I do not think it would mean anything to ask 'whether any such object exists'.[17]

D. Z. Phillips echoes these same sorts of arguments in his own writings. He says:

Despite the fact that one need take no interest in the existence of a planet, an account could be given of the kind of difference the existence of the planet makes, and of how one could find out whether the planet exists or not. But all this is foreign to the question whether there is a God. That is not something anyone could *find out*. It has been far too readily assumed that the dispute between the believer and the unbeliever is over a *matter of fact*. Philosophical reflection on the reality of God then becomes the philosophical reflection appropriate to an assertion of a matter of fact. I have tried to show that this is a misrepresentation of the religious concept, and that philosophy can claim justifiably to show what is meaningful in religion only if it is prepared to examine religious concepts in the contexts from which they derive their meaning.[18]

In his condemnation of the work of Ronald Hepburn and John Hick, Phillips scolds:

Positivism and empiricism have had an obvious influence on their thinking. There is no attempt by them to discuss the difference between believing in a God who may or may not exist, and believing in an eternal God. It is no exaggeration to say that the very possibility of understanding what religion is about depends on this distinction being drawn.[19]

It is important to stress that, according to Phillips, the problem with Hepburn and Hick is not that their view of science is overly restrictive, being too rigidly empiricist. Scientific constraints, no matter how liberally construed, ultimately will result in a denial of the epistemic worthiness of religious discourse. As Phillips puts it:

Despite the protests of these philosophers against an appeal to religious language to find out what is meant by the reality of God, what they have done is to impose the grammar of *another* mode of discourse on religion— namely, our talk about physical objects. Thus, Hick merely begs the whole question by talking about 'the natural and ordinary meaning of words'.

   Once philosophers begin to ignore religious criteria of meaningfulness, epistemological scepticism about religion is inevitable.[20]

This second line of argument, exemplified here in the writings of Rhees and Phillips, has been the concern of the third through the sixth chapters. The argument spanning those chapters was designed to show that epistemological skepticism need not result from a rigid application of scientific standards in religious contexts. Quite to the contrary, it is possible to devise religious explanations in rigid conformity with the models provided by some of the most rigorous of scientific disciplines. Furthermore, at least some of the religious explanations so formulated are worthy of serious consideration. There is even the possibility that certain of these properly formulated accounts should be accepted as the most adequate explanations of specific ranges of phenomena currently available.

The final kind of argument used to support the contention that religious beliefs that are patterned after scientific ones lose their distinctively religious character has yet to be considered. This last category resists any tidy treatment because it is comprised of a loose confederation of diverse argument forms that are bound together only by their common goal. Each argument under this heading is shaped with the intention of showing some marked contrast between the religious life and the activities of science. Obviously, not just any contrast will do. So, features thought to be essential to the religious life, but incompatible with the activities, aspirations, or methods of the sciences are emphasized.

There are two different lines of critical response that might be taken to this sort of argument. First, an attempt might be made to show that features thought to be essential to the religious life really are not so crucial after all. This line will not be pursued here for a variety of reasons. Among the most important is the fact that at least some of these purportedly essential features of the religious life really are central. While some might not be absolutely essential, many would leave the religious enterprise seriously impoverished if they were stripped away. But even if it were true that religion could be stripped of all these supposed essential features without detrimental effect, it would be almost impossible to demonstrate this fact. Given the wide diversity of religious communities, past as well as present, primitive as well as sophisticated, and possible as well as actual, it would be a hopelessly protracted and complicated undertaking to show that even those aspects of the religious life that appear most superficial really are inessential to all believers in all contexts, no matter what the historical or cultural exigencies might be.

Since there appears to be so little promise in the first line of response, the second must be taken. It must be shown that the introduction of religious explanations patterned after the model of the third chapter would not eliminate those aspects of the religious life that are thought to be crucial. While it would certainly be nice to be able to consider each and every characteristic of the religious life that has been thought to be essential, so thorough a treatment is not possible. No complete listing of essential characteristics is available. Differing thinkers have suggested differing lists and controversies continue to rage. Given the unsettled state of this matter, about the best that can be offered is a piecemeal consideration of specific suggestions on a case-by-case basis. Unfortunately, this kind of approach results in a response that is more suggestive than it is exhaustive. However, until some full list of religiously essential characteristics can be generated, this is the best that can be done.

Consider, then, the offerings of Peter Winch. In his discussion of the role that witchcraft plays in a primitive African society, he remarks:

The spirit in which oracles are consulted is very unlike that in which a scientist makes experiments. Oracular revelations are not treated as hypotheses and, since their sense derives from the way they are treated in their context, they therefore *are not* hypotheses. They are not a matter of intellectual interest but the main way in which Azande decide how they should act. If the oracle reveals that a proposed course of action is fraught with mystical dangers from witchcraft or sorcery, that course of action will not be carried out; and then the question of refutation or confirmation just does not arise.[21]

While Winch seems intent upon contrasting the scientific enterprise with that of witchcraft, there does not seem to be anything in this passage that would indicate any radical disanalogy between the two. Certainly, scientists do experiment and they do offer hypotheses for testing, but there are many scientific affirmations that play precisely the role for the scientist that is being played by the oracular pronouncements in this primitive society. Consider, for example, the claim made by physicists that the speed of light is constant. This claim is not treated as an hypothesis and so, by Winch's way of reasoning, is not an hypothesis. It is not open to question or, as Winch puts it, is "not a matter of intellectual interest." Furthermore, this claim determines the behavior of scientists. Any pattern of scientific inquiry or series of hypotheses that can be shown to be at variance with the assumption that the speed of light is constant would be summarily dismissed as misguided. Scientists would never travel such paths and so the possibility of confirming or disconfirming the postulate that the speed of light is constant just never arises. Thus, far from revealing a feature of the practice of witchcraft that is incompatible with a scientific perspective, this passage demonstrates a close similarity between aspects of witchcraft and aspects of science.

A second way in which Winch believes witchcraft differs from science emerges in his discussion of the way in which contradictions are treated by primitive people. He writes:

The Azande, when the possibility of this contradiction about the inheritance of witchcraft is pointed out to them, do *not* then come to regard their old beliefs about witchcraft as obsolete. 'They have no theoretical interest in the subject.' This suggests strongly that the context from which the suggestion about the contradiction is made, the context of our scientific culture, is not on the same level as the context in which the beliefs about witchcraft operate.[22]

This Azande treatment of contradictions suggests nothing of the sort. While old beliefs about witchcraft may be retained in the face of contradiction, it is not uncommon for entrenched scientific commitments similarly to be retained. As Thomas Kuhn has noted there are occasions on which

the problem resists even apparently radical new approaches. Then scientists may conclude that no solution will be forthcoming in the present state of their field. The problem is labelled and set aside for a future generation with more developed tools.[23]

Not every theoretical defect precipitates a crisis out of which can be expected to emerge a new and better alternative. Even contradictions will be tolerated if there is no preferable alternative in sight.

Even were it conclusively shown that the Azande take absolutely no theoretical interest whatever in witchcraft, it would not follow that witchcraft beliefs are ordered conceptually along unscientific or nonscientific lines. Their current lack of theoretical interest does not preclude the possibility of future theoretical interest. Furthermore, the emergence of some future theoretical interest in witchcraft would not alter necessarily the cognitive structure of witchcraft beliefs. Consider the aesthete's purely nontheoretical interest in physics. His interest in the beauty of physical theories does not alter their conceptual structure. Indeed, it is just those structures that he finds so beautiful. Furthermore, were his interests to change from aesthetic to theoretical ones, the conceptual structure of physics would not thereby be altered.

Near the end of his paper on the significance of witchcraft, Winch appears to hint at several other features that might be thought essential to a genuinely religious life. He suggests that religion can have a liberating effect. It can enable the believer to come to grips with the contingency of his existence. The devotee "must see that he can still go on even if he is let down by what is vitally important to him; and he must so order his life that he still *can* go on in such circumstances."[24] He also suggests that a truly religious understanding involves the "recognition that one's life is subject to contingencies, rather than an attempt to control these"[25] and that neither religion nor witchcraft should be misconceived as "a (misguided) technique for producing consumer goods."[26]

None of this appears to be incompatible with the theses of the present study. It cannot be denied, of course, that much of scientific research is motivated by deep desires to control contingencies, alter circumstances, and more efficiently produce coveted material goods. But consider the introduction of an explanation of some range of data that has been modeled after the patterns of the third chapter. Suppose, for the sake of a familiar example, someone were to account for a pattern of constant succor by reference to God's love. Why should the acceptance of this explanation be thought to be incompatible with religious liberation? It would provide no guarantee of such liberation, of course, but what would? Is it not perfectly conceivable that the believer might find such an explanation extremely liberating? The recognition that God has cared so sensitively for his needs in the past might lead him to an increased confidence in the compassion of God, a confidence sufficient to sustain him through even the worst of future times. In fact, the believer's trust in God might be so strengthened that he would continue to believe that God loves him no matter what might happen.

It might be objected that this imagined case is not really one of genuine religious liberation. After all, in this example, while the believer might be enabled to face the future no matter what may come, he is still radically dependent upon the way in which things have gone for him in the past. It is the past pattern of fortunate circumstances that has led to the intensity of this believer's trust in the future love of God. Hence, he is not really liberated from the contingencies of life at all.

This objection can be met easily, however, with a slight alteration in the example. Suppose the believer already was properly liberated by whatever means are religiously appropriate prior to the introduction of this explanation. Subsequent to his religious liberation, then, he is provided with an explanation of constant succor in terms of God's love. There is no reason to suppose that his acceptance of this explanation would destroy his freedom from the contingencies of life. The believer might acknowledge the acceptability of this new explanation but point out that his liberation is neither strengthened nor weakened by it. The crucial point here is, of course, that while this scientifically structured explanation may be irrelevant to the believer's liberation, irrelevance is not incompatibility. This particular aspect of the religious life is not destroyed by the introduction of a bit of discourse modeled on the sciences.

The believer's lack of interest in controlling his environment as well as his concern with matters other than the production of consumer goods can be shown to be compatible with scientifically structured religious explanations by distinguishing explanation from manipulation. It is frequently possible to scientifically explain certain phenomena that cannot be manipulated. For instance, the motions of the planets can be explained, but certainly not controlled or altered in any way. Since the believer might be convinced that a reference to God's love can be used to account for some range of data even though God cannot be controlled or manipulated in any way by his creatures, religious explanations can be generated that provide absolutely no help in either gaining control of anything or producing anything.

In his own work, D. Z. Phillips has found himself in fundamental agreement with the convictions of Winch, but has stressed certain other features of the religious life that he believes to be of crucial importance. For instance, in defense of his interpretation of death and immortality, Phillips wrote in response to a common objection:

He may say that there is no difference between the man who does and the man who does not believe in the life eternal: death is the end of both of them. Neither are going to survive their deaths. This is true, but why should we assume that the difference between the believer and an unbeliever consists in this? The objector may see no point in living according to God's commands unless there is such a difference. In that case, we are back to the desire for compensation.[27]

More generally, he complained:

Certain philosophers . . . have tried to show why religious beliefs are important in much the same way as one might show a certain course of action to be prudential. . . . Such attempts . . . falsify the absolute character of many religious beliefs and values.[28]

In Phillips's view, not only is the believer markedly disinterested in the prudential ramifications of his belief in God, that belief itself is peculiar. Unlike more ordinary beliefs, belief in the reality of God is not open to debate. As Phillips puts it, "A great many believers would not be content to regard the existence of God as an hypothesis, as something which may or may not be true."[29] In other words, "The religious believer is not prepared to say that God might not exist. It is not that *as a matter of fact* God will always exist, but that it *makes no sense* to say that God might not exist."[30]

None of this appears to be incompatible with the introduction of scientifically structured religious explanations. It cannot be denied, of course, that scientists frequently have powerful motives of a prudential sort. Nor can it be denied that science is largely concerned with contingent matters of fact and the testing of hypotheses. Nevertheless, it is not difficult to see that religious explanations can be accepted for reasons other than those of prudence. In fact, many explanations yield no practical compensation whatever. Consider the account of constant succor in terms of God's love. If God cannot be manipulated by believers and if he does not care whether believers accept this particular explanation of succor or not, then this account would have no immediate prudential value to the believer. Furthermore, it might not even have any predictive value. Explanations are not predictions or predictive devices. Though Darwin's evolutionary accounts were certainly explanatory of past biological developments, they were not of a sort that could be used to generate predictions about future evolutionary developments. In similar fashion, though reference to God's love might explain past patterns of succor, the nature of God might be too complicated or the circumstances of his loving behavior too complex to allow any confident prediction of future occasions of divine succor.

It is certainly true that the introduction of God as an explanatory entity in conformity with the patterns of the third chapter is of a hypothetical nature. There can be evidence for and against the explanatory invocation of God. However, the fact that God's role as an explanatory entity can come into dispute should not be confused with the question of his existence. The believer might well be convinced that God's nonexistence is inconceivable, that it is impossible for God to cease to exist, and that the affirmation of his existence is not a hypothesis open to debate, but still wonder whether God can be employed explanatorily in a particular context. The appropriate use of God explanatorily depends upon a number of things, some of which are contingent matters of fact. Presumably, God's existence does not depend upon anything. There is no reason why the believer could not recognize both the contingency of God's use as an explanatory entity and the necessity of his existence.

Probably Winch, Phillips, and similarly minded thinkers would not be particularly impressed with the compatibilities demonstrated thus far. To this point, the feature thought to be most central to religious commitment, the feature that is thought to give rise to nearly all of the other distinctive characteristics of religious life, has yet to be mentioned. Phillips approaches this crucial feature in a number of indirect ways. He asks a series of questions.

Could a philosopher say that he believed that God exists and yet never pray to Him, rebel against Him, lament the fact that he could no longer pray, aspire to deepen his devotion, seek His will, try to hide from Him, or fear and tremble before Him? In short, could a man believe that God exists without his life being touched *at all* by the belief?[31]

He talks about coercing a belief in God.

Certainly, one could not get him to believe by telling him that terrible things will happen to him if he does not believe. Even if it were true that these things are going to happen, and even if a person believed because of them, he would not be believing in God. He would be believing in the best thing for himself. He would have a policy, not a faith.[32]

He contrasts belief in a first cause with belief in God.

Is it by coming to value a theory about the origin of things that one comes to see what is meant by acknowledging God as one's Creator? We might recognize a first cause and ask, 'So what?'. Can one recognize God as one's Creator and ask the same question?[33]

The point that Phillips is trying to make in these passages can be brought to bear upon the question of religious explanation. He might concede that it is possible to formulate explanations along the lines of the third chapter. He might even concede that it is possible to demonstrate, on the criteria offered by Kuhn or Laudan, that some explanations so formulated are worthy of serious investigation and perhaps even of acceptance. Nevertheless, although one might be intellectually coerced into the acceptance of an explanation in terms of God's activities, one would not thereby be coerced into the kingdom of God. Something more is required of the believer beyond a mere assent to specific truth claims.

Phillips has tried to capture this something more by remarking:

Belief in God need not entail a worshipful attitude on the part of the believer. Neither need the believer aspire to attain love of God. On the contrary, he may want to flee from it. Instead of feeling sad because he spurns God's love, he may hate the fact that he cannot rid his life of God.[34]

Whatever the believer's response to God might be, the crucial point is that

the assertion that to know God is to love Him is false if it is taken to imply that everyone who believes in God loves Him. What it stresses, quite correctly, is that . . . 'belief in God involves some affective state or attitude'.[35]

In his positive characterization of this affective state, Phillips noted, "Faith in God does not seem to be simply the recognition of the hidden good there is in life, but a mode of accepting or responding to the good and evil there is in life."[36] Thus, "Religious beliefs are not a class of second-best statements, hypotheses awaiting confirmation. . . . They are a body of truths . . . by which many people still regulate or attempt to regulate their lives."[37] Obviously, as Phillips clearly recognized, not everyone is willing to be so regulated. Still, he argued:

The love of God is the primary form of belief in God if only because the intelligibility of all the other attitudes . . . is logically dependent on it. The rebel must see the kind of relationship God asks of the believer before he can reject and defy it. He sees the story from the inside, but it is not a story that captivates him.[38]

For those who are captivated, however, there is a deep and personal transformation: "Coming to see that there is a God involves seeing a new meaning in one's life, and being given a new understanding."[39] This transformation results in a radical change both in the way the believer perceives himself and in the way he relates to others.

The believer, if his faith is at all deep, is not concerned with his rights. He is not concerned with receiving thanks for the good he does, or recompense for the harm he suffers. What he considers to be advantage, disadvantage, happiness or misery, is determined by his relationship to the love of God.[40]

The key problem here is to determine whether this aspect of the religious life with all that it entails, this something more that has been described so penetratingly by Phillips, is incompatible with the use of religious explanations patterned after scientific ones. It certainly must be admitted that it seems quite unlikely that the generation, evaluation, and increasing refinement of explanations along the lines depicted in the last several chapters ever would play any crucial role in triggering or sustaining such profound human transformations. However, the question at stake here is one only of compatibility. Would the acceptance or use of such explanations destroy this aspect of the religious life? It also must be admitted that a concern with the explanatory aspects of religious belief seems to pale into insignificance when contrasted with these important matters of personal commitment and transformation. But again, the question here is not one of relative value. It is one of compatibility. Are scientifically structured explanations incompatible with this element in the religious life?

There are a number of reasons for believing that there is no problem with compatibility here. In the first place, there are many people, particularly over the course of the last few centuries, who have made science their religion. That is, impressed with the extraordinary rate at which the physical and biological sciences have progressed over the last few hundred years, many people have become disenchanted with their religious heritage. For some, this disenchantment has resulted only in a religious void. For others, salvation has come through replacing the promise of their religion with the promise of science. Of course, a large number of those who have grasped at the promise of science have been led into what Phillips certainly would classify as superficiality. Convinced that their religion cannot guarantee a new life after death and that adherence to religious teachings never will put more food on the table or help the lame to walk, they have turned to the sciences. Perhaps medicine will find ways of prolonging life indefinitely or geneticists will develop new strains of productive wheat or orthopedic surgery will succeed where God has failed. This sort of case manifests nothing but pure selfishness, a groping after material gain. For people of this sort, there is no more chance of finding true peace and joy in the teachings of science than there was of finding them in the teachings of religious leaders.

Nevertheless, there is a second way of taking the promise of science. Some have found sustenance in a scientific vision of the world. Perhaps the orderliness of the world as it is depicted by physics has triggered the transformation. It may have been an appreciation of the interdependence of all creatures stimulated by a study of ecology that has done it. Whatever the stimulus, many people have come to a new appreciation of the unity of all people, have come to understand and accept their place in life, and have been inspired to new levels of giving and caring under the inspiration of a scientific vision of the world. It is absolutely vital that the significance of this fact be understood properly. It very well may be that pure science, as practiced in the cold and metallic laboratories of large universities never could stimulate such a transformation. Perhaps such radical transformations only can be triggered by a romantic and totally unrealistic conception of the sciences. Perhaps it only can be triggered by the influence of misguided and fanatical prophets and preachers of an illusory scientific gospel. All of this is totally irrelevant to the issue at stake. The crucial point is that whatever the stimulus, scientific or nonscientific, the fact of the matter is that in people of this sort the kind of commitment and tranformation depicted by Phillips coexists in harmony with the clear conviction that there are rigorously scientific explanations. While these commitments and transformations may not be caused or stimulated by the recognition of adequate scientific explanations, such commitments and transformations are not destroyed by the introduction or acceptance of adequate scientific explanations.

Another reason for believing that the acceptance of scientifically structured religious explanations will not destroy the possibility of this deeper element in the religious life stems from the relative autonomy of the explanatory enterprise. As has been noted, Winch suggested that a concern to control the circumstances of life or to produce some desired material good can find no place in genuine religious belief. Phillips added that a life of selfishness is incompatible with deep religious belief. Prudential interests are also foreign to this way of life. There is no desire for compensation. But, as has been seen, none of these features thought to be so detrimental to genuine religious belief is connected essentially with the formulation, evolution, or acceptance of religious explanations. There is no reason to believe that the explanation of some range of phenomena by reference to God's activities will yield any increase in control over the environment, more efficient machinery of production, or easier means of acquiring selfish, prudential, or compensatory ends. Thus, there is no reason to believe that the introduction of religious explanations will offer any fertile ground for the cultivation of any of these interests or attitudes thought to be so detrimental to the growth and persistence of a profoundly religious life.

Yet another reason to believe that the adoption of religious explanations is compatible with deep religious commitment comes from an understanding of the nature of this sort of belief. Phillips takes great pains to stress that this profound kind of religious belief and the responses it demands are independent of the contingencies of human life. He is particularly emphatic about this in his discussion of eternal love. He says:

Temporal love . . . is marked by certain characteristics: it depends on how things go. . . . Eternal love . . . is not dependent on how things go, it cannot change. . . . The believer claims that there is a love that will not let one go whatever happens. This is the love of God, the independence of which from what happens is closely bound up with the point of calling it eternal.[41]

If eternal love cannot be destroyed by any of the disappointments life might bring, if it can withstand the betrayal of a lover or even the death of those closest to the believer, it would be rather surprising if it could be demolished by the simple introduction of a religious explanation. This kind of love is not dependent upon anything that happens, although one thing that might happen is the introduction of a religious explanation. So, if the introduction of a religious explanation is incapable of destroying eternal love, then it cannot destroy a true belief in God because to "possess this love is to possess God."[42]

This recitation of reasons why the introduction of religious explanations cannot destroy the sort of religious belief discussed by Phillips and Winch has a somewhat pernicious tendency to obscure the positive contributions such explanations are able to make to the healthy functioning of religious communities. It must be remembered that the formulation of religious explanations along scientific lines can help to fill out the concept of God. Among the other important advantages cited in preceding chapters was the fact that such explanatory attempts can be used to generate criteria for individuating and identifying God. But there is at least one other contribution that religious explanations can make that is significant enough to merit attention.

In their anxiety to illuminate the special and unique features of religious belief, Winch and Phillips focus upon the affective aspects of such belief at the expense of its intentionality. This moves them in the direction of a simplistic caricature. Their interest in the affective side of religious conviction leads them to concentrate on those periods in religious life when the responsiveness of the believer is at its peak. They speak of the passionate devotion of the believer to God. They speak of periods of selfless giving with no expectation of recompense. Even when they discuss more negative religious attitudes, it is defiance or rebellion that they stress. In each of these cases, because the believer is involved so actively in his convictions, the omission of a careful analysis of the intentionality of religious belief is not missed.

There are also periods in the religious life when the believer's responsiveness is at a minimum and the intentional side of his belief becomes critically important. Consider, for example, periods of neglect. Believers frequently neglect God, sometimes only for a few moments or hours, but sometimes for days or even weeks. Neglect, of course, is not defiance, doubt, or disbelief. When neglecting God, the believer is not fighting him, struggling with him, or in any way actively responding to him. If he were doing any of these things, he would not be neglecting God. Nor has the believer lost his faith. A loss of faith or disbelief in God might result eventually from a believer's neglect, particularly if that neglect were to go on for extended periods of time, but it must be noted that such a loss of faith would be the result of neglect, not identical with it. Neglecting God involves continuing to believe in him without the attendant response. During periods of neglect, the believer is just not bothering to pray, worship, or praise.

It must be emphasized that the believer's neglect still is directed toward God even though, during such periods, he is responding neither positively nor negatively. He is not just neglecting in general. He is neglecting something. Furthermore, he is neglecting something in particular. He is not neglecting his spouse, his boss, or his job. He is neglecting God. Thus, there is a specific intentional object of his neglect.

Unfortunately, in their concentration on the affective side of religious belief, Winch and Phillips fail to provide any careful analysis of this intentional object. It is at this point that religious explanations can be introduced profitably. Through the techniques outlined in the preceding chapters, it is possible for the believer to supply characterizations of his intentional object of religious belief. Such characterizations can serve as bases for individuating and identifying God without any dependence upon analyses in terms of the believer's own activities and responses. Of course, there may be other ways of filling out a conception of God beyond those discussed here, but at least the patterns sketched over the last few chapters provide one way for the believer to move toward a clear understanding of the object of his affections.

It might be objected that this attempt to balance the caricature of Winch and Phillips is leading not to a more adequate conception of the religious life, but to an equally dangerous caricature. The believer is envisioned as much more intellectually inclined than he really is. Most believers cannot give any precise characterization of God. Furthermore, they are not even particularly anxious to obtain one. A large proportion of religious devotees are perfectly content to remain in the dark without any sophisticated understanding of their religious commitments whatsoever. In fact, they frequently will make impassioned appeals to the necessity of faith in an effort to avoid any hard, honest intellectual effort. Even at best, believers tend to scrutinize their convictions with only modest energy and leave the really difficult intellectual problems to a few committed theologians who are usually cloistered in some distant seminary.

This intellectual laziness on the part of believers must be admitted to be a rather widespread, if not universal, phenomenon. It is certainly true that very few press hard to understand their faith or the object of their belief. This laziness is perfectly compatible with the role of explanations in religious life that just has been sketched. All that is needed to round out the picture is a twist on Hilary Putnam's conception of the division of linguistic labor. In "The Meaning of 'Meaning'," Putnam introduces his notion of a division of linguistic labor by way of an example. He writes:

We could hardly use such words as 'elm' and 'aluminum' if no one possessed a way of recognizing elm trees and aluminum metal; but not everyone to whom the distinction is important has to be able to make the distinction. Let us shift the example: consider *gold*. Gold is important for many reasons: it is a precious metal, it is a monetary metal, it has symbolic value . . . , etc. Consider our community as a 'factory': in this 'factory' some people have the 'job' of *wearing gold wedding rings*, other people have the 'job' of *selling gold wedding rings*, still other people have the 'job' of *telling whether or not something is really gold*. It is not at all necessary or efficient that everyone who wears a gold ring . . . , or discusses the 'gold standard', etc., engage in buying and selling gold. Nor is it necessary or efficient that everyone who buys and sells gold be able to tell whether or not something is really gold in a society where this form of dishonesty is uncommon (selling fake gold) and in which one can easily consult an expert in case of doubt.[43]

Upon reflection on this example, Putnam goes on to conclude that, like the division of labor in this 'factory,' there also may be

a division of linguistic labor: everyone to whom gold is important for any reason has to *acquire* the word 'gold'; but he does not have to acquire the *method of recognizing* if something is or is not gold. He can rely on a special subclass of speakers. The features that are generally thought to be present in connection with a general name . . . are all present in the linguistic community *considered as a collective body;* but that collective body divides the 'labor' of knowing and employing these various parts of the 'meaning' of 'gold.'[44]

In picturesque summary, Putnam concludes his discussion of the division of linguistic labor by remarking:

There are tools like a hammer or a screwdriver which can be used by one person; and there are tools like a steamship which require the cooperative activity of a number of persons to use. Words have been thought of too much on the model of the first sort of tool.[45]

If these suggestions about a division of linguistic labor were expanded to encompass theoretical activities of a wider scope, the resulting conception of a division of theoretical labor might be used to flesh out the skeletal vision of religious communities being suggested here. It could be argued that most of the members of a religious community are neither interested in nor steeped in the intricacies of theology. These less theologically attuned individuals may possess elaborate behavioral and linguistic skills but they may have only the haziest conception of the meanings of their religious terminology and only the most superficial grasp of the ways in which God might be employed in explanatory or other theoretical contexts. When pressed, they may be able to say little about the content of their beliefs, the meanings of their religious terms, or the theoretical power of reference to God.

Of course, all of this does not mean that a religious community as a whole lacks any theoretical or explanatory expertise. If a division of theoretical labor were taken seriously, a group of intellectually able devotees might be specially organized and provided with the resources and leisure to pursue academic matters. Such an elite group might be expected to bear the intellectual burdens of the entire community. While the bulk of the community might be occupied with the assorted necessities of everyday religious life, a small core of theologians might be entrusted with theorizing and explaining.

Although such a small group of intelligentsia might appear to be sequestered away in blissful isolation from the main body of believers, it would take very little investigation of the religious behavior of the more ordinary members of the community to reveal the central and essential role being played by the theologians. With a modicum of persistent inquiry, the intellectually unsophisticated masses would be forced to admit their lack of theoretical expertise. They would have to concede their inability to define religious terminology precisely. Here their dependence upon the intellectually elite core of theologians would manifest itself. Though the masses themselves might not be able to specify precisely the object of their affections, though they might falter when asked for a clear definition of 'God' or 'God's love', they would be able to say that the object of their affections, the meaning of 'God' and 'God's love', and all other such technical matters are handled by a special subgroup of the community. In short, the masses ride on the linguistic and theoretical competence of trusted theologians. 'God' means whatever the respected authorities mean by it. Various ranges of phenomena can be explained by reference to God in whatever ways the theological specialists do so. The object of religious belief is the God delineated by the theologians. Thus, the point of secluding theologians in specially protected seminaries is to allow them the peace to fulfill their crucial roles in the division of religious labor. Their task is to think, understand, and explain while the task of the masses is to hope, watch, and pray.

With this sketch of the role of religious explanations within certain imaginary communities, the extended attempt to rehabilitate the cognitive integrity of religious discourse in these pages is complete. Beginning with a survey of various types of skeptical objections against the epistemological potential of religious affirmations, attention was turned to one particular explanatory strategy used in the sciences. By patterning religious explanations after this scientific model, it was argued not only that many are capable of epistemologically impeccable formulation, but also that at least some are plausible and, perhaps, even worthy of acceptance. Since the argument presented here was of so limited a scope, should it prove defective at any point, the cognitive rehabilitation of religious discourse might be accomplished through some other argumentative means. All that was argued here was that this one strategy could be used effectively in religious contexts. Even if it were shown that this is not so, it might still be possible to argue that some other explanatory strategy useful to the sciences could be employed religiously. Of course, were it shown that no explanatory enterprise whatever could be implemented effectively within the religious sphere, it still might be possible to show that some other theoretical activity could be undertaken by believers. Should even this be shown to be mistaken and the conclusion drawn that religious activity is completely devoid of theoretical value, it would not necessarily follow that religion should be abandoned as valueless. After all, there are other values besides theoretical ones. Perhaps the most important function of religion is to give meaning to life or to open the way for personally relating to the divine. Religion even might offer assurances of eternal life. None of these possibilities is precluded by either the success or the failure of the argumentation offered here.

Notes

—

I The Problem

1. See Charles Darwin, *The Descent of Man and Selection in Relation to Sex*, 2d ed. (New York: Collier and Son, 1901), chaps. 1–4, 6, 21.
2. Ibid., p. 45.
3. See ibid., pp. 99–102.
4. Ibid., p. 789.
5. Thomas Huxley, "The Origin of Species," in Philip Appleman, ed., *Darwin* (New York: Norton, 1970), pp. 435–36.
6. V. I. Lenin, *Selected Works* (New York: International Publishers, 1935–38), 11: 658.
7. Ibid., p. 661.
8. See ibid., pp. 661–62.
9. See Sigmund Freud, *The Future of an Illusion* (New York: Anchor, 1961), p. 52.
10. Ibid., pp. 52–53.
11. Ibid., p. 49.
12. Ibid., p. 50.
13. Ibid.
14. A. J. Ayer, *Language, Truth, and Logic*, 2d ed. (New York: Dover, 1952), p. 115.
15. Ibid., p. 41.
16. Ibid.
17. Ibid.
18. Ibid., p. 35.
19. Ibid., p. 37.
20. See ibid., pp. 38–39.
21. Ibid., p. 13.
22. Ibid.
23. See Alonzo Church, "A Note on the Entsheidungsproblem," *Journal of Symbolic Logic* 1 (1936), pp. 40–41.

24. This paper, with Hempel's added comments of 1958, may be found collected in A. J. Ayer, ed. *Logical Positivism* (New York: Free Press, 1959), pp. 108–29.

25. A bibliography of published materials by both proponents and critics of the positivist program is available in Ayer, *Logical Positivism*. For a more current bibliography of alternatives to positivist views concerning the nature of scientific theorizing, see Frederick Suppe, ed., *The Structure of Scientific Theories*, 2d ed. (Urbana: University of Illinois Press, 1977). Suppe also offers a more detailed explanation of the development of the positivists and a clear account of the position of their critics.

26. Antony Flew and Alasdair MacIntyre, eds., *New Essays in Philosophical Theology* (New York: Macmillan, 1964), p. 98.

27. Ibid., p. 99.

28. See Kai Nielsen, *Contemporary Critiques of Religion* (New York: Herder and Herder, 1971), pp. 56–61.

29. Alvin Plantinga, *God and Other Minds* (Ithaca: Cornell University Press, 1967), p. 168.

30. Rudolf Carnap, *The Logical Structure of the World*, 2d ed. (Berkeley and Los Angeles: University of California Press, 1969), p. 5.

31. Ibid., p. 10.

32. Ibid., p. 65.

33. Ibid., p. 108.

34. Ibid., pp. 12–13.

35. See ibid., p. 325.

36. Ibid., p. 289.

37. Ibid., p. 308.

38. Ibid., p. 286.

39. Ibid.

40. See ibid., p. 297.

41. Moritz Schlick, "The Foundation of Knowledge," in Ayer, *Logical Positivism*, pp. 209–10.

42. Hempel, "Empiricist Criterion of Meaning," p. 108. See n. 24 of this chap.

43. Otto Neurath, in "Protocol Sentences," was one of the first of the positivists to voice doubts concerning the foundational base needed for the sciences. This paper is collected in Ayer's *Logical Positivism* together with other papers concerned with the same issue. For a persuasive discussion of the problems incurred by foundationalist epistemologies, see also Wilfrid Sellars, "Empiricism and the Philosophy of Mind," in Sellars, ed., *Science, Perception and Reality* (London: Routledge and Kegan Paul, 1963), pp. 127–96.

44. A. J. Ayer, "What I Believe," in Ayer, ed., *What I Believe* (London: George Allyn and Unwin, 1966), p.13.

45. Nielsen, *Contemporary Critiques of Religion*, p. 58.

46. Ibid., p. 57.

47. Carnap, *Logical Structure of the World*, p. 297.

48. Rudolf Bultmann, *Jesus Christ and Mythology* (New York: Scribner's, 1958), p. 38.

49. Ibid., pp. 13–16, 35.
50. Ibid., pp. 35–36.
51. Ibid., p. 36.
52. *New Essays in Philosophical Theology*, p. 101.
53. Ibid., p. 100.
54. Bultmann, *Jesus Christ and Mythology*, p. 36.
55. *New Essays in Philosophical Theology*, p. 101.
56. John Hick, *Faith and Knowledge*, 2d ed. (Ithaca: Cornell University Press, 1966), p. 169.
57. See ibid., pp. 183–84.
58. Ibid., p. 186.
59. Ibid., p. 187.
60. See Nielsen, *Contemporary Critiques of Religion*, pp. 71–79.
61. Basil Mitchell, *The Justification of Religious Belief* (New York: Seabury, 1973), p. 12.
62. Ibid., p. 12.
63. Ibid.
64. See ibid., pp. 12–15.
65. See especially Thomas Kuhn, *The Structure of Scientific Revolutions*, 2d ed. enlarged (Chicago: University of Chicago Press, 1970), as well as an illuminating collection of papers on Kuhnian theses in Imre Lakatos and Alan Musgrave, eds., *Criticism and the Growth of Knowledge* (Cambridge: Cambridge University Press, 1974). Perhaps Quine's most forceful statement of his position on this topic may be found in "Ontological Relativity," collected in W. V. Quine, *Ontological Relativity and Other Essays* (New York: Columbia University Press, 1969). For additional bibliographical materials on this subject and a good summary of recent work in this area of the philosophy of science, see Suppe, *Structure of Scientific Theories*.
66. See Mitchell, *Justification of Religious Belief*, pts. 2–3.
67. Ibid., p. 99.
68. Ibid., p. 95.
69. Ibid., p. 101.

II The Possibility of Religious Explanations

1. Basil Mitchell, *The Justification of Religious Belief* (New York: Seabury, 1973), p. 101.
2. Ian G. Barbour, *Myths, Models and Paradigms* (New York: Harper and Row, 1974), p. 6.
3. Ibid., pp. 6–7.
4. See ibid., pp. 36–42.
5. Ibid., p. 36.
6. Ibid., p. 35.
7. Ibid., p. 37.
8. Ibid., p. 48.

9. Ibid., p. 69.
10. Ibid., p. 16.
11. Ibid., p. 12.
12. Ibid., p. 14.
13. Ibid., p. 13.
14. Ibid., p. 32.
15. Ibid., p. 14.
16. Ibid., p. 16.
17. Ibid., p. 69.
18. Barbour discusses this particular case on p. 31 of ibid.
19. Ibid., p. 16.
20. Ibid., p. 6.
21. Ibid., p. 30.
22. Ibid., pp. 37–38.
23. Ibid., p. 35.
24. Ibid., p. 42.
25. Ibid., p. 31.
26. Ibid., p. 47.
27. Ibid., p. 50.
28. Ibid., p. 178. This same thread of argument can be glimpsed on pp. 7, 8, 38, 53, 55, and 149.
29. For Barbour's extended discussion of the comparative merits of alternative religious models for God, see ibid., pp. 155–70.
30. Ibid., p. 42.
31. Ibid., p. 7.
32. Ibid., pp. 37–38.
33. Ibid., pp. 34–35.
34. Ibid., p. 113. Emphasis in original.
35. Ibid., p. 47.
36. Ibid., p. 16.
37. This seems to be the basic strategy employed by Kai Nielsen in both *Comtemporary Critiques of Religion* (New York: Herder and Herder, 1971) and *Scepticism* (London: Macmillan, 1973). While he is concerned with the general cognitive integrity of religious discourse rather than with its specifically explanatory potential, Nielsen's arguments frequently turn upon the conviction that there is something basically defective about ordinary language when carried over into Christian contexts. Antony Flew argues in a similar fashion in *God and Philosophy* (Atlantic Highlands: Hutchinson University Library, 1966) as does Terence Penelhum in *Survival and Disembodied Existence* (New York: Humanities Press, 1970).
38. For an informal glimpse of some of the ramifications of recent developments in physics and astrophysics, see Albert Einstein and Leopold Infeld, *The Evolution of Physics* (New York: Simon and Schuster, 1938) as well as Steven Weinberg, *The First Three Minutes* (New York: Bantam, 1977).

39. Ludwig Wittgenstein, *Philosophical Investigations*, 2d ed. (New York: Macmillan, 1958), p. 3e.

40. See ibid., p. 5e.

41. Hilary Putnam, "It Ain't Necessarily So," in Putnam, *Mathematics, Matter and Method* (Cambridge: Cambridge University Press, 1975), p. 243.

42. For additional details on this point, see ibid., pp. 243–46.

43. The sorts of objections frequently raised along these lines are catalogued in Nielsen, *Contemporary Critiques of Religion*, chap. 6.

44. J. J. C. Smart, "The Existence of God," in Antony Flew and Alasdair MacIntyre, eds., *New Essays in Philosophical Theology* (New York: Macmillan, 1964), p. 39.

45. Hilary Putnam, "The Logic of Quantum Mechanics," in Putnam, *Mathematics, Matter and Method*, p. 184.

46. Ibid., p. 189. See also Putnam's "Three-valued Logic" in the same volume.

47. See Susan Haack, *Deviant Logic* (Cambridge: Cambridge University Press, 1974) as well as her more recent *Philosophy of Logics* (Cambridge: Cambridge University Press, 1978) for a treatment of some of the issues raised by attempts to develop significant alternative logics. Capsule explanations of alternatives that have been explored actively also may be found in these volumes.

48. Ludwig Wittgenstein, *Lectures and Conversations on Aesthetics, Psychology and Religious Belief*, compiled from notes by Y. Smythies, R. Rhees, and J. Taylor (Berkeley and Los Angeles: University of California Press, 1967), p. 56.

49. Ibid., p. 57.

50. See W. D. Hudson, "Some Remarks on Wittgenstein's Account of Religious Belief," in G. N. A. Vesey, ed., *Talk of God* (London: Macmillan, 1969), esp. pp. 42–45, for a more extended consideration of the problems involved in fully understanding Wittgenstein's work on religion.

51. D. Z. Phillips, *Faith and Philosophical Enquiry* (New York: Schocken, 1970), p. 9.

52. See ibid., pp. 1–5.

53. See ibid., pp. 38–40.

54. See ibid., pp. 85–86.

55. Ibid., p. 127.

56. Ibid., p. 128.

57. Ibid., p. 132.

58. Ibid., p. 26.

59. Ibid., p. 64.

60. Ibid., pp. 67–68.

61. See, for example, Nielsen, *Scepticism*, chap. 2.

62. See, for instance, John Hick, "Skeptics and Believers," in Hick, ed., *Faith and the Philosophers* (New York: St. Martin's, 1964), pp. 235–50.

63. Phillips, *Faith and Philosophical Enquiry*, p. 129.

64. Ibid., pp. 265–66.

65. See, for example, William P. Alston, "Can we Speak Literally of God?" in Axel

Steuer and J. McClendon, eds., *Is God GOD?* (Nashville: Abingdon, 1981), for
a discussion of the purported meaninglessness of conceptions of bodiless agents.
66. Phillips, *Faith and Philosophical Enquiry*, p. 3.
67. Ibid., p. 21.
68. Ibid., p. 159.
69. Ibid., pp. 158–59.
70. Ibid., p. 104.
71. Ibid., pp. 103–4.

III Scientific Explanations

1. Richard Brandt, "Critique of MacIntyre's Starting-Point," in John Hick, ed.,
    Faith and the Philosophers (New York: St. Martin's, 1964), p. 152.
2. Ibid., p. 153. For the general structure of Brandt's pessimism, see pp. 152–53.
3. See Charles Darwin, *The Descent of Man and Selection in Relation to Sex*, 2d.
    ed. (New York: Collier and Son, 1901), pt. 1, esp. chaps. 3–4.
4. A nice example of the use of Malthusian themes can be found in Charles Darwin,
    *The Origin of Species by Means of Natural Selection, or the Preservation of
    Favored Races in the Struggle for Life*, 6th ed. (New York: Collier and Son,
    1902), chap. 3. One prominent place that Malthus is discussed specifically is in
    chap. 2 of *The Descent of Man*, pp. 68ff. For a careful discussion of the influence
    of Thomas Malthus during the time of Darwin, see Sir Gavin de Beer, *Charles
    Darwin: A Scientific Biography* (New York: Doubleday, 1964).
5. Darwin's writing is permeated with the thought of Thomas Malthus. Not only
    are Malthusian convictions discussed in *The Origin of Species* and *The Descent
    of Man*, but Malthus's name appears in numerous lesser-known published and
    unpublished works of Darwin as well.
6. Ernest Nagel, "Goal-directed Processes in Biology," *Journal of Philosophy* 74,
    no. 5 (May 1977), p. 261.
7. Although Nagel's "Teleology Revisited: The Dewey Lectures 1977," *Journal of
    Philosophy* 74, no. 5 (May 1977), pp. 261–301, provides a rather sophisticated
    discussion of the controversy surrounding teleological explanations, chapter 12
    of Ernest Nagel, *The Structure of Science* (New York: Harcourt, Brace and
    World, 1961) offers a fine introduction at a less technical level.
8. Such references frequently show up in such periodicals as *Psychiatry*, *Journal of
    Abnormal Psychology*, and *Journal of Psychoanalytic Nursing and Mental
    Health Services*. Of course, books like Humberto Nagera et al., *Basic Psycho-
    analytic Concepts on the Theory of Dreams* (New York: Basic, 1969) simply are
    awash with them.
9. See the opening pages of B. F. Skinner, *Beyond Freedom and Dignity* (New York:
    Knopf, 1971).
10. Collections like May Brodbeck, *Readings in the Philosophy of the Social Sciences*
    (New York: Macmillan, 1968) provide a good introduction to the controversy
    over the scientific integrity of the human sciences. The writings of Ernest Nagel,

cited in n. 7 of this chap., allow a glimpse of the sort of problems involved in justifying the claim that the teleological explanations of biology are rigorously scientific.

11. Some of the other kinds of explanations that may be offered in the physical sciences are catalogued briefly in Peter Achinstein, *Law and Explanation* (Oxford: Clarendon Press, 1971), pp. 65ff., and in Achinstein, *Concepts of Science* (Baltimore: The Johns Hopkins University Press, 1968), pp. 213–14.

12. Carl Hempel, *Aspects of Scientific Explanation* (New York: Free Press, 1965), p. 247.

13. Ibid.

14. See ibid., p. 278.

15. Basil Mitchell, *The Justification of Religious Belief* (New York: Seabury, 1973), p. 27.

16. Ibid., p. 101.

17. Frederick Ferré, *Language, Logic and God* (New York: Harper and Row, 1961), p. 24. See pp. 23–25 for his full characterization of scientific explanatory structure.

18. See ibid., particularly p. 44, but also chaps. 3 and 4.

19. Ibid., pp. 44–45.

20. Ibid., p. 44.

21. Ian Ramsey, *Religion and Science: Conflict and Synthesis* (London: William Clowes and Sons, 1964), p. 65.

22. Ibid., p. 86.

23. Ibid., pp. 86–87.

24. For just a few of the problems faced by this project, see Michael Scriven, "Explanations, Predictions and Laws," in Herbert Feigl and Grover Maxwell, eds., *Minnesota Studies in the Philosophy of Science* (Minneapolis: University of Minnesota, 1962), vol. 3. Other useful sources are Romano Harré, *The Principles of Scientific Thinking* (Chicago: University of Chicago Press, 1970), chap. 1; and Achinstein, *Law and Explanation*, pp. 99ff.

25. Both Harré, *Principles of Scientific Thinking*, and Achinstein, *Law and Explanation*, provide nice examples of this approach.

26. Dudley Shapere, "Scientific Theories and Their Domains," in Frederick Suppe, ed., *The Structure of Scientific Theories*, 2d ed. (Urbana: University of Illinois Press, 1977), seems to exemplify this cautious type of analysis.

27. Harré, *Principles of Scientific Thinking*, p. 35.

28. See Nicholas Rescher, *Scientific Explanation* (New York: Free Press, 1970), p. 123, for a short list.

29. See William P. Alston, "The Place of the Explanation of Particular Facts in Science," in *Philosophy of Science* 38, no. 1, for an extended discussion of this point.

30. While much of this account of scientific explanations obviously is influenced deeply by the work of Harré in *Principles of Scientific Thinking*, much of it also diverges quite radically from his position. For this reason, it would be unfair to claim his concurrence with any of the analyses presented here, though similarities sometimes will be rather striking.

31. See Harré, *Principles of Scientific Thinking*, for a much fuller, though in numerous ways very different, account.
32. Mitchell, *Justification of Religious Belief*, p. 101.
33. See Hempel, *Aspects of Scientific Explanation*, pp. 247–48.
34. Ibid., p. 248.
35. See Ramsey, *Religion and Science*, p. 65.
36. See Ferré, *Language, Logic and God*, pp. 23–24.

IV Religious Explanations

1. See D. Z. Phillips, *Faith and Philosophical Enquiry* (New York: Schocken, 1970),pp. 127–32 for a typical example of this sort of argument. Wittgenstein's most important comments on the distinctiveness of religious discourse can be found in *Lectures and Conversations on Aesthetics, Psychology and Religious Belief*, compiled from notes by Y. Smythies, R. Rhees, and J. Taylor (Berkeley and Los Angeles: University of California Press, 1967).
2. For the sake of brevity, the present discussion shall be restricted to a consideration of God as an explanatory entity, though other religiously significant beings could be treated similarly.
3. Antony Flew and Alasdair MacIntyre, eds., *New Essays in Philosophical Theology* (New York: Macmillan, 1964), p. 97.
4. See Antony Flew, *God and Philosophy* (Atlantic Highlands: Hutchinson University Library, 1966), esp. chap. 2; and Ronald Hepburn, "From World to God," *Mind* 72, no. 285 (1963), pp. 40–50.
5. Kai Nielsen, *Contemporary Critiques of Religion* (New York: Herder and Herder, 1971), p. 116.
6. Some have argued, of course, that the concept of a bodiless agent is an incoherent one. See Terence Penelhum, *Survival and Disembodied Existence* (New York: Humanities Press, 1970), chaps. 5 and 6, for an extended argument along these lines. But also see William Alston, "Can We Speak Literally of God?" in Axel Steuer and J. McClendon, eds., *Is God GOD?* (Nashville: Abingdon, 1981), for a response to this kind of skeptical argument. Even were no such response as that offered by Alston possible, the religious theorist might take inspiration from the strategy outlined by Hilary Putnam in "The Logic of Quantum Mechanics," in Putnam, *Mathematics, Matter and Method* (Cambridge: Cambridge University Press, 1975). Here it is argued that when all else fails, there is often the possibility of opting for an alternative logic.
7. Thomas Aquinas comes to his conclusion that nothing can be univocally predicated of both God and creatures in *Summa Contra Gentiles*, bk. 1, chap. 32, pp. 143–45. Following Aquinas to a lesser or greater degree are such works as Ralph M. McInerny, *The Logic of Analogy* (The Hague: Martinus Nijhoff, 1971); Gerald B. Phelan, *St. Thomas and Analogy* (Milwaukee: Marquette University Press, 1948); and David B. Burrell, *Analogy and Philosophical Language* (New Haven: Yale University Press, 1973). Matthew C. Menges, *The Concept of Univocity Regarding the Predication of God and Creature according to William*

Ockham (St. Bonaventure: The Franciscan Institute, 1952), develops the position of the main historical opponent of the Thomist position. Moving beyond the original context of this particular debate, Paul Tillich has presented his own arguments against the possibility of univocal predication of both God and creatures. A taste of his argumentation can be found in "The Nature of Religious Language," in Robert C. Kimball, ed., *Theology of Culture* (New York: Oxford University Press, 1959). William P. Alston's "Irreducible Metaphors in Theology" in Eugene T. Long, ed., *Experience, Reason and God* (Washington, D.C.: Catholic University Press, 1980), pp. 129–48, and "Can We Speak Literally of God?" in Steuer and McClendon, *Is God GOD?* contain materials that may be used in support of the claim that univocal predications of God and other things are possible.

8. See Tillich, "The Nature of Religious Language" as well as N. H. G. Robinson, "The Logic of Religious Language" and Frederick Copleston, "Hegel and the Rationalisation of Mysticism." The latter two papers may be found in G. N. A. Vesey, ed., *Talk of God* (London: Macmillan, 1969).

9. John Hick, *Faith and Knowledge*, 2d ed. (Ithaca: Cornell University Press, 1966), p. 189.

10. See especially the first few chapters of B. F. Skinner, *Beyond Freedom and Dignity* (New York: Knopf, 1971).

11. Kai Nielsen, *Scepticism* (London: Macmillan, 1973), p. 10.

12. See ibid., pp. 10ff.

13. Ibid., p. 73.

14. Flew and MacIntyre, *New Essays in Philosophical Theology*, p. 99.

15. Nielsen, *Contemporary Critiques of Religion*, p. 58.

16. Flew and MacIntyre, *New Essays in Philosophical Theology*, p. 103.

17. Again, for the sake of brevity, only God will be discussed. But, as before, the comments made here will apply to other religiously significant entities as well.

V The Plausibility of Religious Explanations

1. Frank B. Dilley, "The Status of Religious Beliefs," *American Philosophical Quarterly* 13, no. 1 (January 1976), p. 41.

2. There is a great body of material that might be cited in support of the inadequacy of Dilley's type of standard. Probably the most famous work along these lines is W. V. Quine, "Two Dogmas of Empiricism," in Quine, *From a Logical Point of View*, 2d ed. rev. (New York: Harper Torchbooks, 1963). For a summary of literature in opposition to Dilley's stance as well as an extensive bibliography, see Frederick Suppe, ed., *The Structure of Scientific Theories* 2d ed. (Urbana: University of Illinois Press, 1977).

3. Quine, "Two Dogmas of Empiricism," p. 43.

4. Ibid., pp. 42–43.

5. Many of these conclusions emerge in W. V. Quine, *Word and Object* (Cambridge, Mass.: MIT Press, 1960) and, more recently, in Quine, "Ontological Relativity," collected in his *Ontological Relativity and Other Essays* (New

York: Columbia University Press, 1969). For a good introduction to the controversy that has been stirred up by all of this, see Donald Davidson and Jaakko Hintikka, eds., *Words and Objections*, rev. ed. (Boston: Reidel, 1975); and Robert W. Shahan and Chris Swoyer, eds. *Essays on the Philosophy of W. V. Quine* (Norman: University of Oklahoma Press, 1979).

6. See especially the discussion, in chapter 4 of this book, of the skeptical challenge raised by Antony Flew and modified by Kai Nielsen.

7. Thomas S. Kuhn, *The Structure of Scientific Revolutions*, 2d ed. enlarged (Chicago: University of Chicago Press, 1970), p. 84.

8. See Hilary Putnam, "Three-valued Logic" and "The Logic of Quantum Mechanics," both of which are collected in Putnam, *Mathematics, Matter and Method* (Cambridge: Cambridge University Press, 1975).

9. Kuhn, *Structure of Scientific Revolutions*, pp. 156–57.

10. Kuhn carefully tried to document this preference for less powerful theories with particular reference to the rise of Copernican over Ptolemaic systems. See especially *The Copernican Revolution* (New York: Vintage, 1957), chaps. 5 and 6. Other, less fully developed cases are discussed in Kuhn, *Structure of Scientific Revolutions*, chap. 12.

11. *Structure of Scientific Revolutions*, p. 158.

12. See ibid., chap. 8, esp. p. 82.

13. Larry Laudan develops his critique of Kuhn's work in *Progress and its Problems* (Berkeley and Los Angeles: University of California Press, 1977). Of particular relevance with regard to the issues under consideration here are pp. 73ff. and pp. 133ff.

14. Ibid., p. 106.

15. Ibid., p. 107.

16. Ibid.

17. Ibid., p. 108. Emphasis in original.

18. Ibid., p. 110. Emphasis in original.

19. Ibid., p. 111.

20. Ibid. Emphasis in original.

21. Ibid., p. 109. Emphasis in original.

22. See Kuhn, *Structure of Scientific Revolutions*, p. 86 and, more pointedly, pp. 155–59.

23. See Laudan, *Progress and its Problems*, pp. 111ff.

24. Ibid., p. 110. Emphasis in original.

25. Kuhn, *Structure of Scientific Revolutions*, p. 103.

26. Ibid.

27. See ibid., p. 113, n. 2 for details.

28. Ibid., p. 113.

29. Ibid., p. 111.

30. Ibid., p. 151.

31. Ibid., p. 159.

32. Ibid., p. 77.

33. Ibid.

34. Ibid., p. 76.
35. See Langdon Gilkey, *Maker of Heaven and Earth* (Garden City, N.Y.: Anchor, 1965), chap. 3, esp. pp. 70ff.
36. See Laudan, *Progress and its Problems*, pp. 78ff., and esp. pp. 95–100.
37. See *Structure of Scientific Revolutions*, chaps. 2 and 3 for Kuhn's discussion of the merits of paradigm-governed research.
38. Strictly speaking, these types of cases may not be capable of arising from within a Kuhnian perspective. If Kuhn's incommensurability doctrines are pressed far enough, it may have to be concluded that ranges of phenomena for which different paradigms account are incommensurable. Hence, it may not be possible for two explanations, springing from divergent paradigm commitments, to be offered in explanatory competition over the same range of data. For the course of the remainder of the present discussion, however, this problem will be put to one side by assuming, perhaps unjustifiably, that such a radical interpretation of Kuhn's incommensurability theses need not be accepted.

VI Plausible Religious Explanations

1. Of course, other religiously significant entities might be used explanatorily. But for the sake of simplification, only the use of God will be considered here. Since the introduction of other religiously significant entities would follow the same patterns used in the introduction of God, this simplifying tactic should not prove to be a detrimental one.
2. See Basil Mitchell, *The Justification of Religious Belief* (New York: Seabury, 1973), p. 101.
3. See Frederick Ferré, *Language, Logic and God* (New York: Harper and Row, 1961), pp. 23–25.
4. See Ian Ramsey, *Religion and Science: Conflict and Synthesis* (London: William Clowes and Sons, 1964), pp. 65, 86–87.
5. David Hume, *Dialogues Concerning Natural Religion*, edited and with a commentary by Nelson Pike (New York: Bobbs-Merrill, 1970), p. 22.
6. Ibid., pp. 108–9.
7. Ibid., p. 63.
8. Ibid., p. 71.
9. Hume's main critique of the reasoning patterns used in the sciences centers about his discussion of knowledge concerning causal relations. Much of what he has to say on this matter is recorded in L. A. Selby-Bigge, ed., *A Treatise of Human Nature* (Oxford: Clarendon Press, 1888), bk. 1, pt. 3.
10. I believe that Hume is incorrect in his argument against the legitimacy of the cognitive structures used in the sciences. This is one reason why I am convinced that any attempt to rehabilitate the cognitive integrity of religious discourse by trying to undermine our faith in the theoretical adequacy of the sciences must fail.
11. Hume, *Dialogues Concerning Natural Religion*, p. 66.
12. Ibid., p. 51.

13. Ibid., p. 38.
14. See ibid., pp. 52–53.
15. See ibid., p. 50.
16. See ibid., pp. 50–51.
17. The conceptual machinery needed for meeting these objections was developed in the third chapter. The application of this machinery to these specifically religious problems was reserved for the fourth chapter.
18. Hume, *Dialogues Concerning Natural Religion*, p. 42.
19. Charles Hartshorne has been one of the leading proponents of this move. His *Man's Vision of God* (Hamden: Archon Books, 1964), for example, is devoted largely to the evolution of a more dynamic conception of God's nature.
20. Hume, *Dialogues Concerning Natural Religion*, p. 64.
21. Ibid., p. 85.
22. See Alvin Plantinga, *God and Other Minds* (Ithaca: Cornell University Press, 1967), chap. 6.
23. Sir Richard Owen published a critical review of Darwin's *Origin of Species* in "Darwin on the Origin of Species," *Edinburgh Review* 111 (1860). Louis Agassiz persistently argued against evolutionists of various stripes. One of his attacks upon Darwin's work may be found in "Evolution and Permanence of Type," *Atlantic Monthly* 33 (1874).
24. Jerry Falwell's militancy is well-known. Among the more prominent organizations devoted to the perpetuation of creationism is the Creation Research Society.
25. Hume, *Dialogues Concerning Natural Religion*, p. 64.
26. Larry Laudan, *Progress and its Problems* (Berkeley and Los Angeles: University of California Press, 1977), p. 109. Emphasis in original.
27. Ibid., p. 111. Emphasis in original.
28. See Gordon W. Allport, *The Individual and His Religion* (New York: Macmillan, 1950).
29. See Acts 7. I am grateful to Professor Ronald A. Veenker of Western Kentucky University for bringing these two biblical examples to my attention.
30. See Thomas Kuhn, *The Structure of Scientific Revolutions*, 2d ed. enlarged (Chicago: University of Chicago Press, 1970), esp. chaps. 2 and 3.
31. See D. Z. Phillips, *Faith and Philosophical Enquiry* (New York: Schocken, 1970), pp. 102ff. and 127ff., for an attempt to argue that the expectation of such divine behavior is more superstitious than it is religious.
32. Officially, of course, this same possibility could arise for religious explanations for natural or broadly historical patterns as well. However, given the development and comprehensive scope of the physical, life, and social sciences, such a possibility is fairly remote. Nevertheless, if it were to arise, the comments made here about religious explanations for more personal patterns would apply to those cases as well.

VII Explanations and Religious Life

1. Wittgenstein's comments on the nature of religious belief are concentrated in *Lectures and Conversations on Aesthetics, Psychology and Religious Belief*, compiled from notes by Y. Smythies, R. Rhees, and J. Taylor (Berkeley and Los Angeles: University of California Press, 1967), pp. 55ff. He also discussed religious issues in his earlier works, particularly in *Notebooks*, trans. G. E. M. Anscombe (New York: Harper Torchbooks, 1969), pp. 72ff; and *Tractatus Logico-Philosophicus*, trans. D. F. Pears and B. F. McGuinness (New York: Routledge and Kegan Paul, 1972), sec. 6.4ff. Whether these earlier notes are compatible with his reflections in *Aesthetics, Psychology and Religious Belief* is subject to debate. Two rather developed interpretations of Wittgenstein's work on religion, both early and late, are W. D. Hudson, *Wittgenstein and Religious Belief* (New York: St. Martin's, 1975) and Patrick Sherry, *Religion, Truth and Language-Games* (New York: Barnes and Noble, 1977).

2. *Aesthetics, Psychology and Religious Belief*, p. 55.

3. Ibid., p. 53.

4. Ibid.

5. Ibid., p. 56.

6. Ibid., p. 54.

7. Ibid., p. 56.

8. Ibid., p. 57.

9. Ibid., p. 56.

10. It is not completely clear that Wittgenstein is actually committed to this strong claim. On pp. 60–61 of *Aesthetics, Psychology and Religious Belief*, he seems to waiver from so universal a commitment when he says that an experience of blood coming out of something in France would not convince him into religious belief, though there might be occasions upon which certain evidence would be convincing. See also Hudson, *Wittgenstein and Religious Belief* (New York: St. Martin's Press, 1975), particularly the later chapters, for an extended discussion of the problems involved in understanding Wittgenstein's position regarding the nature of religious belief. Hudson's paper, "Some Remarks on Wittgenstein's Account of Religious Belief," in G. N. A. Vesey, ed., *Talk of God* (London: Macmillan, 1969), especially pp. 42–45, may prove helpful in this connection as well.

11. Peter Winch, "Understanding a Primitive Society," in D. Z. Phillips, ed., *Religion and Understanding* (New York: Macmillan, 1967), p. 12.

12. D. Z. Phillips, *Faith and Philosophical Enquiry* (New York: Schocken, 1970), p. 64. Emphasis in original.

13. For the full details of this argument, see the second chapter of this book, especially the material following the discussion of Ian Barbour's position.

14. Phillips, *Faith and Philosophical Enquiry*, p. 127.

15. Ibid., p. 128

16. Rush Rhees, *Without Answers* (New York: Schocken, 1969), pp. 6–7.

17. Ibid., p. 131.

18. Phillips, *Faith and Philosophical Enquiry*, p. 17.
19. Ibid., p. 131.
20. Ibid., pp. 131–32.
21. Winch, "Understanding a Primitive Society," p. 19.
22. Ibid.
23. Thomas Kuhn, *The Structure of Scientific Revolutions*, 2d ed. enlarged (Chicago: University of Chicago Press, 1970), p. 84.
24. Winch, "Understanding a Primitive Society," p. 35.
25. Ibid.
26. Ibid., p. 37.
27. D. Z. Phillips, *Death and Immortality* (New York: St. Martin's, 1970), p. 60.
28. Phillips, *Faith and Philosophical Enquiry*, p. 92.
29. Ibid., p.45.
30. Ibid., p. 2. Emphasis in original.
31. Ibid., p. 14.
32. Ibid., pp. 81–82.
33. Ibid., p. 45.
34. Ibid., p. 32.
35. Ibid.
36. Ibid., p. 190.
37. Ibid., p. 159.
38. Ibid., p. 31.
39. Ibid., p. 18.
40. Ibid., p. 52.
41. Ibid., pp. 23–24.
42. Ibid., p. 25.
43. Hilary Putnam, "The Meaning of 'Meaning'," in Putnam, *Mind, Language and Reality* (Cambridge: Cambridge University Press, 1975), p. 227. Emphasis in original.
44. Ibid., pp. 227–28.
45. Ibid., p. 229.

Index

Agassiz, Louis, 161
Allport, Gordon, 166
Augustine, Saint, 168
Ayer, A. J., 4–6, 11–12, 13, 19

Barbour, Ian, 25–34
Biological explanation, 147–48
Bohr, Niels, 92
Brandt, Richard, 51–52
Bultmann, Rudolf, 13–14, 15, 18, 20

Carnap, Rudolf, 8–11, 13, 14, 15, 19
Cognitive meaningfulness: and the role
   of religion, vii, viii, 13–14, 24,
   207–8; and the cognitive rehabilitation of religious discourse, ix,
   22–23; and religious utterances, 5,
   13, 105, 191, 207–8; criteria of,
   5–6, 7–8, 11; and religious belief,
   48; and religious terms, 94, 105,
   122, 127, 146; and religious
   explanations, 181
Copleston, Frederick, 93
Creationism, 109–10, 139, 152, 161–
   64
Critical realism, 25–26

Darwin, Charles, 1–2, 52–53, 153–56,
   160, 161, 198
Data: theory-laden, 31–32; recalcitrant,
   106–7, 108
Design arguments, 153–68

Design explanations, 154–67
Dilley, Frank B., 121, 122

Einstein, Albert, 35
Empiricism, modern: fundamental tenet
   of, 11, 12
Eternal love, 203
Evolutionary explanations. See Explanations, evolutionary
Explanations: diversity of structures,
   52–55, 56–60; teleological, 54; as
   models for religion, 60–61, 64–65;
   of patterns, 151–52
—biological, 147–48
—design, 154–67
—evolutionary: and religious belief, 18,
   109–10, 167
—nonrivalist: and religious traditions,
   139, 152–53; plausibility of,
   143–48, 150, 154, 161, 185;
   reasons for nonrivalry, 143–45; of
   natural patterns, 164–67; of
   historical patterns, 173; of personal
   patterns, 179–83. See also Explanations, religious
—religious: theoretical adequacy of,
   viii; general plausibility of, xi–xii,
   82, 85, 184–85; nonrivalist, xii,
   184; rivalist, xii, 183–84; and
   falsehood, 34–36; constraints
   upon, 43–44; possibility of,
   43–44; evaluation of, 75–76, and

the sciences, 81–83, 84–107;
standards for truth of, 122–23,
124–25; and evidence, 123–24;
and analogy, 125; initial plausibility
of, 125–30, 149, 150; in competition with alternative explanations,
130–32, 133–38, 139–43; ranking
of plausibility criteria for, 132;
without competitors, 132–33,
143–48; and plausibility criteria of
Thomas Kuhn, 133–34, 136–39,
142–43, 150, 164, 172–73,
175–79; and plausibility criteria of
Larry Laudan, 134–36, 138–42,
149–50, 163–64, 167, 172,
175–79; nonepistemic criteria for,
146–47, 150, 165–66, 180–81; of
historical patterns, 152–53, 168–
73, 174; of natural patterns, 152,
153–68, 174; of personal patterns,
153, 174–83; and truth, 184–85.
See also Explanations, nonrivalist;
Explanations, rivalist
—rivalist: and religious traditions, 139,
152–53; their plausibility, 139–43,
146, 148, 149–50, 154, 161–62,
185; of natural patterns, 161–64,
166–67; of historical patterns,
170–73; of personal patterns,
173–79. See also Explanations,
religious
—scientific: as standards for religion, x,
55–56; evaluation of, 75–78; as
models for religion, 81–83, 84–107
Explanatory entities: explanatory
power of, 64–65; existence of,
65–66; nature of, 65–66; refining
conceptions of, 69–72; evaluation
of, 75–78; in religion, 78–79,
95–98; intelligibility of, 94, 131–
32, 159–60; interchangeability of,
108–10; levels of, 147–48. See also
Mechanisms; Theoretical entities
Explanatory overdetermination, xii,
144–46, 164–65

Falsifiability challenge, 6–7, 11, 12, 19,
20, 105–8

Ferré, Frederick, 58, 59, 79–80, 151
Flew, Antony, 6–7, 14, 15, 19, 20, 87,
105, 108
Freud, Sigmund, ix, 3–4, 12, 20, 22, 24,
36, 55, 77, 121, 131–32, 166, 172
Functional definitions: of God, xi, 84,
86–90; in the sciences, 86

Gilkey, Langdon, 139
God: functional definition of, xi, 84,
86–90; as an explanatory entity,
83–120, 149, 196–97, 198–99;
existence of, 83, 105–6; explanatory range of, 84–86, 90–91; as a
bodiless agent, 87–88, 89–90;
identification of, 87–90, 93, 95,
102–3, 191–92, 203, 204; individuation of, 87–90, 93, 191–92,
203, 204; univocal predications of,
87, 92–93; and explanatorily
efficacious properties, 90–98; as
infinite, 95–98, 158; refining
conceptions of, 98–107, 119;
nontheoretical roles of, 99–100;
and sources of analogy, 101;
anthropomorphic conceptions of,
101–2, 158–59; and spatio-
temporal qualities, 103–5; and
recalcitrant explanatory ranges,
106–7; and verification, 108; plausible explanatory ranges for, 110–
19; and corporeality, 158; intelligibility of, 159–60, 162–63, 171–72

Hare, R. M., 14–15
Harré, Romano, 61–63
Hempel, Carl, 6, 11, 56–57, 58, 59,
79–80
Hepburn, Ronald, 87, 192
Hick, John, 19–20, 21, 47, 48, 95–96,
190–91, 192
Hume, David, 63, 153–63, 167, 168,
185
Huxley, Thomas, ix, 2–3, 4, 12, 20, 22,
24, 55, 121

Immortality, 197
Indexical identification, 88–89

Instrumentalism, 25

Kuhn, Thomas, xii, 21, 22, 32, 123–24, 133–34, 135–39, 142–43, 150, 162, 167, 183–84, 195, 199. *See also* Explanations, religious

Laudan, Larry, xii, 134–43, 149–50, 162, 167, 183–84, 199. *See also* Explanations, religious; Research traditions
Lenin, V. I., 3, 4, 12, 24, 121
Logic of discovery, xi

MacIntyre, Alisdair, 51
Malthus, Thomas, 52–53
Mechanisms: governing, x; and analogy, 62, 63–64, 66–71, 72–74, 81; and the sciences, 62, 63–64, 81; and religious explanations, 64–65; explanatory power of, 65; intelligibility of, 65; refining conceptions of, 69–72; levels of, 70–71, 100–101; and spatio-temporal characterizations, 103–5; biological, 106, 117. *See also* Explanatory entities; Theoretical entities
Metaphors, 26–27, 32
Metaphysical sentences, 5
Miracles: confirmation of, 112–16, 128; explanation of, 113–16, 128–29, 152
Mitchell, Basil, 20, 22–23, 24–25, 57–58, 59, 79–80, 107, 151
Models: and Ian Barbour, 25–34; and religion, 28–29, 30; of God, 29, 30
Myth of deductivism, 151

Nagel, Ernest, 54
Naive realism, 25, 27, 31
Newton, Isaac, 35
Nielsen, Kai, 7–8, 11–12, 13, 19, 20, 22, 47, 87, 101–5, 190
Nonrivalist explanations. *See* Explanations, nonrivalist

Oppenheim, Paul, 56–57, 58, 59, 79–80
Owen, Sir Richard, 161

Phillips, D. Z., 45–50, 82, 190–91, 192, 197–98, 199–205
Plantinga, Alvin, 7, 161
Positivism: aftermath of, vii–viii; and standards for religion, x; and Ian Barbour, 31–32; and scientific explanation, 56–57, 59; as influential upon religious studies, 56–59, 79–80, 121, 122, 150–51
Problem of evil, 18, 107–8, 160–61
Putnam, Hilary, 41, 43, 205–6

Quine, W. V., 21, 32, 105, 123

Ramsey, Ian, 58–59, 79, 80, 151
Rational reconstruction, 8–10, 12
Realism: critical, 25–26 naive, 25, 27, 31
Religion as disanalogous to the sciences, 44–49, 189–90, 194–98, 200–203
Religious belief: as regulative, 187–89; intentionality of, 203–205
Religious communities, 36–37, 38, 41, 46, 48, 139–40, 143, 167, 193, 205–7
Religious explanations. *See* Explanations, religious
Religious illusions, 3–4, 36
Religious practice: linguistic, 15–19, 190–92, 205–7; and explanation, 17–19; behavioral, 46–49, 205–7; and cognitive rehabilitation, 83–84
Religious skepticism: general arguments for, ix, 1, 20–21, 24–25, 34–44, 44–50, 55–56, 82, 115, 118–19, 121–22, 126–28, 188, 193, 207–8; traditional forms of, 1–4, 13; positivist forms of, 4–12, 13; and psychology, 36–37; and linguistic studies, 37; and the limits of language, 37–38; and linguistic development, 39–41; and conceptual limitations, 41–42; and logical constraints, 42–44; and true religion, 44–50
Research traditions: their adequacy, 134–35, 140–42; their progress, 134–35, 172; acceptance of, 135,

136, 139–42, 149, 163, 172;
pursuit of, 135, 136, 140–42,
149–50, 164, 172
Revelation and explanation, 91
Rhees, Rush, 191–92
Rivalist explanations. *See* Explanations,
rivalist
Robinson, N. H. G., 93

Schlick, Moritz, 10–11
Science: as standard for religion,
vii–viii, ix–x, 13, 44, 55–56,
121–22, 125; the rise of, viii, ix,
13, 121, 201; explanatory range of,
xii, 61–62, 63–64, 66–69, 72–75,
80, 81; and skepticism, 3, 4;
supremacy of, 3, 13, 25, 51–52, 82;
as theoretically exhaustive, 10–11
Scientific explanations. *See* Explanations, scientific
Skinner, B. F., 55, 101, 172

Smart, J. J. C., 42
Superstition, vii, 2–3, 45, 47, 49,
82
Symbolic language and God, 93

Theologians, 140, 205, 206–7
Theoretical entities: and explanation, x;
and science, 27; levels of, 70–71,
100–101, 147–48. *See also*
Explanatory entities; Mechanisms
Tillich, Paul, 93

Verifiability, 5–6
Verificationism, 151
Vienna Circle, 24

Winch, Peter, 190, 194–197, 199,
202–5
Witchcraft, 194–95
Wittgenstein, Ludwig, xii, 39–40, 45,
82, 186–90